D1024162

New York
2012

WHAT'S NEW | WHAT'S ON | WHAT'S BEST

timeoutnewyork.com

Contents

Published by Time Out Guides Ltd
Universal House
251 Tottenham Court Road
London W1T 7AB
Tel: + 44 (0)20 7813 3000
Fax: + 44 (0)20 7813 6001
Email: guides@timeout.com
www.timeout.com

Managing Director Peter Fiennes
Editorial Director Ruth Jarvis
Business Manager Daniel Allen
Editorial Manager Holly Pick
Management Accountants Margaret Wright, Clare Turner

Time Out Guides is a wholly owned subsidiary of Time Out Group Ltd.

© **Time Out Group Ltd**
Chairman & Founder Tony Elliott
Chief Executive Officer David King
Chief Operating Officer Aksel Van der Wal
Group Financial Director Paul Rakkar
Group General Manager/Director Nichola Coulthard
Time Out Communications Ltd MD David Pepper
Time Out International Ltd MD Cathy Runciman
Time Out Magazine Ltd Publisher/Managing Director Mark Elliott
Group Commercial Director Graeme Tottle
Group IT Director Simon Chappell
Group Marketing Director Andrew Booth

Time Out and the Time Out logo are trademarks of Time Out Group Ltd.

This edition first published in Great Britain in 2011 by Ebury Publishing
A Random House Group Company
Company information can be found on www.randomhouse.co.uk
Random House UK Limited Reg. No. 954009
10 9 8 7 6 5 4 3 2 1

Distributed in the US and Latin America by Publishers Group West (1-510-809-3700)
Distributed in Canada by Publishers Group Canada (1-800-747-8147)

For further distribution details, see www.timeout.com

ISBN: 978-1-84670-234-1

A CIP catalogue record for this book is available from the British Library.

Printed and bound in Germany by Appl.

The Random House Group Limited supports the Forest Stewardship Council® (FSC®),
the leading international forest certification organisation. All our titles that are printed on
Greenpeace approved FSC® certified paper carry the FSC® logo. Our paper procurement
policy can be found at www.randomhouse.co.uk/environment.

Time Out carbon-offsets all its flights with Trees for Cities (www.treesforcities.org).

New York Shortlist

The **Time Out New York Shortlist 2012** is one of a series of annual guides that draws on Time Out's background as a magazine publisher to keep you current with everything that's going on in town. As well as 2012's key sights and the best of its eating, drinking and leisure options, it picks out the most exciting venues to have opened in the last year and gives a full calendar of annual events from September 2011 to August 2012. It also includes features on the important news, trends and openings, all compiled by locally based editors and writers. Whether you're visiting for the first time in your life or the first time this year, you'll find the *Time Out New York Shortlist* contains all you need to know, in a portable and easy-to-use format.

The guide divides central New York into four areas, each containing listings for Sights & Museums, Eating & Drinking, Shopping, Nightlife and Arts & Leisure, and maps pinpointing their locations. At the front of the book are chapters rounding up these scenes city-wide, and giving a shortlist of our overall picks. We also include itineraries for days out, plus essentials such as transport information and hotels.

Our listings give phone numbers as dialled within the US. Within New York you need to use the initial 1 and the three-digit area code even if you're calling from within that area code. From abroad, use your country's exit code followed by the number (the initial 1 is the US's country code).

We have noted price categories by using one to four $ signs

($-$$$$), representing budget, moderate, expensive and luxury. Major credit cards are accepted unless otherwise stated. We also indicate when a venue is **NEW**, and give Event highlights.

All our listings are double-checked, but places do sometimes close or change their hours or prices, so it's a good idea to call a venue before visiting. While every effort has been made to ensure accuracy, the publishers cannot accept responsibility for any errors that this guide may contain.

Venues are marked on the maps using symbols numbered according to their order within the chapter and colour-coded as follows:

❶ Sights & Museums
❶ Eating & Drinking
❶ Shopping
❶ Nightlife
❶ Arts & Leisure

Map Key	
Major sight or landmark	
Hospital or college	
Railway station	
Park	
River	
Freeway	478
Main road	
Main road tunnel	
Pedestrian road	
Airport	✈
Church	✚
Subway station	Ⓜ
Area name	SOHO

Time Out **New York** Shortlist 2012

EDITORIAL
Author Richard Koss
Deputy Editor Claire Boobbyer
Proofreader Mandy Martinez

DESIGN
Art Director Scott Moore
Art Editor Pinelope Kourmouzoglou
Senior Designer Kei Ishimaru
Group Commercial Designer Jodi Sher

Picture Editor Jael Marschner
Acting Deputy Picture Editor Liz Leahy
Picture Desk Assistant/Researcher
  Ben Rowe

ADVERTISING
New Business & Commercial Director
  Mark Phillips
International Advertising Manager
  Kasimir Berger

International Sales Executive
  Charlie Sokol
Advertising Sales (New York)
  Julia Keefe-Chamberlain

MARKETING
Senior Publishing Brand Manager
  Luthfa Begum
Guides Marketing Manager
  Colette Whitehouse
Group Commercial Art Director
  Anthony Huggins

PRODUCTION
Group Production Manager
  Brendan McKeown
Production Controller Katie Mulhern

CONTRIBUTORS
This guide was researched and written by Richard Koss and the writers of *Time Out New York*. The editor would like to thank Claire Boobbyer, previous editor and writer Lisa Ritchie, Will Crow, Joseph Bellis, and Natalya Wells.

PHOTOGRAPHY
Photography by page 9 Adriano Castelli; pages 13, 14, 42, 47, 50 (top left and bottom right), 64, 75, 121 (bottom), 131 Ben Rosenzweig; page 15 Jodie Love; pages 16, 26, 90, 96, 128, 158 Wendy Connett; pages 19, 25, 44, 46, 49, 50 (top right), 68, 101, 110, 128 (bottom), 146, 161, 164 Michael Kirby; page 33 vuwstudio.com / Museum of the Moving Image; page 39 Ken Howard/Metropolitan Opera; page 40 Carl Saytor; page 43 Annie Collinge; pages 50 (bottom left), 121 (top) Jonathan Perugia; pages 52, 102/103, 110 (top), 128 (top) Alys Tomlinson; page 56 Jael Marschner; page 63 Squared Design Lab; page 85 Gurwin Photography; page 95 Catalina Kulczar-Marin; page 113 Andrew Fladeboe; page 117 ċ 2010 8 Legged Productions, LLC; page 125 MOMA; page 134 Jorg Hackemann; page 137 Michael Bodycomb; page 175 Gridley & Graves Photographers; page 163 Leeser Architecture.

The following images were provided by the featured establishments/artists: pages 29, 36, 37, 145, 157, 168, 178.

Cover Photograph: 135th Street at sunset. Credit: 4Corners Images.

MAPS
JS Graphics (john@jsgraphics.co.uk).

About **Time Out**

Founded in 1968, Time Out has expanded from humble London beginnings into the leading resource for those wanting to know what's happening in the world's greatest cities. As well as our influential what's-on weeklies in London, New York and Chicago, we publish nearly 30 other listings magazines in cities as varied as Beijing and Mumbai. The magazines established Time Out's trademark style: sharp writing, informed reviewing and bang up-to-date inside knowledge of every scene.

  Time Out made the natural leap into travel guides in the 1980s with the City Guide series, which now extends to over 50 destinations around the world. Written and researched by expert local writers and generously illustrated with original photography, the full-size guides cover a larger area than our Shortlist guides and include many more venue reviews, along with additional background features and a full set of maps.

  Throughout this rapid growth, the company has remained proudly independent, still owned by Tony Elliott four decades after he started Time Out London as a single fold-out sheet of A5 paper. This independence extends to the editorial content of all our publications, this Shortlist included. No establishment has been featured because it has advertised, and no payment has influenced any of our reviews. And, for our critics, there's definitely no such thing as a free lunch: all restaurants and bars are visited and reviewed anonymously, and Time Out always picks up the bill.
For more about the company, see www.timeout.com.

Don't Miss 2012

KANDINSKY

Solomon R Guggenheim Museum p147

WHAT'S BEST
Sights & Museums

A decade after the attacks of 9/11, New Yorkers are all the more aware of their city's ever-changing nature. The recent economic slump has only heightened Gotham's unpredictability, derailing many of the city's best- (and worst-) laid plans, as countless restaurants, musicals and even museums have opened, only to close over the past few years.

Those that have survived, however, have become indelible parts of the New York landscape, as integral to the city as any of its iconic skyscrapers.

Perhaps the most welcome addition is the High Line (see p94), one of Gotham's more successful public works projects. This 1.5-mile defunct elevated train track on the west side that's being converted into a slender, stylish park, made a

partial debut in summer 2009. The first stretch runs from Gansevoort Street in the Meatpacking District to 20th Street, the gateway to Chelsea's gallery district; the second leg, continuing up to 30th Street, opened in the spring of 2011, while plans for the third and final section remain up in the air.

Right by the High Line, groundbreaking for the downtown branch of the Whitney Museum took place in May 2011. This highly anticipated Renzo Piano-designed museum is expected to open in 2015, with 50,000 square feet of indoor gallery space as well as 13,000 square feet of rooftop exhibition space.

Indeed, museum construction has proceeded apace seemingly unchecked by the recession. In January 2011, the Museum

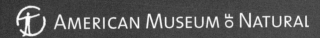

AMERICAN MUSEUM ᴼF NATURAL

Close by.
Worlds away.

Minutes from Midtown, adventure awaits.
Come for an hour or spend the day
time-traveling through space, fossil halls,
ancient cultures, new worlds, and more.

Open daily | Central Park West at 79th Street
212.769.5100 | amnh.org

of the Moving Image (see p166) reopened in an impressive new state-of-the-art facility after several years of renovation. And even stately Museum Mile is evolving. On its northern end, at 110th Street and Fifth Avenue, the Museum for African Art (see p147) has moved into brand new digs in September 2011, the nomadic museum's fourth (and final) home in the city.

Of course, a priority for first-time visitors will be to see some of the world-class collections for which the city is famous. The Metropolitan Museum of Art (see p144) is renowned for its European painting and sculpture, Islamic art, Greek and Roman collection and an ever-changing array of blockbuster travelling shows. The American wing's lovely Engelhard Court, reopened in summer 2009 as a dramatic sculpture court; the entire wing has finally been completed this past year.

The Guggenheim (see p147), whose landmark building is still gleaming from a spruce-up for its big 5-0 in 2009, is another New York essential. If you want a bit of background, the Museum of the City of New York (see p147) provides fascinating insight, while the Lower East Side Tenement Museum (see p76) brings New York's immigrant history to vivid life.

Naturally, with the tenth anniversary of 9/11, attention has turned to Ground Zero. Until a year ago there wasn't much to see, but visible signs of progress have been rising above the hoarding. Construction on the new World Trade Center complex – due to include five office buildings, the National September 11 Memorial & Museum and a transit hub designed by Santiago Calatrava – has been plagued by in-fighting, delays and budget problems. Only the memorial is expected to be

DON'T MISS: 2012

SHORTLIST

Best new
- High Line (see p94)
- Museum for African Art (see p147)
- Museum of the Moving Image (see p166)
- 9/11 Memorial Preview Site (see p63)

Best for local insight
- Lower East Side Tenement Museum (see p76)
- Museum of the Chinese in America (see p73)
- Museum of the City of New York (see p147)

Best free
- Brooklyn Bridge (see p162)
- Governors Island (see p57)
- Staten Island Ferry (see p65)

Best urban oases
- Central Park (see p137)
- The Cloisters (see p159)
- Botanical Garden (see p161)
- Brooklyn Heights Promenade (see p162)

Must-see collections
- Metropolitan Museum of Art (see p144)
- Museum of Modern Art (MoMA) (see p130)

New York icons
- Chrysler Building (see p135)
- Empire State Building (see p129)
- Statue of Liberty (see p65)

Best museum buildings
- American Museum of Natural History (see p150)
- Frick Collection (see p143)
- New Museum of Contemporary Art (see p77)
- Solomon R Guggenheim Museum (see p147)

Discover the city from your back pocket

Essential for your weekend break, over 30 top cities available.

finished by the original anniversary target date, but the new 9/11 Memorial Preview Site (see p63) gives you a glimpse of how it will all eventually look.

Until the completion of its centrepiece, the 1,776-foot 1 World Trade Center (formerly the Freedom Tower) in 2013, the Empire State Building (see p129, remains New York's tallest building. Although there can be long lines to ascend to the observation deck, it's now open until 2am and late-night viewings are usually less crowded (and the illuminated cityscape is spectacular). Another option is the Top of the Rock observation deck, perched above Midtown's Rockefeller Center (see p132). The art deco tower gets one up on the Empire State by allowing a view of that iconic structure. On the subject of spectacular views, the crown of the Statue of Liberty (see p65) is once again open to the public (by advance reservation).

Slicing up the Apple

This book is divided by neighbour hood. Downtown is the oldest part of Manhattan and also the most happening. At the tip of the island is the seat of local government and the epicentre of capitalism in the Financial District. And, over the past decade trendy bars, boutiques and galleries have been moving into the erstwhile immigrant neighbour hood of the Lower East Side. Former bohemian stomping ground Greenwich Village still resounds with cultural associations, but today is more moneyed and has the restaurants to prove it; to the west, leafy, winding streets give way to the Meatpacking District's ware houses, now colonised by designer stores and clubs. The once-radical East Village brims with bars and restaurants. Former art enclave

Soho is now a prime shopping and dining destination, along with well-heeled neighbour Tribeca. And Little Italy is being crowded out by ever-expanding Chinatown and, to the north, boutique-riddled Nolita.

In Midtown, Chelsea contains New York's main gallery district and also the city's most prominent gay enclave. Once mainly commercial, the Flatiron District has evolved into a fine-dining destination and nearby Union Square attracts foodies four days a week to New York's biggest farmers' market. Among the skyscrapers of Midtown's prime commercial stretch are some of NYC's most iconic attractions. Here, Fifth Avenue is home to some of the city's poshest retail, while Broadway is the world's most famous theatreland. Love it or loathe it, garish Times Square (see p122) is a must-gawp spectacle.

DON'T MISS: 2012

Rockefeller Center p132

Uptown, bucolic Central Park (see p137), with its picturesque lakes, expansive lawns and famous zoo, is the green divider between the patrician Upper East Side and the less conservative but equally well-heeled Upper West Side. Between them, these wealthy locales contain the lion's share of the city's cultural institutions: most museums are on the UES – the Metropolitan Museum of Art and others on Fifth Avenue's Museum Mile, in the stately former mansions of the 20th-century elite – but the UWS has the Metropolitan Opera, the New York Philharmonic and the New York City Ballet at Lincoln Center (see p155). Further north, regenerated Harlem offers vibrant nightlife, great soul food and plenty of cultural history.

New York Public Library p130

Making the most of it

First, accept that you can never see it all. The typical week's visit to the city will involve some tough choices. Similarly, it's self-defeating to attempt to hit all the major collections in one visit to an institution as large as the Met or the American Museum of Natural History. So plan, pace yourself and take time to enjoy aimless wandering in picturesque areas like the West Village or Central Park.

Because the city's museums are privately funded, and receive little or no government support, admission prices can be steep. However, these usually include entry to temporary as well as the permanent collections, and many institutions offer one day or evening a week when admission fees are either waived or switched to a voluntary donation (and 'suggested donation' prices are just that). Be warned that many museums are closed on Mondays – except on some holidays, such as Columbus Day and Presidents' Day.

Despite recent budget cuts, the subway (see p184) is still highly efficient and runs 24 hours a day. It is generally well populated, reasonably clean and relatively easy to navigate. It will often get you from one end of the city to another more quickly (not to mention more cheaply) than a cab. Charge up a MetroCard and you can travel seamlessly by subway and bus. Of course, you should keep your wits about you and take basic precautions, but New York these days is a pretty safe place. The best way to get to know the city, however, is by pounding the pavements. Manhattan is a mere 13.4 miles long and 2.3 miles across at its widest point, and once you've mastered the grid, it's easy to find your way (although it gets a little trickier Downtown).

Grand Central Oyster Bar p136

WHAT'S BEST
Eating & Drinking

Dining out is one of New York's truly great passions. Perhaps this is because of the minute, hard-to-cook-in kitchens so many Gothamites have to contend with, or maybe it's because of their relentless craving for variety and novelty. Whatever, the city's restaurants are indispensible sources of nourishment and social pleasure for those who live here. And visitors will find their forays into New York's dining scene one of the surest means of discovering what makes the city (and its inhabitants) tick.

Fierce competition for your dollars ensures restaurateurs are always thinking of creative ways to appeal to your tastebuds, even during the Great Recession – and diners are benefiting from special deals and more solicitous service.

The popular biannual Restaurant Week (see p38), lets you dine at many notable restaurants at $24.07 (a play on 24/7 for lunch and $35 for dinner.

But its creativity in the kitchen that makes the city so unique. The most intriguing spot to open in the past year comes courtesy of Marcus Samuelsson, an Ethiopian-born Swedish chef, who made a name for himself at Aquavit in the mid '90s. In December 2010, he opened Red Rooster (see p159) in Harlem, serving up a compelling fusion of Scandinavian haute cuisine and soul food (think Swedish meatballs accompanied by yam and sweet potato purée). The buzz has been quite extraordinary, even by New York standards, and President Obama has been among the notables to pay the hotspot a visit.

Culinary fusion has an obvious appeal in a city that prides itself as an ethnic melting pot, and few have had as much success in recent years as Korean-American wunderkind David Chang, who opened a Vietnamese-inflected bistro, Má Pêche, in Midtown's Chambers Hotel (see p136) in early 2010. Chang's Momofuku Ko, the East Village showcase for his most refined cuisine, is still nearly impossible to get into. The 13-seat spot requires diners to snare reservations online – a new day opens for booking each morning – at www.momofuku.com. Suffice to say that it's one of the most sought-after tables in town. But, luckily, Chang has two other fine options in the neighbourhood: Momofuku Ssäm Bar and Noodle Bar (for both, see p84).

Legendary restaurateur Keith McNally, a master of nouveau nostalgia, has put his stamp on storied Greenwich Village literary hangout the Minetta Tavern (see p92). The interior, with its long wooden bar and vintage murals, attracts a capacity crowd largely for the scene. The food features solidly executed classics like steak, seafood and a now-famous $26 Black Label burger: a custom premium-beef blend that has upped the city's designer patty ante.

An even more indulgent throwback is the old-world, pubby Breslin Bar & Dining Room (see p112), a charming spot in the Ace Hotel with dark wood panelling and secluded booths. The latest offering from Ken Friedman and chef April Bloomfield, both of the Spotted Pig, takes the recent enthusiasm for hearty cookery to new levels. The uniformly unctuous menu features delicious yet gut-busting fare such as a borderline obscene pork belly for two; the bar and no-reservations restaurant are a zoo most nights. In fact, some of the most buzzed-about new eateries are attached to hotels. Maialino (see p118), Danny Meyer's ode to Rome, is the culinary success story of the Gramercy Park Hotel, and Locanda Verde (see p69), Andrew Carmellini's rustic Italian at the Greenwich, was by many accounts the best restaurant of the year in 2010.

The East Village has a knack for sprouting reasonably priced eateries that draw cult followings. Tiny, white-tiled shop Porchetta (see p86) specialises in prime swine – eaten straight up or in a ciabatta roll – to rival Chang's. Another exceptional

Dirt Candy p83

sandwich comes courtesy of Baoguette (see p82), which peddles some of the city's finest *banh mi*. Outrageously popular Japanese import Ippudo NY (see p84) has fuelled the growing craze for ramen, and Cal Mex transplant Dos Toros (see p83) proves you can get a good burrito in NYC.

If this city is marked by anything, it's an equal vigour for the finest dining and the most down and dirty street food. Madison Square Park's Shake Shack (see p153), which launched a spacious indoor location across from the Museum of Natural History, is several critics' choice for the city's best burger. And the Neapolitan pizza craze has shown no sign of flagging. Newcomer Kesté Pizza & Vino (see p97) creates pies made according to the Italian city's exacting standards, while Motorino (see p84) has expanded to include an East Village storefront in addition to its Williamsburg flagship.

New York's farm-to-table movement is perhaps most robust in Brooklyn, which some people are hailing as the new Berkeley, referring to the West Coast home of Alice Waters (Chez Panisse) and the better-known American foodie revolution. The DIY spirit and devotion to local purveyors and ingredients are arguably the borough's dining culture's most distinguishing features. The nerve centre of the movement is Roberta's in Bushwick (261 Moore Street, at Bogart Street, 1-718 417 1118, www.robertaspizza.com), which has its own rooftop garden and plays host to the Heritage Food Network's sustainable-eats radio station. Enjoy urban-rustic menus and salvaged-wood-furnished environments at the unpretentious Buttermilk Channel in Carroll Gardens (524 Court Street, at Huntington Street, 1-718 852 8490, www.buttermilkchannelnyc.com); or nostalgic Rye in Williamsburg (247

SHORTLIST

Best new
- ABC Kitchen (see p112)
- Fedora (see p97)
- John Dory Oyster Bar (see p114)
- Red Rooster (see p159)

Where to blow the budget
- Daniel (see p149)
- Megu (see p69)
- Per Se (see p153)

Best cheap eats
- Baoguette (see p82)
- Dos Toros (see p83)
- Torrisi Italian Specialties (see p74)

Best American faves
- Amy Ruth's (soul food) (see p159)
- Barney Greengrass (Jewish 'appetizing') (see p152)
- Corner Bistro (burger: cheap) (see p97)
- Crif Dogs (hot dogs) (see p82)

Best cocktail bars
- PDT (see p84)
- The Summit (see p86)
- Vandaag (see p86)

Best dives
- Holiday Cocktail Lounge (see p83)
- International Bar (see p84)
- Rodeo Bar & Grill (see p118)

Best rooftop bars
- The Delancey (see p78)
- Jimmy at the James Hotel (see p67)
- 230 Fifth (see p112)

The classics
- Bemelmans Bar (see p148)
- Grand Central Oyster Bar & Restaurant (see p136)
- Keens Steakhouse (see p119)

South 1st St, between Havemeyer & Roebling Streets, 1-718 218 8047, www.ryerestaurant.com).

Elsewhere, there are cheek-by-jowl Asian restaurants in Chinatown, while Koreatown, the stretch of West 32nd Street between Fifth Avenue and Broadway, is lined with Korean barbecue joints and other eateries. Further afield, Harlem offers soul food and West African cooking, while the melting pot that is Queens counts Greek (in Astoria) and Indian and Latin American (in Jackson Heights) among its globe-spanning cuisines.

Veg out

One of the city's weak spots is the relative dearth of new vegetarian dining options. Dirt Candy (see p83), from former Pure Food & Wine chef Amanda Cohen, serves sometimes sinful, always sophisticated meat-free eats (such as a vibrant and buttery signature carrot risotto). Popular Chelsea mainstay Blossom (187 Ninth Avenue, 1-212 627 1144, www.blossomnyc.com) has now brought its seitan scallopine and Brazilian mock-beef stew to both the Upper West and East Sides. Gramercy Park raw-food specialist Pure Food & Wine (54 Irving Place, between 17th & 18th Streets, 1-212 477 1010, www.purefoodandwine.com) and Counter (105 First Avenue, between 6th & 7th Streets, East Village, 1-212 982 5870, www.counternyc.com) both draw devotees.

The big tipple

The cocktail craze still reigns, spreading to the outer boroughs – mixology master Sasha Petraske's latest venture, Dutch Kills (27-24 Jackson Avenue, at Dutch Kills Street, Long Island City, Queens, 1-718 383 2724), won a *Time Out*

New York Eat Out Award in 2010. A noticeable trend in recent years has been for unmarked, speakeasy-style bars, usually with vintage looks to match. Although locals might be starting to tire of the game, seeking out these 'secret' boozing spots is part of the fun – from the fake phone booth at PDT (see p84) to the fortune teller's front at Employees Only (510 Hudson Street, between Christopher & W 10th Street, 1-212 242 3021, www.employeesonly nyc.com). Raines Law Room (see p114) in the Flatiron District, where several new watering holes – notably, the Flatiron Lounge (see p114) – have popped up, has ditched the bar altogether; instead, the memorable libations are mixed in a semi-hidden cocktail kitchen.

While covert drinking dens are still going strong, the past year has seen the growth of a counter movement. You won't have trouble spotting the new democratic beer gardens, or securing a place. Wine bars are also thriving. Terroir (see p86), the offshoot of East Village restaurant Hearth, recently gained a larger Tribeca sibling (24 Harrison Street, between Greenwich & Hudson Sts, 1-212 625 9463). At more than 150 bottles, the list has been expanded, but as at the original spot, it emphasises wines that best express their *terroir*, or sense of place.

Where there's smoke…

The only legal places to smoke indoors are either venues that cater largely to cigar smokers (and actually sell cigars as well as cigarettes) or spaces that have created areas for smokers. Try Circa Tabac (32 Watts Street, between Sixth Avenue & Thompson Street, Soho, 1-212 941 1781) or Hudson Bar & Books (636 Hudson Street, at Horatio Street, 1-212 229 2642).

Market NYC p76

WHAT'S BEST

Shopping

While it was hard to ignore the appearance of empty storefronts in the city during the initial onslaught of the Great Recession, we're pleased to report that most of our favourite independents are still in business, and there are also unmistakable signs of recovery. In fact, as rents in Manhattan have become more affordable, young designers and boutique-owners from the outer boroughs have started migrating to areas like the Lower East Side that were previously beyond their reach. Shopkeepers are also becoming more creative, launching pop-up shops and hedging their bets with mixed-use businesses, such as the Dressing Room (see p80), which combines a bar and an an impressive boutique. Increasingly, boutiques are selling a combination of goods, and the vintage trend, appealing to the environmentally aware and budget-conscious alike, is stronger than ever. Dear: Rivington (see p79) divides its retail space between designer clothes and vintage home accessories, while Voz (see p88) sells a mix of new and vintage garb, furniture and design objects.

Retail hotspots

Although many of the city's retail-rich districts are within walking distance of each other, and you can zip quickly between others on the subway, because of the dense concentration of shops in some areas (for example, the Lower East Side or Madison Avenue), you might want to limit yourself to a couple of areas in a day out.

Generally speaking, you'll find the most unusual shops Downtown and in parts of Brooklyn.

Although Soho has been heavily commercialised, especially the main thoroughfares, this once edgy, arty enclave still has some idiosyncratic survivors and numerous top-notch shops. Urban fashion abounds on Lafayette Street, while Broome Street is becoming an enclave for chic home design. To the east, Nolita has been colonised by indie designers, especially along Mott and Mulberry Streets.

Once the centre of the 'rag' trade, the Lower East Side used to be associated with bargain outlets and bagels. Now a bar- and boutique-laden patch, it's especially good for vintage, streetwear and local designers, such as Chuck Guarino's rockin' menswear line Thecast (see p80), which has launched a label for the ladies, and Victor Osborne's hip handcrafted hats. Orchard, Ludlow and Rivington Streets are retail hotspots. North of here, in the East Village, you'll find a highly browsable mix of vintage clothing, streetwear and records alongside stylish home and kids' goods, but shops are more scattered than in the Lower East Side.

Over on the other side of the island, the one-time down-at-heel wholesale meat market, stretching south from 14th Street, has become a high-end consumer playground; the warehouses of the Meatpacking District are now populated by a clutch of international designers, including Diane von Furstenberg and Stella McCartney. Meanwhile, the western strip of Bleecker Street is lined with a further cache of designer boutiques.

Most of the city's famous department stores can be found on Fifth Avenue between 42nd and 59th Streets, in the company of big-name designer flagships and chain

S H O R T L I S T

Best new
- Convent (see p79)
- Grast (see p124)
- Lisa Perry (see p149)
- Sigerson Morrison (see p150)

Best vintage
- Cheap Jack's (see p119)
- Chelsea Girl Couture (see p70)
- Housing Works Thrift Store (see p70)
- Vintage Thrift Shop (see p116)

Taste of New York
- Russ & Daughters (see p80)
- Union Square Greenmarket (see p115)
- Zabar's (see p154)

Best books and music
- Other Music (see p88)
- St Mark's Bookshop (see p88)
- Strand Book Store (see p88)

Local labels
- Alexis Bittar (see p70)
- Creatures of Comfort (see p74)
- Rag & Bone (see p99)
- Thecast (see p80)

Most unusual gifts
- Kiosk (see p71)
- Mxyplyzyk (see p93)

Best for emerging designers
- Dressing Room (see p80)
- Market NYC (see p76)

Best accessories
- Dolce Vita (shoes) (see p79)
- Erica Weiner (jewellery) (see p76)
- Fabulous Fanny's (eyewear) (see p87)
- Love, Adorned (jewellery) (see p76)

Best bargain-hunting
- Antiques Garage (see p108)
- Century 21 (see p66)

1000s of
things to do...

1000 Great Holiday Ideas

1000 Time Out things to do in London

1000 things to do in New York

1000 things to do in London for under £10

1000 things for kids to do in the holidays

1000 Time Out things to do in Britain

stores. The exceptions are Bloomingdale's and Barneys, which are both on the Upper East Side. The Uptown stretch of Madison Avenue has long been synonymous with the crème de la crème of international fashion.

It's also well worth venturing across the East River. Williamsburg, one subway stop from the East Village on the L train, abounds with idiosyncratic shops and one-off buys. As well as the main drag, Bedford Avenue, North 6th and Grand Streets are good hunting grounds for vintage clothes, arty housewares and record stores. There are further treasures in Cobble Hill, Carroll Gardens and Boerum Hill, especially on Court and Smith Streets and Atlantic Avenue; the latter has mainly been known for antiques, but cool clothiers have started to move in.

Keep it local

As America's fashion capital, and the site of the prestigious Fashion Institute of Technology and other high-profile art colleges, New York City is a magnet for creative young designers from around the country. Hot local names to look out for in independent boutiques include Mociun, by Brooklyn textile designer Caitlin Mociun, who also creates her own art-influenced prints; Rag & Bone (see p99), a marriage of contemporary style and traditional craftsmanship from Marcus Wainwright and David Neville; Built By Wendy (see p70), a laid-back line by transplanted Midwesterner Wendy Mullin; Hyden Yoo's updated menswear classics; and Nom de Guerre (see p93), a historical-edged, often military-inspired upscale streetwear label designed by a New York collective. There are also opportunities to buy

goods direct from emerging designers at a couple of weekend markets: at Market NYC (see p76), housed in a school gymnasium in Soho, you'll find anything from jewellery to art T-shirts, while at Brooklyn's Artists & Fleas (129 N 6th Street, between Bedford & Berry Streets, Williamsburg, www.artistsandfleas.com), local designers, vintage collectors and craftspeople display clothing, homeware, accessories, jewellery and gifts in a warehouse on Saturdays and Sundays.

Famous names

Of course, many visitors to New York will simply be looking to make the most of the incredible variety of big brands on offer in the city. For young, casual and streetwear labels, head to Broadway in Soho. Fifth Avenue heaves with a mix of designer showcases and mall-level megastores. Madison Avenue is more consistently posh, with a further parade of deluxe labels.

If you prefer to do all your shopping under one roof, famous department stores Macy's (good for mid-range brands), Bloomingdale's (a mix of mid-range and designer), Barneys (cutting-edge and high-fashion) and Bergdorf Goodman (luxury goods and international designer) are all stuffed with desirable goods.

Sniffing out sales

New York is fertile bargain-hunting territory. The traditional post-season sales (which usually start just after Christmas and in early to mid June) have given way to frequent markdowns throughout the year: look for sale racks in boutiques, chain and department stores. The twice-a-year Barneys

Warehouse Sale (see p149) is an important fixture on the bargain hound's calendar. And of course, as New York is home to numerous designer studios and showrooms, there is a weekly spate of sample sales. The best are listed in the Shopping & Style section of *Time Out New York* magazine and www.timeoutnewyork.com.

Top Button (www.topbutton.com) and Clothing Line (1-212 947 8748, www.clothingline.com), which holds sales for a variety of labels – from J Crew and Theory to Tory Burch and Rag & Bone, at its Garment District showroom (Second Floor, 261 W 36th Street, between Seventh & Eighth Avenues) – are also terrific resources.

Chief among the permanent sale stores is the famous Century 21 (see p66) discount trove across the street from the World Trade Center site – it's beloved of rummagers, but detested by those with little patience for sifting through less than fabulous merchandise for the prize finds. Loehmann's (see p108) and Daffy's (www.daffys.com), which has several Manhattan locations, can also come up trumps for cut-price fashion. A branch of Nordstrom Rack, the discount arm of the West Coast-born department store has recently bumped up Union Square's bargains.

Have a rummage

Flea market browsing is a popular weekend pastime among New Yorkers. Chelsea's famous Annex Antiques Fair & Flea Market may be consigned to history, but the area retains the covered market Antiques Garage (see p108) and some worthwhile antiques stores. Also check out the Hell's Kitchen Flea Market (see p108) and the excellent Brooklyn Flea (Bishop Loughlin Memorial High School,

Lafayette Avenue, between Clermont & Vanderbilt Avenues, Fort Greene, www.brooklynflea. com), which has around 150 vendors selling goods in a large schoolyard across the street from a Masonic temple. The market is open on Saturdays from April through November and goods encompass everything from vintage jewellery and crafts to salvage and locally made foodstuffs. For fine antiques, with prices to match, head for Madison Avenue in the 60s and 70s.

Consumer culture

Chains like Barnes & Noble (www.barnesandnoble.com) still dominate the book scene, but well-loved independents, such as St Mark's Bookshop (see p88) and the Strand Book Store, home to 18 miles of books (see p88), have been holding their own in the East Village for years. Housing Works Bookstore Café (see p70) doubles as a popular Soho hangout. For art books, as well as cool souvenirs, don't forget museum shops – MoMA Design & Book Store, attached to the Museum of Modern Art (see p130), the Shop at Cooper-Hewitt (see p143) and the New Museum Store (see p77) are all terrific.

When Other Music (see p88) opened opposite gigantic Tower Records in the East Village in the mid 1990s, it boldly stood as a small pocket of resistance to corporate music. Its Goliath now shuttered, Other Music rolls on, offering a well-curated selection of indie-rock favourites, world music and experimental sounds. Tucked away in a Chinatown basement, the Downtown Music Gallery (see p74) is an essential stop for seekers of avant-garde jazz and new classical.

Sullivan Room p94

Nightlife

Corner a veteran clubber – one, say, who remembers the glory days of hallowed 1970s halls Studio 54 or the Paradise Garage, 1980s alt-clubbing pioneers Danceteria or Area, or even '90s hotspots Twilo and Vinyl – and ask them how they view the Gotham nightlife scene of the new century. Actually, we'll save you the trouble: nine times out of ten, you'll get a response that falls roughly between 'Things aren't like the good old days' and 'What nightlife scene?' And there's a bit of truth to those answers (at least, the first one); compared to previous decades, the current lay of the clubland is a bit flat.

The reasons for that are many, but a crucial one is the city's attitude towards dance clubs. The minutiae of the various laws that impact on clubs could fill this guide, but here's a telling statistic: there are currently roughly 200 venues in NYC with a cabaret licence, the all-important document that allows (legal) dancing. As recently as the 1970s, the number was in the thousands.

But even the old-timers agree that the state of New York nightlife has recently got stronger. Granted, there haven't been any essential new clubs opening lately, but a bad economy can be good for clubland, fostering a more vibrant, underground (and cheaper) side of the scene, rather than spots that serve pedestrian beats and $400 bottles.

To that end, there's been a burst of 'secret-location' shindigs in the past few years, generally held in out-of-the-way warehouses and lofts. By nature, these parties can be a bitch to find out about for those not in the loop, but if you keep your eye on underground-clubbing websites, like www.rhythmism.com and www.residentadvisor.net – and, of course, your indispensable *Time Out New York* weekly clubs listings – you'll be led in the right direction.

Even the old-guard dance clubs, like Sullivan Room (see p94) and Cielo (see p99), have stepped up their games, attracting the world's top DJs. And relative newcomer Santos Party House (see p72) has helped to revitalise the downtown scene.

But it's the regular, seasonal and peripatetic parties that really stand out. P.S.1 Warm Up, a summertime soirée held every Saturday during July and August in the courtyard at MoMA P.S.1 Contemporary Art Center in Queens (see p166), attracts kids who like nothing better than to boogie down to some pretty twisted DJs. The monthly Bunker bash, one of America's top techno get-togethers, takes place in Williamsburg's Public Assembly (70 North 6th Street, between Kent & Wythe Avenues, 1-718 782 5188, www.beyondbooking.com/thebunke r). Competing for the unofficial title

of NYC's best techno party, the Blkmarket crew (www.blkmarket membership.com) hosts nights in established clubs as well as out-of-the-way warehouse spaces. And the wandering Giant Step (www.giant step.net) and Turntables on the Hudson (www.turntablesonthe hudson.com) parties never fail to bring the funk, wherever they are.

The Sunday-night tea dance Body & Soul (www.bodyandsoul-nyc.com), helmed by the DJ holy trinity of Danny Krivit, Joe Claussell and François K, is no longer a weekly affair – nowadays, three editions a year will have to do – but it's still a spectacle, with a few thousand sweaty revellers dancing their hearts out from start till finish.

Live action

The world's economic meltdown has left few industries unscathed, and the music biz is certainly no exception. Yet rock clubs here are still regularly packed and big shows sell out regardless of high ticket prices.

Upright Citizens Brigade p109

For larger seated shows, try the posh theatres further uptown. The palatial art deco Radio City Music Hall (see p135), Harlem's the Apollo Theater (see p160), and of course Carnegie Hall (plus its subterranean baby, Zankel Hall; see p127) lend historic importance to even tedious performances. Jazz at Lincoln Center's Allen Room (see p155), has a million-dollar view that threatens to steal even the *good* shows.

The rock scene's heart, however, beats Downtown and in Brooklyn. The clubs dotting the East Village and Lower East Side are too many to count, but include the Mercury Lounge (see p81), the no-nonsense spot that launched the career of the Strokes, among others. For medium-size acts, the Bowery Ballroom (see p81) remains Manhattan's hub. In recent years, its owners have taken advantage of rock's resurgence by booking larger venues. Under the Bowery Presents rubric, the company regularly books the huge Webster Hall (see p89), as well as Terminal 5 (610 W 56th Street, between Eleventh & Twelfth Avenues, 1-212 260 4700, www.terminal5nyc.com). Bowery has also branched out to Brooklyn with the Music Hall of Williamsburg (66 North 6th Street, between Kent & Wythe Avenues, 1-718 486 5400, www.musichallofwilliamsburg.com), joining such established local venues as Pete's Candy Store (709 Lorimer Street, between Frost & Richardson Streets, 1-718 302 3770, www.petes candystore.com), Public Assembly (70 North 6th Street, between Kent & Wythe Avenues, 1-718 384-4586, www.publicassemblynyc.com) and Union Pool (484 Union Avenue, at Meeker Avenue, 1-718 609 0484, www.unionpool.blogspot.com) to cement Williamsburg's rock-scene status.

While trendspotters' attention has lately been fixed on Brooklyn, the avant-garde tradition still thrives

S H O R T L I S T

Best jazz spots
- Smalls (see p100)
- The Jazz Gallery (see p72)
- The Lenox Lounge (see p160)
- Village Vanguard (see p100)

Hottest dancefloor
- Santos Party House (see p72)
- Cielo (see p99)
- Sullivan Room (see p94)
- Love (see p93)

Most storied venues
- Carnegie Hall (see p127)
- Apollo Theater (see p160)
- Radio City Music Hall (see p135)

Best for rising stars
- Joe's Pub (see p89)
- (Le) Poisson Rouge (see p94)
- Mercury Lounge (see p81)
- Metropolitan Room (see p116)

Best tiny rock clubs
- Cake Shop (see p81)
- Union Pool (see left)
- Music Hall (see left)
- Pete's Candy Store (see left)

Best gay spots
- The Eagle (see p108)
- Henrietta Hudson (see p100)
- Therapy (see p126)

Best cabarets
- Metropolitan Room (see p116)
- Oak Room (see p133)

Best for world music
- SOB's (see p72)
- Nublu (see p89)

Best for laughs
- Comix (see p100)
- Upright Citizens Brigade Theatre (see p109)

Best for partying alfresco
- P.S.1 Warm Up (see p166)

on the island, notably at John Zorn's not-for-profit East Village space the Stone (see p91). (Le) Poisson Rouge (see p94), tucked away in a Village basement, welcomes experimental rock alongside contemporary classical music and other fare.

As in any town, New York's most exciting music tends to emanate from its tiniest spaces. Joe's Pub (see p89), the classy cabaret room tucked inside the Public Theater, continues to present great acts of all genres. Cheaper, grubbier and louder is the Lower East Side's Cake Shop (see p81), which also houses a colourful, vegan-friendly café. The sight lines are ghastly and there are certainly more comfortable places in which to hang out. But the booking is vibrant and on good nights the club has the sticky air of a high-school basement party and so is the ideal setting for a scruffy rock 'n' roll show.

Tears and laughter

The cabaret scene is a confluence of opposites: the heights of polish and the depths of amateurism; intense honesty and airy pretense; earnestness and camp. One thing's for sure, it's a quintessentially New York experience. Classic performance rooms include Café Carlyle in the plush Upper East Side hotel (35 E 76th Street, at Madison Avenue, 1-212 744 1600, www.the carlyle.com) and the Oak Room at the Algonquin (see p133), but cover is high and dinner is often compulsory. A worthy alternative is the Metropolitan Room (see p116), which offers top-notch shows at reasonable prices.

If it's laughs you're after, the city's myriad comedy clubs serve as both platforms for big names and launchpads for the stars of tomorrow. The looming presence of TV sketch giant *Saturday Night Live*, which has been filmed at

Rockefeller Center since 1975, helps to ensure the presence of theatrical comedy; more influential in the day-to-day landscape, however, is the improv and sketch troupe Upright Citizens Brigade, which migrated from Chicago in the 1990s. Its theatre has been the most visible catalyst in New York's current alternative comedy boom, and a second space, in the East Village, is in the works. Other standouts include Comix (see p100) and arts-and-culture venue 92YTribeca (see p71), which is emerging as a comedy hotspot.

It's queer, it's here

New York is home to a huge number of gay subcultures. Promoters throw parties nightly for all sorts of queer scenesters, whether you're an electronica-loving twink, a pumped-up circuit boy, a tattooed trannie or a glammed-out femme. Gay nightspots aren't relegated to just one neighbourhood, either; while the West Village and Chelsea are the most established 'gaybourhoods', there's plenty to pull you to Hell's Kitchen, the East Village, and parts of Brooklyn and Queens too. Mega-clubs are practically extinct because of unfortunate city crackdowns, although a couple of the biggies – Pacha (see p126) and Webster Hall (see p89) – do offer frequent gay blowouts. The best, most consistent parties, though, are more intimate affairs held at spots like Splash (see p116) and the Eagle (see p108). While lesbians definitely get the short end of the stick when it comes to venues – Henrietta Hudson (see p100) and Cubbyhole (281 W 12th Street, at 4th Street, West Village, 1-212 243 9041, www.cubbyholebar.com) pretty much cover it in Manhattan – the girls are, however, always welcome on the boys' turf.

tkts p122

Arts & Leisure

Given the impressive sweep of New York's cultural life, it's easy to be overwhelmed by the number of events on offer. From enormous stadia to tiny Off Broadway stages, from revival cinemas to avant-garde dance venues, the choices are endless. Even lifelong New Yorkers struggle to keep up.

With limited time, however, you can still take in that concert, game, play or ballet that will make your visit all the more memorable. Bargain tickets are often available, if you know where to hunt for them. And it's best to consult *Time Out New York* for all the latest info.

Sports

The professional sports scene has been marked by an edifice complex in the past few years, as several teams have built brand-new stadia. First it was baseball's turn with the 2009 openings of Citi Field in Queens and Yankee Stadium in the Bronx, the respective homes of the hapless Mets (newyork.mets.mlb.com) and the mighty Yankees (newyork.yankees.mlb.com).

Next came American football, when the Giants and Jets kicked off their 2010 seasons in the aptly named New Meadowlands Stadium (www.newmeadowlandsstadium.com) across the river in New Jersey.

Gritty Madison Square Garden (see p120) is still home to basketball's Knicks and hockey's Rangers, but construction is underway for the Barclays Center in Brooklyn, which will become home to basketball's Nets – currently playing in New Jersey – when it opens in 2012.

AT LARGE

CHICAGO
THE MUSICAL

TELECHARGE.COM/CHICAGO or 212-239-6200
CHICAGOTHEMUSICAL.COM · AMBASSADOR THEATRE · 49TH ST. AT BROADWAY

Theatre

The very word 'Broadway' has long been shorthand for American stage success. For decades, however, discerning theatregoers turned their noses up at the Great White Way – insiders knew that the real art was to be found in smaller venues beyond Times Square.

Lately, however, that story has been changing. True, Broadway is still home to long-running hit tuners, such as *Chicago* and *Mamma Mia*, and musical versions of films (such as Elton John's *Billy Elliot*) and cartoons (*The Addams Family*) remain popular. Of late, the much-delayed *Spider-Man: Turn Off the Dark* has garnered most of Broadway's attention, with its costs and on-stage accidents (see p117), but new musicals, like *The Book of Mormon* from the makers of *South Park*, have received rave reviews.

Today, serious straight plays have become increasingly common on Broadway, lit by awesome star wattage; in recent years, Scarlet Johansson, Denzel Washington and Jude Law have all appeared on the local boards. Since tickets for these shows often go fast, you may want to check www.theatermania.com and www.playbill.com for advance information. Nearly all Broadway and Off Broadway shows are served by big ticketing agencies, but for cheap seats, your best bet is the TKTS Discount Booth (see p122).

As fun as big-budget productions are, sometimes you need a bit more intimacy; check out what's playing at Playwrights Horizons (see p129) for quality in a fairly classic mode. The Signature Theatre Company (see p129) is moving into a brand-new Frank Gehry designed complex in 2012. Downtown, the Public Theater (see p91) offers a mix of new plays and classics with excellent production values;

SHORTLIST

Best new or revamped
- Lincoln Center (see p155)
- Museum of the Moving Image (see p166)

Most experimental
- Performance Space 122 (see p91)
- Soho Rep (see p72)
- The Stone (see p91)

Best for unwinding
- Caudalie Vinothérapie Spa (see p135)
- Chelsea Piers (see p109)
- Great Jones Spa (see p91)
- Juvenex (see p120)

Best new Broadway shows
- The Book of Mormon (see p127)
- Rock of Ages (see p129)

Best Off Broadway
- Atlantic Theater Company (see p109)
- New York Theatre Workshop (see p91)
- Public Theater (see p91)

Best free outdoor arts
- Lincoln Center Out of Doors Festival (see p44)
- River to River Festival (see p41)
- Shakespeare in the Park (see p41)

Essential high culture
- Carnegie Hall (see p127)
- Metropolitan Opera House (see p156)
- New York City Center (see p127)

Best cheap tickets
- The Kitchen (see p111)
- Signature Theatre (see p129)
- TKTS (see p122)

Offset your
flight with
Trees for Cities
and make your
trip mean
something for
years to come

www.treesforcities.org/offset

Trees for Cities
Charity registration number 1032154

it also puts up a pair of free Shakespeare in the Park (see p41) productions every summer. Across the East River, the Brooklyn Academy of Music's Harvey Theater (651 Fulton Street, between Ashland & Rockwell Places, Fort Greene, 1-718 636 4100, www.bam.org) stages top-notch international offerings.

If you're looking for something a little more challenging and iconoclastic – and easier on the wallet – head below 14th Street or to Brooklyn, where avant-garde and experimental theatre still thrive. Look for Radiohole (www.radiohole.com), Elevator Repair Service (www.elevator.org), the Nature Theater of Oklahoma (www.oktheater.org) and the Civilians (www.thecivilians.org), which often appear at venues like Performance Space 122 (see p91), Soho Rep (see p72) and New York Theatre Workshop (see p91).

Film

Walking around New York is like entering a film set. Every corner – even the subway – has been immortalised in celluloid, and you might even stumble upon an actual scene being shot (the Queens-based Silvercup Studios has filmed *Gangs* *of New York* and both *Sex and the City* flicks, among many other major motion pictures and TV shows). So it's not surprising that New York has a special relationship with the movies. The calendar is packed with festivals, including Tribeca, the New York Film Festival and several others organised by the excellent Film Society of Lincoln Center (see p155). Summer brings the wonderful tradition of free outdoor screenings at Bryant Park and other parks (www.timeoutnew york.com). Cinephiles love Film Forum (see p100) for its wide range of revivals and new indie features, while Anthology Film Archives (see p89) specialises in experimental programming.

The Museum of Modern Art (see p130) and Lincoln Center's Walter Reade Theater (see p156) also offer imaginatively curated series and impeccable screening conditions; the facilities at Lincoln Center were boosted in June 2011, when the Elinor Bunin-Munroe Film Center opened with two additional screens. Yet perhaps the most eagerly anticipated opening was that of the expanded Museum of the Moving Image in Long Island City, Queens (see p163 **Queens' big screen**) in January 2011.

Museum of the Moving Image p166

Classical music & opera

Change has been the operative word at Lincoln Center (see p155) for the past few years. The renovated Alice Tully Hall has drawn near-unanimous raves for its exceptional acoustics, and with increasingly innovative programming, any sense of fustiness is gradually being shed. The Metropolitan Opera (see p156) forges ahead under the adventurous – and occasionally controversial – guidance of general manager Peter Gelb. The 2011/2012 season boasts new productions of *Don Giovanni* and *Faust* as well as *Siegfried* and *Götterdämmerung*, the third and fourth installments of Robert Lepage's acclaimed Ring Cycle (see box, p39).

Across the plaza at the rechristened David H Koch Theater (see p155), things have settled down after its 2009 budget cuts. The New York City Opera – now led by George Steel – mounts a season blessed with several New York premières (most notably Rufus Wainwright's *Prima Donna*, which will take the stage in the spring of 2012) alongside more canonical works. At the New York Philharmonic, which plays at Lincoln Center's Avery Fisher Hall (see p155), music director Alan Gilbert continues to bring innovation to the forefront without losing sight of the orchestra's past.

Venerable Carnegie Hall (see p127), is under the executive and artistic directorship of Clive Gillinson, formerly of the London Symphony Orchestra. Its three halls continue to set the standard for classical music in New York. Increasingly, however, classical music is also being heard in small, genre-mixing venues, such as (Le) Poisson Rouge (see p94) and the Stone (see p91), bringing it to a new generation of music lovers.

Dance

Tradition and innovation live side by side in New York, where the art form has remarkable breadth. Dance, of course, is not just a pointed foot: choreographers today are intent on exploring the more complex notions of performance and the body. Performance practice is honed within laboratories such as Movement Research (www. movementresearch.org), devoted to the investigation of dance and movement-based forms. In recent years, this intimate, visceral approach has manifested itself at smaller outer-borough performance spaces, such as Brooklyn's Center for Performance Research, Greenbelt, (unit 1, 361 Manhattan Avenue, at Jackson Street, Williamsburg, 1-718 349 1210, www.cprnyc.org). But that's not to suggest that New York is lacking in more established quarters. For ballet fans, there is no greater place to bask in the world of George Balanchine and Jerome Robbins than the New York City Ballet (at the David H Koch Theater, see p155). American Ballet Theatre – joined in 2009 by extraordinary Russian choreographer Alexei Ratmansky – presents a mix of full-length classics with one-act ballets by Twyla Tharp and Antony Tudor (at the Metropolitan Opera House, see p156, in spring and at New York City Center, see p127, in the autumn).

New York is still the centre of modern and postmodern dance, where choreographers like Trisha Brown, Mark Morris and Paul Taylor continue to push their own artistic boundaries. And individual contemporary voices like Sarah Michelson, John Jasperse and Ralph Lemon challenge the notion of what dance means today. Delightfully and defiantly, they prove that there is no right answer.

Calendar

Radio City Christmas Spectacular

Dates highlighted in **bold** are public holidays

September 2011

Ongoing River to River Festival (see June); P.S.1 Warm Up (see July)

4-6, 10, 11 **Washington Square Outdoor Art Exhibit**
Greenwich Village (see p92)
www.washingtonsquareoutdoorart exhibit.org
See art in streets around the park.

5 **West Indian-American Day Carnival**
Brooklyn (see p162)
www.wiadca.org
Costumed dancers parade to calypso and soca music at this colourful cultural celebration.

6 **Labor Day**

9-11 **Howl!**
East Village (see p81)
www.howlfestival.com
A reading of Allen Ginsberg's seminal poem kicks off this three-day arts fest.

15-25 **Feast of San Gennaro**
Little Italy (see p72)
www.sangennaro.org
Eleven-day street fair with a marching band and plenty of Italian eats.

mid Sept **Broadway on Broadway**
Times Square (see p122)
www.broadwayonbroadway.com
Stars perform their Broadway hits for free in Times Square.

23-25 **Dumbo Arts Festival**
Various locations in Dumbo, Brooklyn
www.dumboartsfestival.com
Concerts, forums, a short-film series and studio visits by the Dumbo artists.

25 **Atlantic Antic**
Brooklyn
www.atlanticave.org
Entertainment, ethnic food, children's activities and the inimitable World Cheesecake-Eating Contest.

30-16 Oct **New York Film Festival**
Lincoln Center (see p155)
www.filmlinc.com

October 2011

Ongoing New York Film Festival
(see Sept)

8-9 **Open House New York**
Various locations
www.ohny.org
Architectural sites acros the city that
are normally off-limits open their doors
to the public for two days.

early Oct-mid Dec **Next Wave Festival**
Brooklyn
www.bam.org
Showcasing the very best in avant-
garde music, dance, theatre and opera.

11 **Columbus Day**

15-19 **CMJ Music Marathon & FilmFest**
Various locations
www.cmj.com
Showcase for new musical acts.

27 Siegfried at the Met
www.metoperafamily.org/metopera.
See box, p39.

31 **Village Halloween Parade**
Sixth Avenue, from Spring to
21st Streets, Midtown-Downtown
www.halloween-nyc.com

November 2011

Ongoing Next Wave Festival
(see Oct)

2-6 **New York Comedy Festival**
Various locations
nycomedyfestival.com
Presented in association with Comedy
Central, this five-day laugh fest
features big names and up-and-comers.

6 **ING New York City Marathon**
Various locations
www.ingnycmarathon.org
Starting on Staten Island, the runners'
course weaves through Brooklyn,
Queens and the Bronx before finishing
in Central Park.

11 **Veterans' Day**

Mid Nov-late Dec **Radio City Christmas Spectacular**
Radio City Music Hall, Midtown
www.radiocity.com
Dance troupe the Rockettes and an
onstage nativity scene with live
animals are the kitsch attractions at
this annual festive show.

Village Halloween Parade

23, 24 Macy's Thanksgiving Day Parade & Balloon Inflation
Central Park West
www.macysparade.com
Gigantic balloons and elaborate floats.

25 Thanksgiving Day

December 2011

Ongoing Next Wave Festival
(see Oct); Radio City Christmas
Spectacular (see Nov)

early Dec **Rockefeller Center Tree-Lighting Ceremony**
Rockefeller Center, Midtown
www.rockefellercenter.com
The giant evergreen is illuminated
following a star-studded line-up.
There's also a festive outdoor ice rink.

mid Dec **Unsilent Night**
Washington Square Arch,
Fifth Avenue.
www.unsilentnight.com
Phil Kline's boom box chorale parade
is one of the loveliest new music experiences you'll ever witness.

mid Dec **National Chorale Messiah Sing-In**
Avery Fisher Hall, Lincoln Center,
Upper West Side
www.lincolncenter.org,
www.messiahsingalong.com
Hallelujah! Rehearse and perform on
the spot. Novices welcome.

25 Christmas Day

31 Emerald Nuts Midnight Run
Naumburg Bandshell,
middle of Central Park
www.nyrrc.org
See in the new year with a four-mile jog
through Central Park, organised by the
New York Road Runners.

31 New Year's Eve in Times Square
Times Square, Theater District
www.timessquarenyc.org/nye
See the giant illuminated ball
descend plus celebrity performers.

January 2012

1 New Year's Day

1 New Year's Day Marathon Benefit Reading
Poetry Project, St Mark's Church-in-
the-Bowery, East Village
www.poetryproject.org
Big-name bohos step up to the mic
in this spoken-word spectacle.

17 Martin Luther King, Jr Day

27 Götterdämmerung at the Met
www.metoperafamily.org/metopera.
See box, right.

late Jan-early Feb **Winter Restaurant Week**
Various locations
www.nycvisit.com/restaurantweek
Sample delicious gourmet food at
highly palatable prices.

February 2012

Ongoing Winter Restaurant Week
(see Jan)

3 Chinese New Year
Around Mott Street, Chinatown
www.explorechinatown.com
Parades, performances and food, all
reflecting Chinese culture, during the
two weeks of the Lunar New Year.

21 Presidents' Day

late Feb-early Mar **ADAA: The Art Show**
Seventh Regiment Armory,
Upper East Side
www.artdealers.org/artshow
This vast fair, presented by the
Art Dealers Association of America,
offers the chance to peruse some of
the world's most impressive, museum-
quality pieces on the market across
70 exhibitions.

March 2012

Ongoing ADAA: The Art Show
(see Feb)

Rewiring the Ring

The Met brings Wagner into the digital age.

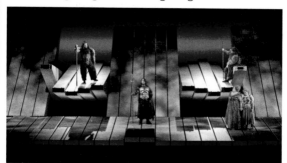

When Austrian director Otto Schenk's *Ring Cycle* opened at the Metropolitan Opera House in 1987, it was derided in Europe for being too traditional and literal and welcomed in the US for its storybook depiction of Wagner's epic culled from German and Norse myth. Yet, in the 20-plus years that it ran consistently at Lincoln Center, Wagnerites from around the globe gathered to see any or all of the four operas – *Das Rheingold*, *Die Walküre*, *Siegfried* and *Götterdämmerung*.

Since the Met's founding in 1880, the house has been a haven for the German composer. It was the first to stage the *Ring* in the US in 1889 and has been leaving audiences wired ever since. Which is why when Schenk's Valhalla fell for the last time, the idea of mounting a new *Ring* was a cause of controversy among the die-hards. Yet, if Schenk's *Ring* was a storybook, Canadian director Robert Lepage's new production is like a series of YouTube videos. Lepage's previous production for the Met, Berlioz's *La Damnation de Faust*, made use of interactive video triggered by live sound and movement and Cirque du Soleil-style acrobatics. Such innovations – and more – have been brought to the stage again. 'It's a way of dealing with this story in a way that's never been seen before,' observes the Met's music director James Levine.

Das Rheingold kicked off the 2010/11 season with singers going off the wall – with the help of bungee cords – while negotiating an intricate 45-tonne set made of 24 aluminum planks rotating on a single axis (think clothes pins on a washing line). Despite an opening-night malfunction that sabotaged the closing entrance to Valhalla, the opera was rapturously received by and large, as was *Die Walküre*, which opened in spring 2011.

The third and fourth installments of the Ring, *Siegfried* (with Deborah Voigt, Gary Lehman and Bryn Terfel) and *Götterdämmerung* (with Voigt, Lehman, Waltraud Meier and Hans-Peter König), debut during the 2011/12 season. True fans have the chance to see complete cycles of the *Ring* in April and May 2012.

Mermaid Parade p42

Mar **Ringling Bros and Barnum & Bailey Circus Animal Walk**
Midtown
www.ringling.com
True circus freaks make the trek to see elephants and zebras march on to the streets of Manhattan.

1-4 **Armory Show**
Piers 92 & 94, Hell's Kitchen
www.thearmoryshow.com
A huge contemporary art mart.

17 **St Patrick's Day Parade**
Fifth Avenue, from 44th to 86th Streets
www.saintpatricksdayparade.com
March of green-clad merrymakers.

April 2012

8 **Easter Parade**
Fifth Avenue, from 49th to 57th Streets
Admire the myriad creative Easter bonnets on show at this one-day event.

mid-late Apr **SOFA New York**
Seventh Regiment Armory, Upper East Side
www.sofaexpo.com
Giant show of Sculptural Objects and Functional Art.

late Apr-early May **Sakura Matsuri (Cherry Blossom Festival)**
Brooklyn Botanic Garden
www.bbg.org
The climax to the cherry blossom season celebrates Japanese culture with concerts, traditional dance, sword demonstrations and tea ceremonies.

late Apr-early May **Tribeca Film Festival**
Various locations
www.tribecafilm.com/festival/
Two-week festival of films organised by Robert De Niro. There's also a Family Film Festival too.

May 2012

Ongoing **Sakura Matsuri** (Cherry Blossom Festival) (see April)

6 **Bike New York: Five Boro Bike Tour**
Battery Park to Staten Island
www.bikenewyork.org
Thousands of cyclists take part in a 42-mile Tour de New York.

26-28, 2, 3 June **Washington Square Outdoor Art Exhibit**
See Sept.

Late May **Lower East Side Festival of the Arts**
Theater for the New City, 155 First Avenue, between 9th & 10th Streets
www.theaterforthenewcity.net/les.htm
Three days of theatre, poetry readings, and family-friendly programming.

30 **Memorial Day**

June 2012

Ongoing **Washington Square Outdoor Art Exhibit** (see May and Sept)

June-Aug **Central Park SummerStage**
Rumsey Playfield, Central Park
www.summerstage.org
Rockers, orchestras, authors and dance companies take to the stage.

June-Aug **Shakespeare in the Park**
Delacorte Theater, Central Park
www.publictheater.org
Join the queue for free alfresco theatre.

June-mid Sept **River to River Festival**
Various venues along the West Side & southern waterfronts of Manhattan
www.rivertorivernyc.org
More than 400 free events.

early June **National Puerto Rican Day Parade**
Fifth Avenue, from 44th to 86th Streets
www.nationalpuertoricandayparade.org
Celebrate the city's largest Hispanic community, and its culture.

early June **Red Hook Waterfront Arts Festival**

Various locations in Red Hook, Brooklyn
www.bwac.org
Neighbourhood cultural bash including dance, music and spoken word.

10 **Egg Rolls & Egg Creams Festival and Block Party**
Eldridge Street Synagogue, Lower East Side
www.eldridgestreet.org
Celebrate the convergence of Jewish and Chinese traditions with acrobats, yarmulke makers and Torah scribes.

Mid June **Museum Mile Festival**
Fifth Avenue, from 82nd to 105th Streets, Upper East Side
www.museummilefestival.org
Nine major museums are free of charge for one day every year.

mid June-late Aug **Celebrate Brooklyn!**
Prospect Park Bandshell, Brooklyn
www.bricartsmedia.org
Brooklyn's premier summer offering of music, dance, film and spoken word.

17 **Broadway Bares**
Roseland Ballroom, Theater District
www.broadwaycares.org/broadwaybares
Some of Broadway's hottest bodies *sans* costumes feature in this fundraiser.

mid June **Mermaid Parade**
Coney Island, Brooklyn
www.coneyisland.com/mermaid
Decked-out mermaids, mermen and elaborate, kitschy floats.

late June **NYC LGBT Pride March**
From Fifth Avenue, at 52nd Street, to Christopher Street
www.hopinc.org
Downtown becomes a sea of rainbow flags for the annual Pride event.

late June-early July **Summer Restaurant Week**
Various locations
www.nycvisit.com/restaurantweek
See Jan Winter Restaurant Week.

Mid June-mid July **Midsummer Night Swing**
Lincoln Center Plaza, Upper West Side
www.lincolncenter.org
Dance under the stars to salsa, Cajun, swing and other music for three weeks.

July 2012

Ongoing Shakespeare in the Park (see June); River to River Festival (see June); Midsummer Night Swing (see June); Summer Restaurant Week (see June)

Macy's Fourth of July Fireworks p44.

Tis the season...

...to blitz your gift list at the city's festive markets.

Festive fare at the Bryant Park fair

The Holiday Shops at Bryant Park
Where Bryant Park, between Fifth & Sixth Avenues and 40th & 42nd Streets (1-212 661 6640, www.theholidayshopsat bryantpark.com).
When Late Oct-early Jan
Why go Clustered around a seasonal skating rink, the 125 glassed-in shoplets are part of an entire festive microcosm.
What to buy Although some of the wares skirt tourist-craft-shop territory, there are plenty of unusual finds: jewellery and accessories, toys, foodstuffs and household devices.

Gifted
Where Location varies (www.brooklynflea.com).
When Late Nov-late Dec.
Why go This isn't your grandma's holiday market. As it's run by the folks behind the cult phenomenon Brooklyn Flea, you won't find any cheesy reindeer tree ornaments here – unless they're of the ironic variety.
What to buy Unsurprisingly, the market has a prominent vintage strand, but it's also strong on cool home design, handmade jewellery and other arty wares.

Grand Central Holiday Fair
Where Grand Central Terminal, Lexington Avenue, at 42nd Street (1-212 340 2345, www.grandcentralterminal.com).
When Late Nov-late Dec.
Why go Featuring more than 70 microboutiques, this elegant affair gives you a peek inside Vanderbilt Hall, the station's main former waiting room.
What to buy Handpicked goods range from contemporary jewellery and art objects to African crafts and Christmas ornaments.

Union Square Holiday Market
Where South-west corner of Union Square, at 14th Street (1-212 529 9262, www.urbanspacenyc.com).
When Late Nov-late Dec.
Why go This traditional outdoor market encompasses around 150 decorated, tented booths.
What to buy Toys, toiletries, jewellery, accessories and home goods are all in the diverse mix.

4 Independence Day

July-Aug **New York Philharmonic Concerts in the Parks**
Various locations
www.nyphil.org

July-Sept **P.S.1 Warm Up**
MoMA P.S.1, 22-25 Jackson Avenue, at 46th Avenue, Long Island City
www.ps1.org
Thousands of dance fans make the pilgrimage to Long Island City on summer Saturdays to drink and dance at this resolutely underground clubbing event.

4 Macy's Fourth of July Fireworks
Waterfront locations
World-famous annual display.

4 Nathan's Famous Fourth of July International Hot Dog Eating Contest
Outside Nathan's Famous, corner of Surf & Stillwell Avenues, Coney Island, Brooklyn
www.nathansfamous.com
Eaters gather from all over the world for the granddaddy of all pig-out contests.

mid July-Aug **Harlem Week**
Various Harlem locations
www.harlemweek.com

'Week' is a misnomer; you'll find live music, art and food on tap for around a month. Great going for a culture fest, which began in 1974 as a one-day event celebrating all things Harlem.

August 2012

Ongoing Shakespeare in the Park (see June); River to River Festival (see June); New York Philharmonic Concerts in the Parks (See July); P.S.1 Warm Up (see July); Harlem Week (see July)

Aug **Lincoln Center Out of Doors**
Lincoln Center, Upper West Side
www.lincolncenter.org
Several weeks of free family-friendly classical and contemporary works.

mid-late Aug **New York International Fringe Festival**
Various locations
www.fringenyc.org
Wacky, weird and sometimes wonderful, Downtown's Fringe Festival – inspired by the Edinburgh original and due to have celebrated its 15th anniversary in 2011 – shoehorns hundreds of arts performances into 16 theatre-crammed days. Check Time Out New York magazine during the festival as it is committed to reviewing each and every event.

NYC LGBT Pride March p42

Itineraries

Woolworth Building

High Points

In *Here is New York*, EB White wrote that the city's iconic skyline 'is to the nation what the white church spire is to the village – the visible symbol of aspiration and faith, the white plume saying that the way is up.' Despite the irrevocable damage to the skyline from the 9/11 attacks, the comment still resonates with locals and visitors. From City Hall's neo-classical rotunda (1811) to the impressive International style slab of Chase Manhattan Plaza (1960) to the shifting surfaces of Frank Gehry's 8 Spruce Street (2011), New York's architecture never ceases to awe.

Above all, this is a city of skyscrapers, so the logical starting point is an early-morning visit to the **Skyscraper Museum** in the Financial District (see p56). Here you can see large-scale photographs of lower Manhattan's skyscrapers from 1956, 1974 and 2004, a 1931 silent film documenting the construction of the Empire State Building, as well as

fascinating architectural artefacts, like original models of the Twin Towers and the 1,776-foot (541-metre) tall 1 World Trade Center, currently under construction.

Head out the door, make a left and follow Battery Place across West Street and along the northern edge of Battery Park. Turn left up Greenwich Street, and at Morris Street walk along Trinity Place to make a brief stop at **Trinity Church** (see p62). In stark contrast to the skyscrapers that surround it, Trinity – the third church to stand on this spot – remains frozen in Gothic Revival style designed by Richard Upjohn, but it was the island's tallest structure when it was completed in 1846, thanks to its 281-foot (86-metre)-tall spire. The churchyard, which dates back to 1697, is one of New York's oldest cemeteries. Alexander Hamilton (the nation's first secretary of the treasury – you can check out his mug on the $10 bill) is buried here.

Afterwards, it's time to visit one of the most powerfully moving sites in recent history: Ground Zero, the spot where the mighty Twin Towers once stood. From the church, continue to walk up Trinity Place for two more blocks and cross over Liberty Street. The fenced-off World Trade Center construction site is to your left. At the time of writing, the **National September 11 Memorial & Museum** is on track to debut by September 2011, and you can view models of the entire planned development at the 9/11 Memorial Preview Site (see p63 **After the fall**) on Vesey Street.

From the place where New York's tallest towers fell, it's onwards and upwards to the spot where the race to the heavens began. Walk up Vesey Street, then north on Broadway to the **Woolworth Building** (No. 233, at Barclay Street). Note the flamboyant Gothic terracotta cladding designed by Cass Gilbert in 1913. The 55-storey, 793-foot (242-metre) 'Cathedral of Commerce' was the world's tallest structure for 16 years until it was topped by 40 Wall Street.

The Woolworth Building overlooks City Hall Park. Walk through the park and aim for the foot of the **Brooklyn Bridge** (see p162). Our sojourn is about buildings, not bridges – but we wouldn't mind if you made a detour here; it takes an hour to walk out to the middle of the bridge and back, allowing plenty of time to gaze upon the East River and marvel at the web of steel cables.

Back to the current plan: once you've passed through the park (bordered to the east by Park Row), look for a subway entrance to your left. Board the Uptown 4 or 5 train to Grand Central-42nd Street. On the subway, consider this: it took ten years of unflagging effort for Jacqueline Kennedy Onassis and others to save **Grand Central Terminal** (see p135), your next destination. After the glorious (original) Pennsylvania Station was demolished in 1963, developers unveiled plans to wreck Grand Central, which opened in 1913, and erect an office tower in its place. Jackie O would have none of it and rallied politicians and celebrities to her cause. In 1978, her committee won a Supreme Court decision affirming landmark status for the beloved Beaux Arts building. When you exit the subway, head upstairs and take in the thrilling main concourse. Curiously, the constellations on the ceiling are drawn in reverse, as if you were staring down from space.

By now you'll likely be famished. Head back downstairs to one of Manhattan's most famous eateries, the **Grand Central Oyster Bar & Restaurant** (Lower Concourse; see p136), for a late lunch. Before heading inside, linger a moment under the low ceramic arches, dubbed the 'whispering gallery'. Instruct a friend to stand in an opposite, diagonal corner from

Empire State Building

ITINERARIES

you and whisper sweet nothings to each other – they'll sound as clear as if you were face to face.

Revitalised, you're ready for the next stop: **Columbus Circle**. Either hop back on the subway (S to Times Square, transfer to the Uptown 1 train and get off at 59th Street-Columbus Circle) or, preferably, you can hoof it there in about 30 minutes. Exit Grand Central on 42nd Street and head west. At Fifth Avenue, you'll pass by another Beaux Arts treasure from the city's grand metropolitan era, the **New York Public Library** (see p130); the sumptuous white-marble façade recently underwent a restoration for its centennial in May 2011. Built on a former Revolutionary War battleground, the library now sits on the greensward known as Bryant Park. When you get to Broadway, make a right and head north into Times Square. Imposing, sentinel-like skyscrapers mark the southern entry to the electric carnival here; the 2000 **Condé Nast Building** (4 Times Square) and the 2001 **Reuters Building** (No.3), both by Fox & Fowle, complement Kohn Pedersen Fox's 2002 postmodern **5 Times Square** and the David Childs' 2004 **Times Square Tower** (No.7). Take a detour if you want to see Renzo Piano's sparkling 2007 **New York Times Building** (620 Eighth Avenue, between W 40th & 41st Streets), one block west and a couple of blocks' south. The glass-walled design is a representation of the newspaper's desire for transparency in reporting the news.

Back on Broadway, walk north on the pedestrian-packed sidewalks until you spot Christopher gazing out from his perch in the centre of Columbus Circle at 59th Street. The renovated traffic circle, with its ring of fountains and benches, is the perfect place to contemplate another set of twin towers, the 2003 **Time Warner Center**, also designed by David Childs.

Increasingly, skyscrapers are incorporating green design, to minimise the impact of construction on the environment. Lord Norman Foster's extraordinary 2006 **Hearst Magazine Building** (959 Eighth Avenue, at W 57th Street) is a shining example. Look south-west and you can't miss it; it's the one that resembles a giant greenhouse.

At this point you have two options. The first is to end the day at the Time Warner Center and enjoy the staggering view from a leather chair in the **Mandarin Oriental Hotel**'s Lobby Lounge, perched 35 floors in the air. The drinks prices here are equally staggering, but the Fifth Avenue and Central Park South skylines make it worth the splurge. Alternatively, you can hail a cab and top off a day of skyscraper gazing with a panoramic view from either New York's tallest tower, the **Empire State Building** (see p129), or the **Top of the Rock** observation deck at **Rockefeller Center** (see p132). The latter has an edge as it affords a great view of the former. Also look out for William Van Alen's silver-hooded **Chrysler Building** (see p135). The acme of art deco design, it was part of a madcap three-way race to become the world's tallest building just before the Depression. The competitors were **40 Wall Street** (now the Trump Building) and the Empire State Building. Van Alen waited for the first to top out at 927 feet before unveiling his secret weapon – a spire assembled inside the Chrysler's dome and raised from within to bring the height to 1,046 feet (319 metres). At 102 storeys and 1,250 feet (381 metres), the Empire State Building surpassed it only 11 months later.

Central Park

Garden Variety

Smack in the middle of Manhattan, **Central Park** (see p137) serves as the city's year-round playground, nature reserve, fitness centre and meat market. Its 843 acres (3.4 square kilometres) were opened to the public in 1857, and, a year later, the newly formed Central Park Commission hired landscape designer Frederick Law Olmsted and architect Calvert Vaux to turn what was a vast tract of rocky swampland into a rambling oasis of lush greenery. The Commission, inspired by the great parks of London and Paris, imagined a place that would provide city dwellers with a respite from the crowded streets. Finally completed in 1873, it became the first man-made public park in the US.

This gentle two-hour stroll takes in the park's iconic sights and film locations. Enter the park at Scholars' Gate, at 60th Street and Fifth Avenue, and head north along the path past the portrait painters and souvenir vendors to the Central Park Wildlife center. A collection of animals has been kept in Central Park since the 1860s, but in its current form, the **Central Park Zoo** dates only from 1988. Neither as large nor as celebrated as the Bronx Zoo (see p161), it is home to some 130 species who inhabit its 6.5-acre corner of the park. The sombre brick building across from the zoo's entrance spent time as the American Museum of Natural History's first home from 1869 to 1877 and is now the administrative centre of the Parks Department.

North of the zoo, you'll encounter one of New York's most beloved attractions. The **Delacorte Musical Clock** springs to life on the half hour, when a menagerie of bronze animals – look for the violin-playing hippo and the drum-beating penguin – take their turn just beneath the clock, while two monkeys sound the bell at the top. The troupe has 44 tunes in its repertoire, which changes with the

Central Park Zoo p49

season, but you can generally count on a rendition of 'Three Blind Mice'.

Continue north, passing through the Denesmouth Arch (completed in 1859), and you'll come to the modest **Tisch Children Zoo**. The Lehman Gates at the entrance were designed by Paul Manship, whose iconic *Atlas* and *Prometheus* statues grace Rockefeller Center (see p132).

Just beyond the next overpass, the path forks. Veer left until you reach the bronze statue of **Balto**, a malamute who led a team of sled dogs transporting the diphtheria serum to Nome, Alaska, during a horrendous blizzard in January 1925 to prevent a potential epidemic. Although the dog's death was

mistakenly reported in the press, he was in fact brought to New York ten months later and was actually present at the statue's unveiling.

Continue past the statue and under the archway, then turn left until you reach **the Mall**, an elm-lined promenade that attracts in-line skaters, street performers and strolling couples who recall Billy Crystal and Meg Ryan's autumn turn here in *When Harry Met Sally* (1989). A host of statues survey the human parade. At the Mall's southern end, Christopher Columbus is perched across from William Shakespeare. This bronze Bard was sculpted in 1872 by John Quincy Adams Ward, most famous for his rendition of George Washington on the steps of Wall Street's Federal Hall. As you make your way north, you'll encounter Robert Burns seated on a tree stump (1880) and Sir Walter Scott, an 1872 statue based on Edinburgh's Memorial.

Heading further north along the Mall brings you to the **Naumberg Bandshell**, which has been staging concerts since 1923. Acts as varied as Benny Goodman, Duke Ellington and the Grateful Dead have graced the stage, and it has served as the backdrop for scenes of numerous films, notably *Breakfast at Tiffany's* (1961) and *Hair* (1980).

At the northern end of the Mall, follow the central staircase down to the subterranean **Bethesda Terrace Arcade**. Erected in 1860, it is the work of an obscure Englishman named Jacob Wrey Mould. He designed the *trompe l'oeil* paintings on the arcade's marble-paneled walls as well as the colourful ceiling, composed of tiles made by the English firm of Mintons (who were also responsible for the floor of the United States Capitol building). More than 15,000 ceramic tiles grace the arcade.

Beyond the arcade lies the Moorish-styled **Bethesda Terrace**. One of the city's true gems, it attracts an eclectic array of street musicians, models and photographers engaged in fashion shoots, and jugglers and gawkers; it's easy to see why Woody Allen and Diane Keaton enjoyed people watching here in *Annie Hall* (1977). The terrace's centrepiece is the iconic **Angel of the Waters** fountain, created by Emma Stebbins in 1873. It depicts an angel blessing the Pool of Bethesda from the Gospel of John and commemorates the Croton water system, which began transporting fresh water to the city from upstate New York in 1842. The statue comes to life at the beginning of Tony Kushner's *Angels in America* (2003) and is evoked at the end of the film as a symbol of hope.

Duly inspired, retrace your steps up one of the staircases on the outer sides of the Bethesda Terrace Arcade and pause to appreciate the intricate sandstone carvings.

Reaching the top, you're at the 72nd Street cross-town tranverse. Olmsted and Vaux planned four sunken roadways that were intended to cross the park unobtrusively, but this particular transverse is actually quite a stately avenue. Follow it west for about 200 yards and you'll note the bronze statue of **The Falconer** perched on a rock on your left. This 1875 replica of a George Blackall Simonds sculpture that was shown at the Royal Academy exhibition in London earlier that year is a true survivor. Both the falcon and the arm holding it aloft have been targets of thieves, but the current version was repainted in 1995.

About 150 feet (46 metres) further on, the 72nd Street transverse intersects the West Drive, which courses up the length of the park. Cross just above the intersection and you'll find a rising path that leads through **Strawberry Fields**. A tribute to John Lennon, who lived in, and was shot in front of, the nearby Dakota Building, on December 8, 1980, Strawberry Fields is a 2.5 acre area landscaped in the shape of a teardrop. More than 160 species of flowers and plants bloom here, including strawberries. Further up the path, you'll find the circular, black-and-white **Imagine** mosaic that was designed by artists from Naples. Leaving the park at 72nd Street and Central Park West, you'll see the Dakota Building on the northwest corner, where Lennon lived the last years of his life. The building was also the home of Mia Farrow in the film *Rosemary's Baby* (1968).

ITINERARIES

Washington Square

Literary Greenwich Village

Although its genteel townhouses and upscale restaurants might seem at odds with its bohemian reputation, Greenwich Village was once the city's answer to Paris' Left Bank. As the rich moved uptown following World War I, free thinkers and artists – most notably writers – from all over the world began to move in, taking advantage of the cheap rents and large apartments. In the 1950s the Beat poets made the area their own. You'd need a lot more than a struggling writer's salary to inhabit its leafy streets today, but many of the literary landmarks remain.

We suggest taking this half-day outing in the afternoon. Start with an espresso at the oldest coffeehouse in the village, **Caffe Reggio** (119 MacDougal Street, between Bleecker & W 3rd Streets, 1-212 475 9557), open since 1927. The carved wooden chairs and relaxed vibe maintain the cosy feel that appealed to Jack Kerouac, native Villager Gregory Corso and other Beat poets.

Sadly, the **San Remo Café** has not survived. Formerly located on the northwest corner of Bleecker and MacDougal Streets, it was one of literary bohemia's hotspots during the 1950s and '60s. Tennessee Williams, James Baldwin, Dylan Thomas and assorted Beats were habitués at this bar, which Dawn Powell, novelist and satirist of Village life, regarded as one of four bars that marked the boundaries of 'the cultural and social hub of New York City'. Kerouac is rumoured to have picked up Gore Vidal here.

Heading north, you'll pass the recently renovated **Provincetown Playhouse** (133 MacDougal Street, between W 3rd & 4th Streets), former home to the Provincetown Players (1916-29), a seminal group that introduced the works of leading members Eugene O'Neill, Djuna Barnes and Edna St Vincent Millay, among others. Although the Players didn't survive the Crash of 1929, the Playhouse continued as one of America's foremost independent theatres, premiering the works of David Mamet and John Guare, as well as the first NYC production of Edward Albee's **Zoo Story**, the city's quintessential drama.

Just across the street, at **Nos 130-132**, Louisa May Alcott lived from 1867 to 1870. It was here, while convalescing from typhoid she contracted as a nurse during the Civil War, that she finished her masterpiece *Little Women*.

If the stately townhouses along the northern fringe of **Washington Square** still evoke Henry James' novel of that name, it's no small tribute to their preservation. Although the actual inspiration for the novel (James' grandmother's home at No.18) has not survived, the townhouses along Washington Square North provide a good indication of its august world. Edith Wharton lived at No.7 in 1882, while John Dos Passos commenced work on his *Manhattan Transfer* while briefly living in No.3 in 1925. At No.38 Washington Square South, Eugene O'Neill consecrated his first New York residence by having an affair with journalist Louise Bryant, while her husband, John Reed (author of *Ten Days That Shook the World*) was in hospital.

Leave the square via Fifth Avenue and head north, turning left on 10th Street, which brings you to Sixth Avenue and the Jefferson Market Library. Just behind it, off 10th, lies **Patchin Place**, former home to some of the leading luminaries of New York's literary pantheon. This cul-de-sac lined with brick houses built during the mid-19th century is off-limits to the public, but through the gate you can make out No.1,

which Reed and Bryant made their home; No.4, where the poet and foe of capitalisation e.e. Cummings resided from 1923 to 1962; and No.5, where Djuna Barnes, author of *Nightwood*, lived from 1940 to 1982. Ezra Pound, Theodore Dreiser and John Cowper Powys also lived here briefly.

Dylan Thomas, the self-destructive Welsh poet whose final years living in the Chelsea Hotel were marked by prodigious bouts of drinking, found liquid solace in the Village. His favourite watering hole – the **White Horse Tavern** (567 Hudson Street, at W 11th Street, 1-212 243 9260) – was also beloved of Kerouac, Anaïs Nin, Baldwin and Norman Mailer. Thomas made the place his own, and a portrait of the poet hangs over his favourite table – although the story of him drinking 18 straight whiskys and expiring on the premises is a myth. He gave his mistress that highly unlikely figure upon returning from the White Horse on 4 November 1953, then slept it off before heading back to the bar for two glasses of beer. Returning to the Chelsea, he collapsed and later died.

If you've made reservations, head straight down Bleecker Street, taking a left at Carmine Street, on to Minetta Lane and back to MacDougal. Here, revived hotspot the **Minetta Tavern** (see p92) was once a haunt for literati of the calibre of Ernest Hemingway and F Scott Fitzgerald, as well as the famously blocked – like Joe Gould, whose dry spell was recounted in Joseph Mitchell's *Joe Gould's Secret*. If you can't secure a table, or if the celebrated $28 Black Label burger seems a tad steep, head north to the **Corner Bistro** (see p97) at the junction of W 4th and Jane Streets, where the burgers are consistently rated among the city's best.

ITINERARIES

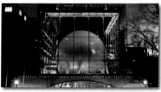

New York by Area

Financial District

Downtown

The southern tip of Manhattan has always been the city's financial, legal and political powerhouse. It's where New York began, and it's where the 19th-century influx f immigrants infused the city with new energy. Yet with much of it off the Big Apple's orderly grid, Downtown doesn't conform to the standard. The landscape shifts rom block to block. In the Financial District, gleaming skyscrapers rub shoulders with 18th-century landmarks; Tribeca's haute cuisine dining spots are only a short hop from Chinatown's frenetic food markets and restaurants; and around the corner from the clubs of the Meatpacking District, impeccably dressed matrons tend to the delicate gardens of their West Village brownstones. The character of these diverse neighbourhoods is constantly changing, but while the counterculture that erupted in Greenwich Village and the Lower East Side may have been tamed by development, iconoclastic art, music and retail still thrive.

Financial District

Commerce has been the backbone of New York's prosperity since its earliest days. The southern point of Manhattan quickly evolved into the Financial District because, in the days before telecommunications, various banks established their headquarters near the port. Wall Street, which took its name from a defensive wooden wall built in 1653 to mark the northern limit of Nieuw Amsterdam, is synonymous with the world's greatest den of capitalism. On the eastern shore of lower Manhattan, old buildings in the disused South Street Seaport area were redeveloped in the mid 1980s into restaurants, bars and stores. Also check out the views of Brooklyn Bridge (see p162).

Sights & museums

City Hall

City Hall Park, from Vesey to Chambers Streets, between Broadway & Park Row (1-212 639 9675, www. nyc.gov/designcommission). Subway J, M, Z to Chambers Street; R to City Hall; 2, 3 to Park Place; 4, 5, 6 to Brooklyn Bridge-City Hall. **Open** *Tours* (individuals) noon Wed, 10am Thur; (groups) 10am Mon, Tue, Wed, Fri. **Admission** free. **Map** p58 C2 ❶
Designed by French émigré Joseph François Mangin and native New Yorker John McComb Jr, the fine, Federal-style City Hall was completed in 1812. Tours take in the rotunda, with its splendid coffered dome; the City Council Chamber; and the Governor's Room, which houses a collection of 19th-century American political portraits as well as historic furnishings (including George Washington's desk). Individuals can book for the Thursday-morning tour (at least two days in advance); alternatively, sign up at the Heritage Tourism Center at the southern end of City Hall Park on the east side of Broadway, at Barclay Street, for Wednesday's first-come, first-served tour at noon.

Fraunces Tavern Museum

2nd & 3rd Floors, 54 Pearl Street, at Broad Street (1-212 425 1778, www. frauncestavernmuseum.org). Subway J, M, Z to Broad Street; 4, 5 to Bowling Green. **Open** noon-5pm Mon-Sat. **Admission** $10; free-$5 reductions; free under-6s. **Map** p58 C4 ❷
True, George Washington slept here, but the Colonial Revival building before you was actually constructed in 1907 in the style of the general's era. The actual 18th-century tavern that was favoured by Washington during the Revolution has long since disappeared. The museum itself features a collection of flags, paintings devoted to events of the Revolutionary War, and such Washington relics as one of his

false teeth and a lock of his hair. It was here, after the British had finally been defeated, that Washington took tearful farewell of his troops and vowed to retire from public life. Luckily, he had a change of heart six years later and became the country's first president.

Governors Island

1-212 440 2202, www.govisland.com. Subway R to Whitehall Street; 1 to South Ferry; 4, 5 to Bowling Green; then take ferry from Battery Maritime Building at Slip no.7. **Open** *late May-late Sept* 10am-5pm Fri; 10am-7pm Sat, Sun. **Admission** free. **Map** p58 C5 ❸
A seven-minute ride on a free ferry takes you to this seasonal island sanctuary, a scant 800 yards from lower Manhattan. Thanks to its strategic position in the middle of New York Harbor, Governors Island was a military outpost and off-limits to the public for 200 years. It finally opened to summer visitors in 2006. The verdant, 172-acre isle still retains a significant chunk of its military-era architecture, including Fort Jay, started in 1776, and Castle Williams, completed in 1812 and for years used as a prison. Today, as well as providing a peaceful setting for cycling (bring a bike on the ferry, or rent from Bike & Roll once there), the island hosts a programme of events (see website for schedule). And where else can you have a picnic directly across from the Statue of Liberty?

Museum of American Finance

48 Wall Street, at William Street (1-212 908 4110, www.financialhistory. org). Subway 2, 3, 4, 5 to Wall Street;1 to Rector Street. **Open** 10am-4pm Tue-Sat. **Admission** $8; free-$5 reductions; free under-7s. **Map** p58 C4 ❹
Situated in the old headquarters of the Bank of New York, the Museum of American Finance's permanent collection traces the history of Wall Street and America's financial markets. Displays in the august banking hall

NEW YORK BY AREA

Downtown 1

THE BOWERY

D

FORSYTH ST
CHRYSTIE ST
ELDRIDGE ST
ALLEN ST
ORCHARD ST
HESTER ST
LUDLOW ST
ESSEX ST

See
p61
Seward
Park

E EAST BROADWAY

HENRY ST
MADISON ST

F

East
River
Park

CANAL ST
45
51 Eldridge St
Synagogue

JEFFERSON ST
CLINTON ST
MONTGOMERY ST
GOUVERNEUR ST

WATER ST

1

Confucius
Plaza

BAYARD ST
PELL ST

DIVISION ST

MADISON ST
RUTGERS ST

CHERRY ST

CHATHAM
SQ 43

HENRY ST

PIKE ST

Rutgers
Park

PARK ROW

CATHERINE ST
OLIVER ST

MONROE ST 46

MARKET ST

First Shearith
Israel Graveyard

WATER ST

ST JAMES PL

SOUTH ST

2

MANHATTAN BRIDGE

WAGNER PL

FRANKLIN D ROOSEVELT DR

DOVER ST
PECK SLIP
WATER ST 15
13
BEEKMAN ST

BROOKLYN BRIDGE

South Street
Seaport

19

8 South St
Seaport
Museum

18

17

3

16

15

DEPEYSTER ST
14

New York City
Police Museum

13

BROOKLYN

FRANKFURT LN 11

9

0   200 m

0   200 yds

© Copyright Time Out Group 2011

4

5

❶ Sights & museums

❶ Eating & drinking

❶ Shopping

❶ Nightlife

❶ Arts & leisure

include a bearer bond made out to President George Washington and ticker tape from the morning of the stock market crash of 1929. Perhaps the highlight of the collection is the ongoing 'Tracking the Credit Crisis' exhibit, a concise timeline that follows the collapse of the American finanical system from the housing bubble's burst in 2006 to the 2009 bailout.

National Museum of the American Indian

George Gustav Heye Center, Alexander Hamilton Custom House, 1 Bowling Green, between State & Whitehall Streets (1-212 514 3700, www.nmai. si.edu). Subway R to Whitehall Street; 1 to South Ferry; 4, 5 to Bowling Admission free. **Map** p58 C4 ❺
The National Museum of the American Indian's George Gustav Heye Center, a branch of the Smithsonian, displays its collection on the first two floors of Cass Gilbert's grand 1907 Custom House, one of the finest Beaux-Arts buildings in the city. On the second level, aspects of the life and culture of Native Americans are presented in rotating exhibitions in galleries radiating out from the rotunda. Craft demonstrations, native dances, films and other events take place in the Diker Pavilion for Native Arts & Culture on the ground floor.

St Paul's Chapel & Trinity Church

St Paul's Chapel 209 Broadway, between Fulton & Vesey Streets (1-212 233 4164, www.saintpauls chapel.org). Subway A, C to Broadway-Nassau Street; J, M, Z, 2, 3, 4, 5 to Fulton Street. **Open** *10am-6pm Mon-Fri; 10am-4pm Sat; 7am-3pm Sun. Trinity Church 89 Broadway, at Wall Street (1-212 602 0800, www.trinitywallstreet.org). Subway R to Rector Street; 2, 3, 4, 5 to Wall Street.* **Open** *7am-6pm Mon-Fri; 8am-4pm Sat; 7am-4pm Sun. Both* **Admission** *free.* **Map** p58 B3 ❻

Trinity Church was the island's tallest structure when it was completed in 1846 (the original burned down in 1776; a second was demolished in 1839). A set of gates north of the church on Broadway allows access to the adjacent cemetery, where tombstones mark the final resting places of dozens of past city dwellers, including such notable New Yorkers as Founding Father Alexander Hamilton, business tycoon John Jacob Astor and steamboat inventor Robert Fulton. The church museum displays an assortment of historic diaries, photographs, sermons and burial records. Six blocks away, Trinity's satellite, St Paul's Chapel, is more important architecturally. The oldest building in New York still in continuous use (it dates from 1766), it is one of the nation's most valued Georgian structures. Trinity Church also hosts the inexpensive lunchtime Concerts at One series (see website for details).
Event highlights Concerts at One, at Trinity Church, 1pm Thur.

Skyscraper Museum

39 Battery Place, between Little West Street & 1st Place (1-212 968 1961, www.skyscraper.org). Subway 4, 5 to Bowling Green. **Open** *noon-6pm Wed-Sun.* **Admission** *$5; $2.50 reductions.* **Map** p58 B4 ❼
The only institution of its kind in the world, this modest space explores highrise buildings as objects of design, products of technology, real-estate investments and places of work and residence. A large portion of the single gallery (a mirrored ceiling gives the illusion of verticality) is devoted to temporary exhibitions, for example the 2009 China Prophecy examined Shanghai as a model of 21st-century urban development. A substantial chunk of the permanent collection relates to the World Trade Center, including original models of the Twin Towers and the new skyscraper, 1 World Trade Center (*see right*).

After the fall

Ten years on from 9/11, the new WTC site is taking shape.

Plans for the World Trade Center's redevelopment were announced in 2003, but there was little sign of progress until spring 2010. The National September 11 Memorial is on track to be completed by the tenth anniversary of the attacks, while the museum and the 1,776-foot tall (105-floor) centrepiece skyscraper, 1 World Trade Center, are expected to be finished by 2013. At the time of writing, steel construction had risen to the 62nd floor of 1 WTC, while glass panelling had reached the 28th storey. Visitors to the 9/11 Memorial Preview Site (20 Vesey Street, at Church Street (1-212 267 2047, www.national911 memorial.org) can survey an architectural model and live webcam images of construction.

Surrounded by a plaza with 400 swamp white oak and sweetgum trees, the memorial, *Reflecting Absence*, designed by Michael Arad and Peter Walker, will comprise two one-acre 'footprints' of the destroyed towers, with 30-foot waterfalls cascading down their sides. Bronze parapets around the edges will be inscribed with the names of the dead. 'When people approach these pools and see the names of the 2,982 victims arrayed around them they will get a sense of what was here and what is no longer with us – that they're standing at a spot where ten years ago these buildings stood and now there is only a void and sky,' says Joe Daniels, president of the National September 11 Memorial.

The museum's atrium will house two steel columns salvaged from the base of the Towers. Inside, visitors can descend to the original foundations alongside a remnant of the Vesey Street staircase known as the 'Survivors' Stairs'.

'We're building an eight-acre green roof that will introduce this area of lower Manhattan back into lower Manhattan,' explains Daniels. 'Beneath it will be the heart of the Memorial Museum. When you go down to bedrock, you'll be able to walk on the space where the Twin Towers stood.'

Ellis Island Immigration Museum

South Street Seaport Museum

Visitors' centre, 12 Fulton Street, at South Street (1-212 748 8786, www. southstreetseaportmuseum.org). Subway A, C to Broadway-Nassau Street; J, M, Z, 2, 3, 4, 5 to Fulton Street. **Open** *Apr-Dec* 10am-6pm Tue-Sun. *Jan-Mar* 10am-5pm Thur-Sun. **Admission** $15; free-$12 reductions. **Map** p59 D3 ❽

Occupying 11 blocks along the East River, this museum is an amalgam of galleries, historic ships, 19th-century buildings and a visitors' centre. Wander around the rebuilt streets and pop in to see an exhibition on marine history before climbing aboard the four-masted 1911 barque *Peking* or the 1930 tug *WO Decker*. Although, in spring 2011, the museum's finanical struggles sparked rumours that it might have to close, efforts were being made to save it.

Staten Island Ferry

Battery Park, South Street, at Whitehall Street (1-718 727 2508, www.siferry. com). Subway 1 to South Ferry; 4, 5 to Bowling Green. **Tickets** free. **Map** p58 C5 ❾

During this commuter ferry's 25-minute crossing, you'll see superb panoramas of lower Manhattan and the Statue of Liberty. Boats leave South Ferry at Battery Park, and run 24 hours daily.

Statue of Liberty & Ellis Island Immigration Museum

Liberty Island & Ellis Island (1-212 363 3200, www.nps.gov/stli, www.ellisisland. org). Subway R to Whitehall Street; 1 to South Ferry; 4, 5 to Bowling Green; then take Statue of Liberty ferry (1-877 523 9849, www.statuecruises.com), departing roughly every 30mins from gangway 4 or 5 in southernmost Battery Park. **Open** ferry runs 9.30am-3.30pm daily. Purchase tickets online, by phone or at Castle Clinton in Battery Park. **Admission** $13; free-$10 reductions. **Map** p58 B5 ❿

The sole occupant of Liberty Island, *Liberty Enlightening the World* stands 305ft tall from the bottom of her base to the tip of her gold-leaf torch. Intended as a gift from France on America's 100th birthday, the statue was designed by Frédéric Auguste Bartholdi (1834-1904). Construction began in Paris in 1874, her skeletal iron framework crafted by Gustave Eiffel (the man behind the Tower), but only the arm with the torch was finished in time for the centennial. In 1884, the statue was finally completed – only to be taken apart to be shipped to New York, where it was unveiled in 1886. It served as a lighthouse until 1902 and as a welcoming beacon for millions of immigrants. These 'tired…poor…huddled masses' were evoked in Emma Lazarus's poem 'The New Colossus', written in 1883 to raise funds for the pedestal and engraved inside the statue in 1903. With a free Monument Pass, only available with ferry tickets reserved in advance, you can enter the pedestal and view the statue's interior through a glass ceiling. The crown opened to the public for the first time since 9/11 in July 2009; tickets cost an extra $3 and must be reserved in advance.

A half-mile across the harbour from Liberty Island is 32-acre Ellis Island, gateway to the country for over 12 million people who arrived between 1892 and 1954. In the Immigration Museum, photos and exhibits pay tribute to the hopeful souls who made the voyage, and the nation they helped transform. Visitors can also search the archives and print copies of an ancestor's records.

Tribute WTC Visitor Center

120 Liberty Street, between Church & Greenwich Streets (1-866 737 1184, www.tributewtc.org). Subway A, C to Broadway-Nassau Street; E to World Trade Center; J, M, Z, 2, 3, 4, 5 to Fulton Street; 1, R to Rector Street. **Open** 10am-6pm Mon, Wed-Sat; noon-6pm Tue; noon-5pm Sun. **Admission** $10; free-$5 reductions. **Map** p58 B3 ⓫

Created by a not-for-profit organisation started by families of the 9/11 victims, this centre serves several functions: a collective memorial; a historical testament of the events and aftermath; and a repository of artefacts from that day. Ground-floor galleries contain a timeline of the tragedy on panels the same width as the Twin Towers' windows, along with recovered objects; a strangely unharmed paper menu from the 106th-floor Windows on the World restaurant contrasts sharply with a twisted steel beam from the wreckage. The final gallery contains photographs and names of the dead. Downstairs, visitors are invited to write down their own memories or feelings, a selection of which are posted.

Eating & drinking

Adrienne's Pizzabar

54 Stone Street, between Coenties Alley and Mill Street (1-212 248 3838, www. adriennespizzabar.com). Subway R to Whitehall Street; 2, 3 to Wall Street. **Open** 11am-midnight Mon-Sat; 11am-10pm Sun. **$**. **Café**. Map p58 C4 ⑫

It feels like you're ducking out of the city for a while when eating at this bright, modern pizzeria on quaint Stone Street. The kitchen prepares nicely charred specimens featuring delectable toppings like the rich quattro formaggi. You can eat your pie at a standing-room-only bar, but we recommend stopping by for dinner, when you can savour your meal – small plates and entrées like baked sea scallops and ravioli al formaggio – in the sleek, wood-accented dining room.

Bin No. 220

220 Front Street, between Beekman Street & Peck Slip (1-212 374 9463, www.binno220.com). Subway A, C to Broadway-Nassau; J, M, Z, 2, 3, 4, 5 to Fulton Street. **Open** 4pm-4am daily. **$$**. **Wine bar**. Map p59 D3 ⑬

See box p85.

Financier Pâtisserie

62 Stone Street, between Hanover Square & Mill Lane (1-212 344 5600, www.financierpastries.com). Subway 2, 3 to Wall Street. **Open** 7am-8pm Mon-Fri; 8.30am-6.30pm Sat. **$**. **Café**. Map p58 C4 ⑭

Tucked away on a cobblestoned street, this sweet gem offers tasty café fare to those seeking a pleasant alternative to the Financial District's pubs and delis. Hot pressed sandwiches (try the croque-monsieur), salads, tarts and quiches are all good. But the pastries are where it excels, including miniature financiers, which are free with each coffee.

Other locations 35 Cedar Street, at William Street (1-212 952 3838); 3-4 World Financial Center (1-212 786 3220).

Jack's Stir Brew Coffee

222 Front Street, between Beekman Street & Peck Slip (1-212 227 7631, www.jacksstirbrew.com). Subway A, C to Broadway-Nassau Street. **Open** 7am-7pm Mon-Sat; 8am-7pm Sun. **$**. No credit cards. **Café**. Map p59 D3 ⑮

Java fiends convene at this award-winning caffeine spot that offers organic, shade-grown beans and a homely vibe. Coffee is served by espresso artisans with a knack for oddball concoctions, such as the super-silky Mountie latte, infused with maple syrup.

Shopping

Century 21

22 Cortlandt Street, between Broadway & Church Street (1-212 227 9092, www. c21stores.com). Subway R to Cortlandt Street. **Open** 7.45am-9pm Mon-Wed; 7.45am-9.30pm Thur, Fri; 10am-9pm Sat; 11am-8pm Sun. Map p58 C3 ⑯

A Gucci men's suit for $300? A Marc Jacobs cashmere sweater for less than $200? No, you're not dreaming – you're shopping at Century 21. You may have to rummage around to unearth a treasure, but with savings from 25% to 75% or more off regular prices, this is a gold mine for less-minted fashion addicts.

Tribeca & Soho

A former industrial wasteland, Tribeca (the Triangle Below Canal Street) is now one of the city's most expensive areas. Likewise, Soho (the area South of Houston Street) was once a hardscrabble manufacturing zone with the derisive nickname Hell's Hundred Acres.

Earmarked for destruction in the 1960s by over-zealous urban planner Robert Moses, its signature cast-iron warehouses were saved by the artists who inhabited them. Although the large chain stores and sidewalk-encroaching street vendors along Broadway create a crush at weekends, there are some fabulous shops, galleries and eateries in the locale.

Sights & museums

Museum of Comic & Cartoon Art

594 Broadway, Suite 401, between Houston & Prince Streets (1-212 254 3511, www.moccany.org). Subway B, D, F to Broadway-Lafayette Street; N, R, to Prince Street; 6 to Bleecker Street. **Open** noon-5pm Tue-Sun. **Admission** suggested donation $5; free under-12s. **Map** p60 C4 ⓱

Batman, Wolverine, Watchmen... No longer just for pre-pubescent kids and ageing geeks, comic books have made a major comeback on the cultural scene. But the Museum of Comic & Cartoon Art doesn't stop there: the institution embraces every genre of comic and cartoon art and hosts regular lectures and events with creators and experts. Revolving exhibitions in its two galleries feature anime, cartoons, comic strips, political satire and graphic novels, among other strands. Each spring, the museum organises the MoCCA Festival, bringing together established and emerging artists and fans for two days.

Eating & drinking

Balthazar

80 Spring Street, between Broadway & Crosby Street (1-212 965 1414, www.balthazarny.com). Subway N, R, to Prince Street; 6 to Spring Street. **Open** 7.30-11am, noon-5pm, 6pm-midnight Mon-Thur; 7.30-11am, noon-5pm, 6pm-1am Fri; 10am-4pm, 6pm-1am Sat; 10am-4pm, 5.30pm-midnight Sun. **$$**. **French**. **Map** p60 C4 ⓲

At dinner, this iconic eaterie is perennially packed with rail-thin lookers dressed to the nines. But it's not only fashionable – the kitchen rarely makes a false step and the service is surprisingly friendly. The $115 three-tiered seafood platter casts an impressive shadow, and the roast chicken on mashed potatoes for two is délicieux.

Corton

239 West Broadway, between Walker & White Streets (1-212 219 2777, www.cortonnyc.com). Subway A, C, E to Canal Street; 1 to Franklin Street. **Open** 5.30-10.30pm Mon-Thur; 5.30-11pm Fri, Sat. **$$$**. **French**. **Map** p58 B1 ⓳

When it opened in 2008, Corton was given the highest possible star rating by *Time Out New York* magazine's critics. A meal here is an extraordinary experience. Restaurateur Drew Nieporent's white-on-white sanctuary focuses all attention on chef Paul Liebrandt's finely wrought food. The presentations, in the style of the most esteemed modern kitchens of Europe, are Photoshop flawless: sweet bay scallops, for example, anchor a visual masterpiece featuring wisps of radish, marcona almonds and sea urchin.

Jimmy

NEW *15 Thompson Street, between Canal and Grand Streets (1-212 201 9118). Subway A, C, E to Canal Street.* **Open** 4pm-1am Mon-Wed, Sun; 4pm-2am Thur-Sat. **Bar**. **Map** p60 C4 ⓴

NEW YORK BY AREA

Hot on the heels of opening his buzzy Lamb's Club restaurant (see p180) at the Chatwal Hotel, nightlife impresario David Rabin debuts this top-floor drinkery at the James New York. In warm months, the space will open directly onto a rooftop pool and deck; when it's cold out, cluster around a fireplace in one corner or perch on benches upholstered in herringbone fabric. Cocktails will feature syrups made from house-grown herbs, as in the Mexican Bee Hive (silver tequila, honey, lavender syrup, lime juice and a honeycomb garnish.)

Locanda Verde

W 1377 Greenwich Street, at North Moore Street (1-212 925 3797, www.locandaverdenyc.com). Subway 1 to Franklin Street. **Open** 8-11am, 11.30am-3pm, 5.30-11pm Mon-Fri; 8am-3pm, 5.30-11pm Sat, Sun. $$. **Italian**. Map p60 B5 ㉑

Owner Robert De Niro swapped his train-wreck trattoria, Ago, for this blockbuster replacement helmed by chef Andrew Carmellini (A Voce). Carmellini's bold family-style fare is best enjoyed as a bacchanalian banquet. A single charred octopus tentacle served with tangy romesco won't last long in the middle of the table. Nor will the chef's ravioli – as delicate as silk and oozing pungent *robiola*. Locanda is the rare Italian restaurant where the desserts are worth saving room for: try the rich, crumbly brown-butter plum cake.

M1-5

52 Walker Street, between Broadway & Church Street (1-212 965 1701, www.m1-5.com). Subway J, M, N, Q, R, Z, 6 to Canal Street. **Open** 4pm-4am Mon-Fri; 8pm-4am Sat; 11am-midnight Sun. **Bar**.

Map p58 C1/p60 C5 ㉒

The name of this huge, red-walled hangout refers to Tribeca's zoning ordinance, which permits trendy restaurants to co-exist with ware-houses. The mixed-use concept also applies to M1-5's crowd: suited brokers, indie musicians and baby-faced screenwriters play pool and order from the full, well-stocked bar specialising in stiff martinis.

Megu

62 Thomas Street, between Church Street & West Broadway (1-212 964 7777, www.megunyc.com). Subway A, C, 1, 2, 3 to Chambers Street. **Open** 5.30-11pm Mon-Wed, Sun; 5.30pm-midnight Thur-Sat. $$$.

Japanese. Map p58 B2 ㉓

Since the day this awe-inspiring temple of Japanese cuisine opened in 2004, diners have criticised its overblown prices and unwieldy, complicated menu. But critics often forget to mention that this is one of the most thrilling meals you'll find in New York. Opt for the tasting menu: a parade of ingenious little bites and surprising presentations.

Osteria Morini

NEW *218 Lafayette Street, between Broome and Spring Streets (1-212 965 8777). Subway 6 to Spring Street.* **Open** 7am-1am daily. $$. **Italian**. Map p61 D4 ㉔

Chef Michael White (Alto, Marea) is one of New York's most prolific and successful Italian-American chefs, and this terrific downtown homage to a classic Bolognese tavern is the most accessible restaurant in his stable. The toque spent seven years cooking in Italy's Emilia-Romagna region, and his connection to the area surfaces in the rustic food. Handmade pastas – frail ricotta gnocchi in light tomato cream, fat *tortelli* bundles oozing an absurdly rich mix of braised meats – are fantastic across the board. Heart-stopping meats, meanwhile, include porchetta with crisp, crackling skin and potatoes bathed in pan drippings. With so much butter and cream, you might skip dessert, but don't miss head barman Eben Freeman's riffs on classic *aperitivi*.

Pegu Club

77 W Houston Street, at West Broadway (1-212 473 7348, www. beguclub.com). Subway B, D, F, M to Broadway-Lafayette Street; N, R to Prince Street. **Open** 5pm-2am Mon-Wed, Sun; 5pm-3am Thur; 5pm-4am Fri, Sat. **Bar**. Map p60 C4 ㉕

Audrey Saunders, the drinks maven who turned Bemelmans Bar (see p148) into one of the city's most respected cocktail lounges, is behind this sleek liquid destination. It has just the right element of secrecy without any awkward faux-speakeasy trickery. Tucked away on the second floor, it was inspired by a British officers' club in Burma (Myanmar). The cocktail list features classics culled from decades-old booze bibles. Gin is the key ingredient, and these are serious drinks for grown-ups.

Savoy

70 Prince Street, at Crosby Street (1-212 219 8570, www.savoynyc.com). Subway N, R to Prince Street; 6 to Spring Street. **Open** noon-10pm Mon-Thur; noon-10.30pm Fri, Sat; 6-10pm Sun. **$$$**. **American creative**. Map p60 C4 ㉖

Chef Peter Hoffman maintains his reputation as one of the godfathers of the local foods movement at this comfortable Soho stalwart, outfitted with a wood-burning fireplace (and a congenial, semicircular bar). Hoffman makes daily pilgrimages to the Union Square Greenmarket to assemble Savoy's farm-forward, aggressively seasonal menus, which include the likes of flaky halibut perched over a verdant fava bean purée; or duck, vibrantly pink within and sporting a slightly crunchy salted crust.

Shopping

Alexis Bittar

465 Broome Street, between Greene & Mercer Streets (1-212 625 8340, www.alexisbittar.com). Subway N, R

to Prince Street; 6 to Spring Street. **Open** 11am-7pm Mon-Sat; noon-6pm Sun. Map p60 C4 ㉗

Alexis Bittar, the jewellery designer who started out selling his designs from a humble Soho street stall now has three shops in which to show off his art-object designs, including his trademark sculptural Lucite cuffs and oversized crystal-encrusted earrings. All of them are handcrafted in his Brooklyn atelier.

Built by Wendy

7 Centre Market Place, at Grand Street (1-212 925 6538, www.builtbywendy. com). Subway B, D to Grand Street; J, N, Q, R, M, Z, 6 to Canal Street. **Open** noon-7pm Mon-Sat; noon-6pm Sun. Map p61 D4 ㉓

Wendy Mullin started selling handmade clothes and guitar straps in record stores in 1991. Today, her youthful men's and women's garb still maintains a homespun look and Midwestern vibe, via men's plaid flannel shirts and girlish dresses, as well as cool graphic T-shirts.

Other locations 46 North 6th Street, at Kent Avenue, Williamsburg, Brooklyn (1-718 384 2882).

Chelsea Girl Couture

186 Spring Street, between Sullivan & Thompson Streets (1-212 343 7090, www.chelsea-girl.com). Subway A, C, E, 1 to Canal Street. **Open** noon-7pm daily. Map p60 C4 ㉙

Owner Elisa Casas fills her jewel box of a space with pristine, on-trend, upscale garb from the 1920s to the '80s, including YSL, Diane Von Furstenberg and Pucci. No matter what your period proclivity, glam girls can find everything from 1950s Doris Day-style prom dresses to a ruched leopard-print frock fit for Alexis Carrington.

Housing Works Thrift Store

130 Crosby Street, between Houston & Prince Streets (1-646 786 1200, www.housingworks.org). Subway B, D,

F, M to Broadway-Lafayette Street; R to Prince Street; 6 to Bleecker Street. **Open** 11am-7pm Mon-Sat; noon-5pm Sun. **Map** p60 C4 ⑳

It's cool to donate your old duds and furniture to Housing Works, so the shelter-oriented charity's thrift stores are among the city's best. The prices aren't the lowest, but the stock is quality. If you're lucky, you can score designer pieces (in clothes and furnishings) you'd never be able to afford new. You just have to do a little rummaging.

Kiki de Montparnasse

79 Greene Street, between Broome & Spring Streets (1-212 965 8150, www. kikidm.com). Subway R to Prince Street; 6 to Spring Street. **Open** 11am-7pm Mon, Sun; 11am-8pm Tue-Sat. **Map** p60 C4 ㉛

This erotic boutique channels the spirit of its namesake, a 1920s sexual icon and Man Ray muse, with a posh array of tastefully provocative contemporary lingerie in satin and French lace. Bedroom accoutrements, including molten crystal 'dilettos' and tastefully packaged 'intimacy kits', give whole new meaning to the expression 'satisfied customer'.

Kiosk

95 Spring Street, between Broadway & Mercer Street (1-212 226 8601, www.kioskkiosk.com). Subway 6 to Spring Street. **Open** 1-7pm Mon-Sat. **Map** p60 C4 ㉜

Don't be put off by the unprepossessing, graffiti-covered stairway that leads up to this gem of a shop. Alisa Grifo has collected an array of inexpensive items – mostly simple and functional but with a strong design aesthetic – from around the world, such as Finnish chalk, colourful net bags from Germany and hairpins in a cool retro box from Mexico.

Opening Ceremony

35 Howard Street, between Broadway & Lafayette Street (1-212 219 2688, www.openingceremony.us). Subway J,

M, N, Q, R, Z, 6 to Canal Street. **Open** 11am-8pm Mon-Sat; noon-7pm Sun. **Map** p60 C5 ㉝

The name references the Olympic Games; each year Opening Ceremony assembles a group of hip US designers (Band of Outsiders, Alexander Wang, Patrik Ervell, Rodarte) and pits them against the competition from abroad in its chandelier-lit warehouse-size space. The store also features high-profile collaborations, including Chloë Sevigny's line, which channels preppy style.

Phillip Lim

115 Mercer Street, between Prince & Spring Streets (1-212 334 1160, www.31philliplim.com). Subway N, R to Prince Street; 6 to Spring Street. **Open** 11am-7pm Mon-Sat; noon-6pm Sun. **Map** p60 C4 ㉞

Since Phillip Lim debuted his collection back in 2005, he has attracted a devoted international following, who appreciate his simple yet strong silhouettes and beautifully constructed tailoring-with-a-twist. His boutique gathers together his award-winning womens- and menswear and accessories under one roof.

Nightlife

92YTribeca

200 Hudson Street, between Canal & Desbrosses Streets (1-212 601 1000, www.92ytribeca.com). Subway A, C, E, 1 to Canal Street. **Map** p60 B5 ㉟

The downtown outpost of the 92nd Street Y, 92YTribeca is ostensibly a cultural centre for hip young Jews. It hosts regular evenings of stand-up, plus storytelling and singalong musical film screenings. The club – which houses a performance space, screening room, art gallery and café – has become one of the most daring music venues in Manhattan. Its breadth is impressive, featuring obscure indie-rock, world music, country and mixed-media shows.

Santos Party House

*96 Lafayette Street, at Walker Street
(1-212 584 5492, www.santosparty
house.com). Subway J, M, N, Q, R, Z,
6 to Canal Street.* **Open** usually 7pm–
4am daily. **Map** p58 C1 ③⑥
Launched by a team that includes rocker
Andrew WK, Santos Party House – two
black, square rooms done out in a bare-
bones, generic club style – was initially
hailed as a scene game-changer. While
those high expectations didn't exactly
pan out, it's still a solid choice, featuring
hip hop to underground house.

SOB's

*204 Varick Street, at Houston Street
(1-212 243 4940, www.sobs.com).
Subway 1 to Houston Street.*
Map p60 B4 ③⑦
The titular Sounds of Brazil (SOB, ged-
dit?) are just some of the many global
genres that keep this spot hopping. Hip
hop, soul, reggae and Latin beats all figure in the mix, with BLK JKS, Gil Scott-
Heron and Eddie Palmieri each
appearing of late. The drinks are expensive, but the sharp-looking clientele
doesn't seem to mind.

Arts & leisure

HERE

*145 Sixth Avenue, between Broome
& Spring Streets (1-212 647 0202,
Smarttix 1-212 868 4444, www.
here.org). Subway C, E to Spring
Street.* **Map** p60 C4 ③⑧
This recently renovated Soho arts complex, dedicated to not-for-profit arts
enterprises, has been the launch pad
for such well-known shows as Eve
Ensler's *The Vagina Monologues*. It
has also showcased the talents of pup-
peteer Basil Twist, singer Joey Arias
and playwright-performer Taylor Mac.

Jazz Gallery

*290 Hudson Street, between Dominick
& Spring Streets (1-212 242 1063,
www.jazzgallery.org). Subway A, C, E
to Spring Street.* **Map** p60 B4 ③⑨

The fact that there's no bar here should
be a tip-off: the Jazz Gallery is a place
to witness true works of art, from the
sometimes obscure but always interesting jazzers who play the club (Lee
Konitz and Steve Coleman, to name a
couple) to the photos and artefacts
displayed on the walls. The diminutive
room's acoustics are sublime.

Soho Rep

*46 Walker Street, between Broadway
& Church Street (Smarttix 1-212 868
4444, www.sohorep.org). Subway A,
C, E, N, R, 6 to Canal Street; 1 to
Franklin Street.* **Map** p58 C1/p60 C5 ④⓪
Although this Off-Off mainstay has
moved to an Off Broadway contract,
tickets for most shows have remained
cheap. Artistic director Sarah Benson's
programming is diverse and adventurous. Recent productions have included
works by Dan LeFranc, Sarah Kane
and the Nature Theater of Oklahoma.

Chinatown, Little Italy & Nolita

Take a walk in the area south
of Broome Street and east of
Broadway, and you'll feel as though
you've entered a different continent.
New York's Chinatown is one of
the largest Chinese communities
outside Asia. The crowded streets
are lined by fish-, fruit- and
vegetable-stocked stands, and Canal
Street is infamous for its (illegal)
knock-off designer handbags,
perfumes and other goods among
the numerous cheap gift shops. But
the main attraction is the food: Mott
Street, between Kenmare and Worth
Streets, is lined with restaurants.

Little Italy once stretched from
Canal to Houston Streets, between
Lafayette Street and the Bowery,
but these days a strong Italian
presence can only truly be
observed on the blocks immediately
surrounding Mulberry Street.

Ethnic pride remains, though: Italian-Americans flood in from across the city during the 11-day Feast of San Gennaro (see p36). Nolita (North of Little Italy) became a magnet for pricey boutiques and trendy eateries in the 1990s. Elizabeth, Mott and Mulberry Streets, between Houston and Spring Streets, in particular, are home to hip designer shops.

Sights & museums

Museum of Chinese in America

NEW *215 Centre Street, between Grand & Howard Streets (1-212 619 4785, www.mocanyc.org). Subway J, M, N, Q, R, Z, 6 to Canal Street.* **Open** 11am-5pm Mon, Fri; 11am-9pm Thur; 10am-5pm Sat, Sun. **Admission** $7; free-$4 reductions; free to all Thur. **Map** p59 D1/p61 D5 ④

Designed by prominent Chinese-American architect Maya Lin, MoCA has reopened in an airy former machine shop. Its interior is loosely inspired by a traditional Chinese house, with rooms radiating off a central courtyard and areas defined by screens. MoCA's core exhibition traces the development of Chinese communities in the US from the 1850s to the present through objects, images and video. Innovative displays (drawers open to reveal artwork and documents, and portraits are presented in a ceiling mobile) cover the development of industries such as laundries and restaurants in New York, Chinese stereotypes in pop culture, and the suspicion and humiliation Chinese-Americans endured during World War II and the McCarthy era. A mocked-up Chinese general store evokes the feel of these multipurpose spaces, which served as vital community lifelines for men severed from their families under the 1882 Exclusion Act, which restricted immigration. A gallery is devoted to temporary exhibitions.

Eating & drinking

Café Habana

17 Prince Street, at Elizabeth Street (1-212 625 2001, www.ecoeatery.com). Subway N, R to Prince Street; 6 to Spring Street. Open 9am-midnight daily. **$**. **Cuban**. **Map** p61 D4 ④

Trendy Nolita types storm this chrome corner fixture for the addictive grilled corn: golden ears doused in fresh mayo, chargrilled, and generously sprinkled with chilli powder and grated *cotija* cheese. Staples include a Cuban sandwich of roasted pork, ham, melted swiss and pickles, and beer-battered catfish with spicy mayo. At the takeout annexe next door (open May-Oct), you can get that corn-on-a-stick to go.

Dim Sum Go Go

5 East Broadway, between Catherine & Oliver Streets (1-212 732 0797). Subway F to East Broadway. **Open** 10am-10.30pm daily. **$**. **Chinese**. **Map** p59 D2 ④

A red and white colour scheme spruces up this Chinatown dim sum restaurant, where dumplings (more than 24 types) are the focus. A neophyte-friendly menu is divided into categories that include 'fried', 'baked' and 'steamed'. To avoid tough decisions, order the dim sum platter, whose artful array of ten items includes juicy steamed duck and mushroom dumplings, and the offbeat, slightly sweet pan-fried dumplings filled with pumpkin.

Ed's Lobster Bar

222 Lafayette Street, between Kenmare & Spring Streets (1-212 343 3236, www.lobsterbarnyc.com). Subway B, D, F, M to Broadway-Lafayette Street. **Open** noon-3pm, 5-11pm Tue-Thur; noon-3pm, 5pm-midnight Fri; noon-midnight Sat; noon-9pm Sun. **$$**. **Seafood**. **Map** p61 D4 ④

Chef Ed McFarland (formerly of Pearl Oyster Bar) is behind this tiny seafood joint. If you secure a place at the 25-seat marble bar or one of the few tables in

NEW YORK BY AREA

the whitewashed eaterie, expect superlative raw-bar eats, delicately fried clams and lobster served every which way: steamed, grilled, broiled, chilled, stuffed into a pie and – the crowd favourite – the lobster roll. Here, it's a buttered bun stuffed with premium chunks of meat and just a light coating of mayo.

Peking Duck House

28 Mott Street, between Mosco & Pell Streets (1-212 227 1810, www.peking duckhousenyc.com). Subway J, M, N, Z, Q, R, 6 to Canal Street. **Open** 11.30am-10.30pm Mon-Thur, Sun; 11.30am-11.30pm Fri, Sat. **$ Chinese.** **Map** p61 D5 ⓭

Your waiter parades the roasted duck past your party before placing it on the center show table. A chef brandishes his knives dramatically, then slices the aromatic, crisp-skinned, succulent meat with great flair. Select the 'three-way,' and your duck will yield the main course (complete with pancakes and plum sauce for rolling up the goods), a vegetable stir-fry with left-over bits of meat and a cabbage soup made with the remaining bone. Yes, the menu lists many dishes besides Peking duck, but reading it will only delay the inevitable.

Torrisi Italian Specialties

NEW *250 Mulberry Street, between Prince and Spring Streets (1-212 965 0955, www.piginahat.com). Subway N, R to Prince Street; 6 to Spring Street.* **Open** 11am-4pm, 6-11pm Tue-Sun. **$ Italian.** **Map** p61 D4 ⓰

Rich Torrisi and Mario Carbone (both formerly of Café Boulud) traded in their chef's whites for deli-man hats at this homage to Italian sub shops. Their pristine antipasti include a sweet-and-spicy potato salad flecked with minced pepperoni. Their cold-cut sandwiches are outstanding throwbacks filled with herb-rubbed roasted turkey or the classic combo of provolone, salami, ham, soppressata and

pepperoni. Even better is the chicken Parmesan hero, featuring a succulent cutlet, chunky tomato *ragù*, mozzarella and basil. Although $45 prix-fixe dinners are available, the sandwiches are the real draw.

Shopping

Creatures of Comfort

NEW *205 Mulberry Street, between Kenmare & Spring Streets (1-212 925 1005, www.creaturesocomfort.com). Subway 6 to Spring Street; N, R to Prince Street..* **Open** 11am-7pm Mon-Sat; noon-7pm Sun. **Map** p61 D4 ⓱

It may be the former home of the 12th police precinct, but the only thing criminal about Jade Lai's Nolita store would be passing up its hip merch. A spin-off of the five-year-old Los Angeles boutique, Creatures of Comfort has made a name for itself by scouting up-and-coming labels from near and far. Now that it has expanded to the East Coast, you can browse pricey but oh-so-cool statement pieces from avant-garde lines such as MM6 and Zucca, plus bohemian basics from Lai's Creatures of Comfort in-house collection. Don't forget to sashay on back to the swanky garden patio after your plastic cools off.

Downtown Music Gallery

13 Monroe Street, between Catherine & Market Streets (1-212 473 0043, www.downtownmusicgallery.com). Subway J, M, Z to Chambers Street; 4, 5, 6 to Brooklyn Bridge-City Hall. **Open** noon-6pm Mon; noon-8pm Thur-Sun; also by appt. **Map** p59 D2 ⓳

Many landmarks of the so-called Downtown music scene have closed, but as long as DMG exists, the community will have a sturdy anchor. The shop, which moved from a plum Bowery spot to a Chinatown basement in 2009, stocks the city's finest selection of avant-garde jazz, contemporary classical, progressive rock and related styles.

Downtown trails

Neighbourhood tours for the urban explorer.

Chinatown

New York can be a daunting place to navigate – even if you're armed with this trusty guide. There are simply too many must-see sights to cram into a single visit. The following Downtown tours are available to help you peel away the layers of several neighbourhoods and attractions. Also check out the Own This Town section of *Time Out New York* magazine, which offers listings for urban outings.

If **Chinatown** whets your appetite, the Museum of Chinese in America leads tours (www.moca nyc.org/visit/tours/walking_tours; 1-212 619 4785; $15, free-$12 reductions) from May to December. 'Chinatown: A Walk Through History' takes you from the neighbourhood's early days as a Native American settlement to its turn-of-the-century period of rapid immigration, while 'From Coffeehouses to Banquet Halls' is a tantalising food-themed tour including several stops to eat.

New York was known as the Big Onion before it became the Big Apple, and the guides at Big Onion Walking Tours (1-212 439 1090; www.bigonion.com; $15, $12 reductions) are happy to tell you why. They also lead engaging tours of the **Financial District**, tracing the development of Wall Street from colonial boundary to international banking centre, and the **'Official' Gangs of New York Tour**, which explores the former Five Points neighbourhood that inspired Herbert Asbury's 1927 classic book as well as Martin Scorsese's 2002 film.

Things are busy atop the **High Line**, as the elevated park has just opened its second section, running from 20th Street to 30th Street. Explore the new half as well as the old on various Saturday-morning tours with the High Line (1-212 206 9922; www.thehighline.org; $15) throughout the spring and summer, when the Friends of the High Line recount the trestle's industrial history and tie it all in to the area's meatpacking past. You can see the old meat hooks on some of the buildings that you pass.

Erica Weiner

NEW *173 Elizabeth Street, between Kenmare & Spring Streets (1-212 334 6383, www.ericaweiner.com). Subway C, E, 6 to Spring Street.* Open noon-8pm daily. **Map** p61 D4 ⓐ

Seamstress-turned-jewelry-designer Erica Weiner sells her own bronze, brass, silver and gold creations alongside vintage and reworked baubles in her first-ever, eponymous boutique. With a painted tin ceiling and white-tiled floors accented by early-20th-century furnishings, the store resembles an old-fashioned dress shop. Weiner combs estate sales and New England auction houses to line the shelves of her cozy shop with antique engagement rings, earrings, necklaces and bracelets, all of which have unique stories behind them. Her wares are often casts or modified versions of old objects, such as 1930s cocktail stirrers from the Waldorf-Astoria Hotel that she fashioned into polished brass necklaces.

Love, Adorned

NEW *269 Elizabeth Street, between Houston & Prince Streets (1-212 431 5683, www.loveadorned.com). Subway C, E, 6 to Spring Street.* **Open** noon-8pm Mon-Sat; noon-7pm Sun. **Map** p61 D4 ⓑ

Lori Leven, owner of sister tattoo parlors, New York Adorned has expanded her brand to include a new jewelry haven: Love, Adorned. The third spin-off chainlet houses a treasure trove of baubles, home goods and trinkets. Stark white walls, glass and wood display cases, and a warehouselike lofted ceiling play backdrop to the store's offbeat mix of goods. A kitschy selection of Santa Fe Stoneworks patterned pocket knives and rainbow vintage ashtrays spruce up a bulky wooden table, while super-pricey Lindsay Thornburg billowy, handmade cloaks hang from the walls.

Market NYC

268 Mulberry Street, between Houston & Prince Streets (no phone, www.the marketnyc.com). Subway B, D, F, M to Broadway-Lafayette Street; N, R to Prince Street; 6 to Bleecker Street. **Open** 11am-7pm Sat, Sun. No credit cards. **Map** p61 D4 ⓑ

Every weekend, independent clothing and accessories designers set up shop in the gymnasium of a church's youth centre, giving shoppers the chance to buy direct from the makers.

Lower East Side

Once better known for bagels and bargains, this old immigrant area is now brimming with vintage and indie-designer boutiques, speakeasy-style bars and, since the New Museum of Contemporary Art opened a $50 million building on the Bowery in late 2007, dozens of storefront galleries.

Sights & museums

Lower East Side Tenement Museum

Visitors' centre: 108 Orchard Street, Delancey Street (1-212 982 8420, www.tenement.org). Subway F to Delancey Street; J, M, Z to Delancey-Essex Streets. **Open** *Museum shop & ticketing* 10am-6pm daily. *Tours* 10.30am-5pm (every 30mins) Mon-Fri; 10.30am-5pm (every 15mins) Sat, Sun. **Admission** $20; $15 reductions. **Map** p61 E4 ⓑ

This fascinating museum – actually a series of restored tenement apartments at 97 Orchard Street – is accessible only by guided tour. Tickets can be purchased at the visitors' centre at 108 Orchard Street or online and tours often sell out, so it's wise to book ahead.

'Getting By' visits the homes of an Italian and a German-Jewish clan; 'Piecing It Together' explores the apartments of two Eastern European Jewish families as well as a garment shop where many of the locals would have found employment; 'The Moores' unfurls the life of an Irish family coping with the loss of their child; and the

'Confino Family Living History Program' takes in the homes of Sephardic Jewish occupants with the help of an interpreter in period costume. From April to December, the museum also conducts themed daily 90-minute walking tours of the Lower East Side.

Museum at Eldridge Street (Eldridge Street Synagogue)

12 Eldridge Street, between Canal & Division Streets (1-212 219 0302, www. eldridgestreet.org). Subway F to East Broadway. **Open** 10am-5pm Mon-Thu, Sun; 10am-3pm Fri. *Tours* every 30mins 10am-4pm. **Admission** $10; free-$8 reductions. **Map** p59 D1/63 E5 🖸

With an impressive façade that combines Moorish, Gothic and Romanesque elements, the first grand synagogue on the Lower East Side is now surrounded by dumpling shops and Chinese herb stores. As Jews left the area the building fell into disrepair. However, a recently completed 20-year facelift has restored its splendour; the soaring main sanctuary features hand-stencilled walls and a resplendent stained-glass rose window incorporating Star of David motifs. A new window, designed by artist Kiki Smith and architect Deborah Gans, was installed in 2010. Downstairs, touchscreen displays highlight the synagogue's architecture, aspects of worship and local history, including other Jewish landmarks.

New Museum of Contemporary Art

235 Bowery, between Prince & Stanton Streets (1-212 219 1222, www.new museum.org). Subway F to Lower East Side-Second Avenue. **Open** 1am-6pm Wed, Fri-Sun; 11am-9pm Thur. **Admission** $12; free-$10 reductions; free to all 7-9pm Thur. **Map** p61 D4 🖸

After 30 years of occupying various sites around town, New York City's only contemporary art museum finally got its own purpose-built space in late 2007. Dedicated to emerging media and

under-recognised artists, the seven-floor space is worth a look for the architecture alone – a striking, off-centre stack of aluminium-mesh-clad boxes designed by the cutting-edge Tokyo architectural firm Sejima + Nishizawa/SANAA. On weekends, don't miss the fabulous views from the minimalist, seventh-floor Sky Room.

Event highlights The Generational (Spring 2012), a triennial showcase of new artists curated by Eungie Joo.

Eating & drinking

Back Room

102 Norfolk Street, between Delancey & Rivington Streets (1-212 228 5098). Subway F, J, M, Z to Delancey-Essex Streets. **Open** 7.30pm-3am Tue-Thur, Sun; 7.30pm-4am Fri, Sat. **Bar**. **Map** p61 E4 🖸

For access to this ersatz speakeasy, look for a sign that reads 'The Lower East Side Toy Company'. Pass through the gate, walk down an alleyway, up a metal staircase and open an unmarked door to find a convincing replica of a 1920s watering hole. Cocktails come in teacups, and bottled beer is brown-bagged before being served. Patrons must be 25 or older on Fridays and Saturdays.

Clinton Street Baking Company

4 Clinton Street, between Houston & Stanton Streets (1-646 602 6263, www.clintonstreetbaking.com). Subway F to Delancey Street; J, M, Z to Delancey-Essex Streets. **Open** 8am-4pm, 6-11pm Mon-Fri; 9am-4pm, 6-11pm Sat; 9am-4pm Sun. **$**. **Café**. **Map** p61 E4 🖸

The warm buttermilk biscuits and fluffy pancakes at this pioneering little eaterie give you reason enough to face the guaranteed brunch-time crowds. If you want to avoid the onslaught, however, the homely spot is just as reliable at both lunch and dinner; drop in between 6pm and 8pm for the daily $12 beer-and-burger special (6-8pm Mon-Thur), consisting of 8oz of Black Angus topped with Swiss cheese and caramelised onions, served with a Brooklyn Lager.

The Delancey

168 Delancey Street, at Clinton Street (1-212 254 9912, www.thedelancey. com). Subway F to Delancey Street, J, M, Z to Delancey-Essex Streets. **Open** 5pm-4am daily. **Bar**. Map p61 E4 ⑤⑦

The rooftop is what keeps crowds coming back to this LES rock club – it's got potted palms, a fishpond and a margarita machine. When the party ends at midnight, head to the ground level for deejayed music or into the basement for a live show. Tuesdays from 7 to 10pm, hot dogs and burgers are served for five bucks per plate – so no need to worry about boozing on an empty stomach.

Freemans

2 Freeman Alley, off Rivington Street, between Bowery & Chrystie Street (1-212 420 0012, www.freemans restaurant.com). Subway F to Lower East Side-Second Avenue; J, M, Z to Bowery. **Open** 11am-4pm, 6-11.30pm Mon-Fri; 10am-4pm, 6-11.30pm Fri, Sat. $$. **American**. Map p61 D4 ⑤⑧

Up at the end of a graffiti-marked alley, Freemans' appealing colonial-tavern-meets-hunting-lodge style is still a hit with retro-loving Lower East Siders. Garage-sale oil paintings and moose antlers serve as backdrops to a curved zinc bar, while the menu recalls a simpler time – devils on horseback (prunes stuffed with stilton and wrapped in bacon); rum-soaked ribs, the meat falling off the bone with a gentle nudge of the fork; and stiff cocktails that'll get you good and sauced.

Katz's Delicatessen

205 E Houston Street, at Ludlow Street (1-212 254 2246, www.katzdeli.com). Subway F to Lower East Side-Second Avenue. **Open** 8am-9.45pm Mon, Tue; 8am-10.45pm Wed, Thur, Sun; 8am-2.45am Fri, Sat. $. **American**. Map p61 E4 ⑤⑨

A visit to Gotham isn't complete without a stop at a quintessential New York deli, and this Lower East Side survivor is the real deal. You might get a kick out of the famous faces (from Bill Clinton to Ben Stiller) plastered to the panelled walls, or the spot where Meg Ryan faked it in When Harry Met Sally…, but the real stars of this cafeteria are the thick-cut pastrami sandwiches and the crisp-skinned all-beef hot dogs – the latter are a mere $3.10.

Schiller's Liquor Bar

131 Rivington Street, at Norfolk Street (1-212 260 4555, www.schillersny.com). Subway F to Delancey Street; J, M, Z to Delancey-Essex Streets. **Open** 11am-1am Mon-Wed; 11am-2am Thur; 11am-3am Fri; 10am-3am Sat; 10am-1am Sun. $. **Eclectic**. Map p61 E4 ⑥⓪

The menu at Schiller's is a mix of French bistro (steak-frites), British pub (fish and chips) and good ol' American (cheeseburger), while the wine menu famously hawks a down-to-earth hierarchy: Good, Decent, Cheap. As at Keith McNally's other establishments, Balthazar (see p67) and Pastis, folks pack in for the scene, triple-parking at the bar for cocktails and star sightings.

Spitzer's Corner

101 Rivington Street, at Ludlow Street (1-212 228 0027, www.spitzerscorner. com). Subway F to Delancey Street; J, M, Z to Delancey-Essex Streets. **Open** 4pm-3am Mon, Tue; 4pm-4am Wed, Thur; noon-4am Fri; 10am-4am Sat; 10am-3am Sun. **Bar**. Map p61 E4 ⑥①

Referencing the Lower East Side's pickle-making heritage, the walls at this rustic gastropub are made from salvaged wooden barrels. The formidable beer list – 40 ever-rotating draughts – includes Bear Republic's fragrant Racer 5 IPA. Mull over your selection, with the help of appetising tasting notes, at one of the communal tables. The gastro end of things is manifest in the menu of quality pub grub – pan-seared foie gras, for example, or *panko*-encrusted asparagus.

Shopping

Alife Rivington Club

158 Rivington Street, between Clinton & Suffolk Streets (1-212 375 8128, www.rivingtonclub.com). Subway F to Delancey Street; J, M, Z to Delancey-Essex Streets. **Open** noon-7pm daily. **Map** p61 E4 ⏣

Whether you're looking for a simple white trainer or a trendy graphic style, you'll want to gain entry to this 'club', which stocks a wide range of major brands including Nike, Adidas and New Balance, along with less mainstream names. Shoes that get sneaker freaks salivating include retro styles such as Warrior Footwear, an athletic shoe line that originated in China in the 1930s, and the Nike Air Jordan 1.

BBlessing

181 Orchard Street, between Houston & Stanton Streets (1-212 378 8005, www.bblessing.com). Subway F to Lower East Side-Second Avenue. **Open** noon-8pm daily. **Map** p61 D4 ⏣

The interior of this men's shop, which frequently doubles as a gallery space, is as elegant as the clothing displayed within it. New York designers that put a current spin on classic American style – Thom Browne, Patrik Ervell and the store's own line – are the central focus. You can also pick up CDs, DVDs and accessories that reflect owner Nicholas Kratochvil's enviable aesthetic.

Convent

NEW *179 Stanton Street, between Attorney & Clinton Streets (1-212 673 0233). Subway F to Lower East Side-Second Avenue.* **Open** Noon-8pm Tue-Sat; noon-5pm Sun. **Map** p61 E4 ⏣

Industrial, dark and eccentric are the three words freelance stylist turned shop owner Travis Wayne uses to describe his Stanton Street boutique, a 300-square-foot shop outfitted with racks Wayne built himself using industrial piping. Convent offers men's and women's styles for every budget

(Cheap Monday, Motel, Geronimo, Postmodertease, Sally LaPointe, etc.). One standout is Miiche's collection of jersey, raw silk and merino-wool-blend men's vests ($180-$200), which look just as good cloaking the fairer sex.

Dear: Rivington

5 Rivington Street, between Ludlow & Orchard Streets (1-212 673 3494, www.dearrivington.com). Subway F to Delancey Street; J, M, Z to Delancey-Essex Streets. **Open** noon-7pm daily. **Map** p61 E4 ⏣

The glass storefront is a stage for Moon Rhee and Hey Ja Do's art installation-like displays; inside the white bi-level space, head downstairs for their own Victorian-inspired line and select pieces by avant-garde Japanese labels such as Comme des Garçons and Yohji Yamamoto. Upstairs is a fascinating archive of vintage homewares, objects and contemporary art, including framed antique silhouettes, old globes and tins.

Doyle & Doyle

189 Orchard Street, between Houston & Stanton Streets (1-212 677 9991, www.doyledoyle.com). Subway F to Lower East Side-Second Avenue. **Open** 1-7pm Tue, Wed, Fri; 1-8pm Thur; noon-7pm Sat, Sun. **Map** p61 D4 ⏣

Whether your taste is art deco or nouveau, Victorian or Edwardian, gemologist sisters Pam and Elizabeth Doyle, who specialise in estate and antique jewellery, will have that one-of-a-kind item you're looking for, including engagement and eternity rings. The artfully displayed pieces within wall-mounted wood-frame cases are just a fraction of what they have in stock.

Dolce Vita

149 Ludlow Street, between Rivington and Stanton Streets (1-212 529 2111, www.shopdolcevita.com). Subway F to Delancey Street; J, M, Z to Delancey-Essex Streets. **Open** noon-8pm Mon-Sat; noon-7pm Sun. **Map** p61 E4 ⏣

In-the-know fashionistas have a secret: When *Vogue* features an haute shoe, chances are you can find a similar, less-expensive version by Dolce Vita or diffusion line DV. The trendy footwear ranges from $50 to $198, and includes oh-so-right-now flats, pumps, sandals, wedges and boots. The neighbouring shops are just a few doors apart and also carry glam women's threads (dresses, skirts, cardigans, tops and more) by Mara Hoffman, Sass & Bide, Minkpink and Torn by Ronny Kobo.

Dressing Room

75A Orchard Street, between Broome & Grand Streets (1-212 966 7330, www.thedressingroomnyc.com). Subway B, D to Grand Street; F to Delancey Street; J, M, Z to Delancey-Essex Streets **Open** 1pm-midnight Tue, Wed, Sun; 1pm-2am Thur-Sat. **Map** p61 E4 ⑥⑧

At first glance, the Dressing Room may look like any Lower East Side lounge, thanks to a handsome wood bar, but stylist and designer Nikki Fontanella's quirky co-op cum watering hole rewards the curious. The adjoining room displays designs by indie labels, which rotate every four months, while downstairs is a vintage and second-hand clothing exchange.

Honey in the Rough

161 Rivington Street, between Clinton & Suffolk Streets (1-212 228 6415, www.honeyintherough.com). Subway F to Delancey Street; J, M, Z to Delancey-Essex Streets. **Open** noon-8pm Mon-Sat; noon-7pm Sun. **Map** p61 E4 ⑥⑨

Looking for something sweet and charming? Hit this cosy, ultra-femme boutique. Owner Ashley Hanosh fills the well-worn spot with an excellent line-up of local indie labels, including Samantha Pleet, Thread Social and Nomia, alongside carefully selected accessories, some of which are exclusive to the shop. In the downstairs beauty studio, Rosie Rodriguez offers eyebrow sculpting, make-up application and more.

Reed Space

151 Orchard Street, between Rivington & Stanton Streets (1-212 253 0588, www.thereedspace.com). Subway F to Delancey Street; J, M, Z to Delancey-Essex Streets. **Open** 1-7pm Mon-Fri; noon-7pm Sat, Sun. **Map** p61 D4 ⑦⓪

Reed Space is the brainchild of Jeff Staple (Staple Design), who has worked on product design and branding with the likes of Nike and Timberland. It stocks local and international urban menswear brands (10.Deep, Mishka, Crooks & Castle), footwear (including exclusive Staple collaborations), and hard-to-get accessories, such as Japanese Head Porter nylon bags and pouches. Art books and culture mags are shelved on an eye-popping 'chair wall' – four stacked rows of white chairs fixed to one wall.

Russ & Daughters

179 E Houston Street, between Allen & Orchard Streets (1-212 475 4880, www.russanddaughters.com). Subway F to Lower East Side-Second Avenue. Open 8am-8pm Mon-Fri; 9am-7pm Sat; 8am-5.30pm Sun. **Map** p61 D4 ⑦①

The daughters in the name have given way to great-grandchildren, but this Lower East Side survivor, established in 1914, is still run by the same family. Specialising in smoked and cured fish and caviar, it sells ten varieties of smoked salmon, eight types of herring and many other Jewish-inflected Eastern European delectables. Bagels are available to take away.

Thecast

71 Orchard Street, between Broome & Grand Streets (1-212 228 2020, www.thecast.com). Subway F to Lower East Side-Second Avenue. **Open** 11am-8pm Mon-Sat; noon-7pm Sun. **Map** p61 E4 ⑦②

Owner Chuck Guarino has traded his (literally) underground location for a sliver of a storefront on Orchard Street, but the new shop maintains the neo-gothic vibe with ghoulish knickknacks, such as a human skull. At the core of the unabashedly masculine collection is the trinity of well-cut denim, superior leather jackets based on classic motorcycle styles, and the artful T-shirts that launched the label in 2004. Model and Brit 'it' girl Agyness Deyn was so smitten she bought some pieces for herself, but now the ladies get their own line, Aloha From Hell.

Victor Osborne
160 Orchard Street, between Rivington & Stanton Streets (1-212 677 6254, www.victorosborne.com). Subway F to Lower East Side-Second Avenue. **Open** noon-8pm daily. **Map** p61 4 ⓐ
Milliner Victor Osborne moved his shop-atelier from Williamsburg to the Lower East Side in 2009. The 27-year-old FIT graduate says most of his customers – Rihanna among them – are between 20 and 35. Designs encompass funky patterned caps, vintage-inspired cloches and fedoras.

Nightlife

Bowery Ballroom
6 Delancey Street, between Bowery & Chrystie Street (1-212 533 2111, www.boweryballroom.com). Subway B, D to Grand Street; J, M, Z to Bowery; 6 to Spring Street. **Map** p61 D4 ⓐ
It's probably the best venue in the city for seeing indie bands, either on the way up or holding their own. Still, the Bowery also manages to bring in a diverse range of artists from home and abroad. Expect a clear view and bright sound from any spot. The spacious downstairs lounge is a great place to relax and socialise between (or during) sets.

Cake Shop
152 Ludlow Street, between Rivington & Stanton Streets (1-212 253 0036, www.cake-shop.com). Subway F to Lower East Side-Second Avenue. **Open** 5pm-2am Mon-Thur, Sun; 5pm-4am Fri, Sat. **Map** p61 E4 ⓐ

It can be hard to see the stage in this narrow, stuffy basement, but Cake Shop gets big points for its keen indie and underground-rock bookings, among the most adventurous in town. True to its name, the venue sells vegan pastries and coffee upstairs, and record-store ephemera in the street-level back room.

Mercury Lounge
217 E Houston Street, between Essex & Ludlow Streets (1-212 260 4700, www.mercuryloungenyc.com). Subway F to Lower East Side-Second Avenue. **Map** p61 E4 ⓐ
The unassuming, boxy Mercury Lounge is both an old standby and pretty much the number-one indie rock club in town, with solid sound and sight lines. There are four-band bills most nights, though they can seem stylistically haphazard and set times are often later than advertised. It's a good idea to book bigger shows in advance.

Arts & leisure

Dixon Place
161 Chrystie Street, at Delancey Street (1-212 219 0736, www.dixonplace.org). Subway F to Lower East Side-Second Avenue; J, M, Z to Bowery-Delancey Streets. **Map** p61 D4 ⓐ
Over two decades after Ellie Covan started hosting experimental performances in her living room, this plucky organisation finally opened a state-of-the-art space on the Lower East Side. Along with a mainstage theatre, there's a pub – perfect for post-show discussions. Dixon Place supports emerging artists and works in progress; summer events include the annual Hot! festival of lesbian and gay arts.

East Village

The area east of Broadway between Houston and 14th Streets has a long history as a countercultural hotbed. From the 1950s to the '70s,

St Marks Place (8th Street, between Lafayette Street & Avenue A) was a hangout for artists, writers, radicals and musicians. It's still packed until the wee hours, but these days it's with crowds of college students and tourists browsing for bargain T-shirts, used CDs and pot paraphernalia. While legendary music venues such as CBGB are no more, a few bohemian hangouts endure, and the East Village has also evolved into a superior cheap-eats hotspot. In the neighbourhood's renovated green space, Tompkins Square Park, bongo beaters, guitarists, yuppies and the homeless all mingle.

Eating & drinking

Back Forty
190 Avenue B, between 11th & 12th Streets (1-212 388 1990, www.back fortynyc.com). Subway L to First Avenue. **Open** 6-11pm Mon-Thur; 6pm-midnight Fri, Sat; noon-3.30pm, 6-10pm Sun. **$$. American. Map** p61 E2 **⑦**
Chef-restaurateur Peter Hoffman (of Savoy fame; see p70) is behind this East Village seasonal-eats tavern, where modern farmhouse chic prevails both in the decor and on the menu. House specialities include juicy grass-fed burgers, stout floats made with beer from New York-area breweries, and golden pork-jowl nuggets. The spacious back garden is a bonus during the warmer months.

Baoguette
37 St Marks Place, at Second Avenue (1-212 380 1487, www.baoguette.com). Subway 6 to Astor Place. **Open** 11am-midnight Mon-Thur, Sun; 11am-2am Thur-Sat. **$. Vietnamese. Map** p61 D3 **⑦**
If the Vietnamese *banh mi* is a study in contrasts, then Baoguette's signature is the definitive text. Three forms of sweet and juicy pork (pâté, terrine and pulled) are stuffed into a crusty French loaf, their fatty flavour offset by bright strands of pickled carrot and daikon radish, and enhanced by fresh cilantro (coriander leaves), garlicky aïoli and hot *sriracha* sauce. Other variations include a vegetarian version, and catfish with cucumber relish, pickled red onions and honey-mustard sauce.

Bourgeois Pig
111 E 7th Street, between First Avenue & Avenue A (1-212 475 2246, www. bourgeoispigny.com). Subway F to Lower East Side-Second Avenue; 6 to Astor Place. **Open** 6pm-2am Mon-Thur, Sun; 6pm-3am Fri, Sat. **Wine bar. Map** p61 E3 **㉚**
See box p85.

Caracas Arepa Bar
91 E 7th Street, between First Avenue & Avenue A (1-212 228 5062, www. caracasarepabar.com). Subway F to Lower East Side-Second Avenue; 6 to Astor Place. **Open** noon-11pm Tue-Sat; noon-10pm Sun. **$. Venezuelan. Map** p61 D3 **㉛**
This endearing spot, with flower-patterned, vinyl-covered tables, zaps you straight to Caracas. The secret is in the *arepas* themselves: each corn-meal patty is made from scratch daily before it's stuffed with a choice of 18 fillings, such as chicken and avocado or mushrooms with tofu. Top off your snack with a *cocada*, a thick and creamy milkshake made with freshly grated coconut and cinnamon.

Crif Dogs
113 St Marks Place, between First Avenue & Avenue A (1-212 614 2728). Subway L to First Avenue; 6 to Astor Place. **Open** noon-2am Mon-Fri; noon-4am Sat; noon-1am Sun. **$. American. Map** p61 D3 **㉜**
You'll recognise this place by the giant hot dog outside, bearing the come-on 'Eat me'. Crif offers the best Jersey-style dogs this side of the Hudson: handmade smoked-pork tube-steaks that are deep-fried until they're burst-

ing out of their skins. While they're served in various guises, among them the Spicy Redneck (wrapped in bacon and covered in chilli, coleslaw and jalapeños) and the Chihuahua (wrapped in bacon and served with sour cream and avocado), we're partial to the classic with mustard and kraut.

DBGB Kitchen & Bar

299 Bowery, at 1st Street (1-212 933 5300, www.danielnyc.com). Subway B, D, F, M to Broadway-Lafayette Street; 6 to Bleecker Street. **Open** 5.30pm-midnight Mon; noon-midnight Tue-Thur; 11am-1am Fri, Sat; 11am-11pm Sun. $$. **French**. **Map** p61 D3 ㉝
Even in a city awash in unruly menus, the one at DBGB – chef Daniel Boulud's most populist venture – stands out for its kitchen-sink scope. There's high-end junk food in the form of sausages (the best of the bunch is the Beaujolaise, infused with red wine, bacon and mushrooms). And there's haute bistro fare such as pink duck breast with boozy cherries and marcona almonds. The best way to get your head around the schizophrenic enterprise is to bring a large group and sample the range – including a sundae, layered with cherry-flavoured kriek beer ice-cream and speculoos cookies, for dessert.

Death & Company

433 E 6th Street, between First Avenue & Avenue A (1-212 388 0882, www.death andcompany.com). Subway F to Lower East Side-Second Avenue; 6 to Astor Place. **Open** 6pm-1am Mon-Thur, Sun; 6pm-2am Fri, Sat. **Bar**. **Map** p61 E3 ㉞
The nattily attired mixologists are deadly serious about drinks at this pseudo speakeasy with Gothic flair (don't be intimidated by the imposing wooden door). Black walls and cushy booths combine with chandeliers to set the luxuriously sombre mood. Patrons bored by shot-and-beer bars as well as top-notch grub including bacon-swaddled filet mignon bites.

Dirt Candy

430 E 9th Street, between First Avenue & Avenue A (1-212 228 7732, www.dirtcandynyc.com). Subway L to First Avenue; 6 to Astor Place. **Open** 5.30-11pm Tue-Sat. $$. **Vegetarian**. **Map** p61 E2 ㉟
The shiny, futuristic surroundings here look more like a chic nail salon than a restaurant. Chef-owner Amanda Cohen has created an unlikely space to execute her less-likely ambition: to make people crave vegetables. She mostly succeeds. Elaborate dishes might include a spicy asparagus paella served with a crisped-rice cake on top, or a pungent portobello mousse accompanied by shiitake mushrooms and fennel-peach compote.

Dos Toros

137 Fourth Avenue, between 13th & 14th Streets (1-212 677 7300, www. dostorosnyc.com). Subway L to Third Avenue; N, Q, R, 4, 5, 6 to 14th Street-Union Square. **Open** 11.30am-11pm Mon-Sat; noon-10pm Sun. $. **Mexican**. **Map** p60 C2 ㊱
This bright little Cal-Mex taqueria just off Union Square won a 2010 *Time Out New York* Eat Out Award for its bangin' burritos and has not lost a step. The fillings – juicy flap steak, moist grilled chicken, smooth guacamole – are the best in town.

Holiday Cocktail Lounge

75 St Marks Place, between First and Second Avenues (1-212 777 9637). Subway L to First Avenue, 6 to Astor Place. **Open** 6pm-1am daily. **Bar**. **Map** p61 D2 ㊲
No-nonsense barkeep Stefan Lutak has been running the show since before Warhol and his gang commandeered the Polish National Home down the street for their "Exploding Plastic Inevitable" multimedia show. Lutak, unmoved by such things, still ensures that trendiness stops at the door. Drinks are equally no-frills: Bottles of Bud go for $3; imports are $3.50. Expect a cross

section of East Village types to filter in; the night lasts until Lutak figures everybody's had enough fun.

In Vino

215 E 4th Street, between Avenues A and B (1-212 539 1011). Subway 6 to Astor Place. **Open** 5.30pm-midnight Mon-Thur; 5.30pm-1am Fri, Sat; 5.30-11pm Sun. **Bar**. Map p61 E3 ⑱
See box p85.

International Bar

1202 First Avenue, between St Marks Place & E 7th Street (1-212 777 1643). Subway F to Lower East Side-Second Avenue; L to First Avenue. **Open** 1pm-4am daily. **Bar**. Map p61 D3 ⑲
The walls have been cleared of graffiti, but the second coming of this legendary saloon stays true to its dive bar roots (the original closed in 2005 after more than 40 years of business). A scuffed mahogany bar and vintage film posters make up the decor, and the jukebox is still killer (Black Flag, Nina Simone). The cheap booze and grimy vibe foster the feeling that I-Bar never left.

Ippudo New York

65 Fourth Avenue, between 9th & 10th Streets (1-212 388 0088). Subway 6 to Astor Place. **Open** 11am-3.30pm, 5-11.30pm Mon-Thur; 11am-3.30pm, 5pm-12.30am Fri, Sat; 11am-10.30pm Sun. Ramen $13. **Japanese**. Map p61 D2 ⑳
This outrageously popular Japanese import has fuelled the growing craze for ramen. Sample the Akamura Modern, a steaming bowl of tonkotsu broth (a creamy pork-bone brew) with pork belly, spring onions and wheat noodles; a complex, filling meal for a mere $13.

Momofuku Ssäm Bar

207 Second Avenue, at 13th Street (1-212 254 3500, www.momofuku.com). Subway L to First or Third Avenues; L, N, Q, R, 4, 5, 6 to 14th Street-Union Square. **Open** 11.30am-midnight Mon-Thur, Sun; 11.30am-2am Fri, Sat. $$. **Korean**. Map p61 D2 ㉑

At chef David Chang's second restaurant, waiters hustle to noisy rock music in the 50-seat space, which feels expansive compared with its Noodle Bar predecessor's crowded counter dining. Try the wonderfully fatty pork-belly steamed bun with hoisin sauce and cucumbers or one of the ham platters, but you'll need to come with a crowd to sample the house speciality, *bo ssäm* (a slow-roasted hog butt that is consumed wrapped in lettuce leaves, with a dozen oysters and other accompaniments); it serves six to eight people and must be ordered in advance. David Chang has further expanded his E Vill empire with a sweet annexe at this location, Momofuku Milk Bar.

Other locations Momofuku Ko, 163 First Avenue, at 10th Street (no phone); Momofuku Noodle Bar, 171 First Avenue, between 10th & 11th Streets (1-212 777 7773).

Motorino

349 E 12th Street, between First & Second Avenues (1-212 777 2644, www.motorinopizza.com). Subway L to First Avenue. **Open** 5pm-midnight Mon-Thur, Sun; 5pm-1am Fri, Sat. $. **Pizza**. Map p61 D2 ㉒
In addition to Motorino chef Mathieu Palombino's expertly baked Neapolitan-style pies, sweet with pools of molten mozzarella, there's a selection of to-die-for appetisers, like roasted strips of porky mortadella with cherry tomatoes, olives and basil.

PDT

113 St Marks Place, between First Avenue & Avenue A (1-212 614 0386). Subway L to First Avenue; 6 to Astor Place. **Open** 6pm-2am Mon-Thur, Sun; 6pm-4am Fri, Sat. **Cocktail bar**. Map p61 D3 ㉓
Word has got out about 'Please Don't Tell', the faux speakeasy inside gourmet hot dog joint Crif Dogs (see p82), so it's a good idea to reserve a booth in advance. Once you arrive, you'll notice people lingering outside an old wooden

New York uncorked

Downtown winebars are offering hip sips.

Terroir p86

The city that never sleeps is so awash in noisy beerhalls, trendy cocktail lounges, louche dive bars and faux speakeasies that it's easy to overlook Gotham's winebars. These watering holes are by no means new, but their quality has definitely improved in the last decade, as serious oenophiles and casual drinkers have increasingly sought out a quiet spot for a pre- or post prandial drink – or simply a place to make an evening of it. We have selected several downtown spots well worth seeking out.

While the Financial District is rather devoid of decent drinking destinations, **Bin No. 220** (see p66) is a notable oasis. This sleek, Italian-style wine bar offers refuge from the tourist scene with a selection of 60 wines (20 available by the glass). It features cast-iron columns, a polished walnut bar and a nifty metal wine rack showcasing the horizontally stowed bottles.

In the East Village, ornate mirrors and antique chairs give the small, red-lit **Bourgeois Pig** (see p82), a wine and fondue joint, a decadent feel. The wine list is well chosen, and although harder liquor is *verboten*, mixed concoctions based on wine, champagne or beer cater to cocktail aficionados. At **Terroir** (see p86), oeno-evangelist Paul Grieco preaches the powers of *terroir* – grapes that express a sense of place – at this sparse wine haunt. The knowledgeable waitstaff adroitly help patrons navigate the 50 by-the-glass options. At **In Vino** (see left), you'll savour Southern Italian wines paired with tasty pitted fried green olives stuffed with beef. The cavelike space offers hundreds of regional Italian wines.

Over in the West Village, at **Gottino** (see p97) Morandi chef Jody Williams and owner Michael Bull have opened a new 40-seat enoteca. Fifty Italian wines are paired with bites like wine marinated baked beets with horseradish. *Salute!*

phonebooth near the front. Slip inside, pick up the receiver and the host opens a secret panel to the dark, narrow space. The cocktails surpass the gimmicky entry: try the house old-fashioned, made with bacon-infused bourbon, which leaves a smoky aftertaste.

Porchetta

110 E 7th Street, between First Avenue & Avenue A (1-212-777-2151, www. porchettanyc.com). Subway F to Lower East Side-Second Avenue; L to First Avenue; 6 to Astor Place. **Open** 11.30am-10pm Mon-Thur, Sun; 11.30am-11pm Fri, Sat. **Pork parlour.** **Map** p61 E3 🥩

This small, subway-tiled space has a narrow focus: central Italy's classic boneless roasted pork. The meat – available as a sandwich or a platter – is amazingly moist and tender, having been slowly roasted with rendered pork fat, seasoned with fennel pollen, herbs and spices, and flecked with brittle shards of skin. The other menu items (a mozzarella sandwich, humdrum sides) seem incidental; the pig is the point.

The Summit Bar

133 Avenue C, between 8th and 9th Streets (1-212 253 0470 , www.the summitbar.net). Subway L to First Avenue, 6 to Astor Place. **Open** 5.30pm-3am Mon, Sun; 5.30pm-4am Tue-Sat. **Bar**. **Map** p61 E3 🍸

Mixologist Greg Seider is behind this democratic lounge – handsome with blue-velvet banquettes and a black-granite bar – for serious drinkers. The menu includes classics like a peppery old-fashioned cocktail, and more-creative tipples, including the whisky-driven Gov'ner (*yuzu*, orange juice and cardamom-infused agave syrup). As much as Seider's inventiveness succeeds, it can also go off the rails, as in the She Loves Mei She Loves Mei Not, overly perfumed with rose petals and Szechuan-peppercorn-infused agave. Nonetheless, the bar's willingness to experiment sets it apart in the crowded cocktail field.

Terroir

413 E 12th Street, between First Avenue & Avenue A (no phone, www. wineisterroir.com). Subway L to First Avenue; L, N, Q, R, 4, 5, 6 to 14th Street-Union Square. **Open** 5pm-2am Mon-Sat; 5pm-midnight Sun. **Bar**. **Map** p61 D2 🍷

See box p85.

Vandaag

NEW *103 Second Avenue, at E 7th Street (1-212 253 0470, www. vandaagnyc.com). Subway F to Lower East Side-Second Avenue, 6 to Astor Place.* **Open** 9am-midnight Mon, Tue; 9am-1.30am Wed-Sat; 11am-midnight Sun. **Bar**. **Map** p61 D3 🍴

Northern European fare is underexposed in NYC, but this trailblazing bistro and bar makes a strong case for its appeal. The minimalist interior sets the scene for cutting-edge cocktails from barkeep Katie Stipe, who uses unusual ingredients (beer, *jenever*) in tipples like the beautifully balanced Turf War (aquavit, Lillet, maraschino juice, orange bitters, absinthe). Chef Phillip Kirschen-Clark (wd~50) offers great bites to match – bright seasonal pickles, crisp *bitterballen* (meaty croquettes) and crunchy sweetbread nuggets served with a lush Concord grape dipping sauce. The sweet treats (like warm caramel wafers) deliver an inspired finale.

Shopping

Bespoke Chocolates

6 Extra Place (off E 1st Street), between Bowery & Second Avenue (1-212 260 7103, www.bespoke chocolates.com). Subway F to Lower East Side-Second Avenue. **Open** 11am-7pm Tue-Fri; noon-8pm Sat, Sun. **Map** p61 D3 🍫

See box p95.

Bond No.9

9 Bond Street, between Broadway & Lafayette Street (1-212 228 1732, www.bondno9.com). Subway B, D, F, M

to Broadway-Lafayette Street; 6 to
Bleecker Street. **Open** 11am-8pm Mon-
Sat; noon-6pm Sun. **Map** p61 D3 🟢
The collection of scents here pays
olfactory homage to New York City.
Choose from 34 'neighbourhoods' and
'sensibilities', including Wall Street,
Park Avenue, Eau de Noho, even
Chinatown (but don't worry, it smells
of peach blossom, gardenia and
patchouli, not fish stands). A scent celebrating NYC's newest park, the High
Line, debuted in 2010. The arty bottles
and the neat, colourful packaging are
highly gift-friendly.

Bond Street Chocolate

63 E 4th Street, between Bowery &
Second Avenue (1-212 677 5103,
www.bondstchocolate.com). Subway
6 to Bleecker Street. **Open** noon-8pm
Tue-Sat. **Map** p61 D3 🟢
See box p95.

Dave's Quality Meat

7 E 3rd Street, between Bowery &
Second Avenue (1-212 505 7551,
www.davesqualitymeat.com). Subway
F to Lower East Side-Second Avenue.
Open 11.30am-7.30pm Mon-Sat;
11.30am-6.30pm Sun. **Map** p61 D3 🟢
Dave Ortiz – formerly of ghetto urban
threads label Zoo York – and professional skateboarder Chris Keefe stock
a range of top-shelf streetwear in their
wittily designed shop. In addition to a
line-up of the latest sneaks by Adidas,
Nike and Vans, DQM sells its own-
label graphic tees and hoodies.

Fabulous Fanny's

335 E 9th Street, between First &
Second Avenues (1-212 533 0637,
www.fabulousfannys.com). Subway L to
First Avenue; 6 to Astor Place. **Open**
noon-8pm daily. **Map** p61 D2 🟢
Formerly a Chelsea flea market booth,
this two-room shop is the city's best
source of period glasses, stocking more
than 30,000 pairs of spectacles, from
Jules Verne-esque wire rims to 1970s
rhinestone-encrusted Versace shades.

Future Perfect

55 Great Jones Street, between Bowery
& Lafayette Street (1-212 473 2500,
www.thefutureperfect.com). Subway
6 to Bleecker Street. **Open** noon-7pm
Mon-Sat; noon-6pm Sun.
Map p61 D3 🟢
Championing avant-garde interior
design, this innovative design store
showcases international and local
talent. Heather Dunbar's 'Graf'
pillows ($175) employ folksy needle-
point to recreate Brooklyn graffiti,
while Parsons graduate Sarah Cihat's
'rehabilitated' china is reglazed
with appealing retro-vibe images
including phonographs, astronauts,
and anchors.

INA

15 Bleecker Street, between Bowery
& Lafayette Street (1-212 228 8511,
www.inanyc.com). Subway B, D, F, M
to Broadway-Lafayette Street, 6 to
Bleecker Street. **Open** noon-8pm
Mon-Sat; noon-7pm Sun.
Map p61 D3 🟢
For more than 15 years, INA has been
a leading light of the designer-resale
scene. A string of five consignment
shops offers immaculate, bang-on-
trend items (Christian Louboutin and
Manolo Blahnik shoes, Louis Vuitton
and Marc Jacobs bags, clothing by
Alexander McQueen and Marni) at a
fraction of their original prices. This
branch caters to both sexes.

Kiehl's

109 Third Avenue, between 13th
& 14th Streets (1-212 677 3171,
www.kiehls.com). Subway L to Third
Avenue; N, Q, R, 4, 5, 6 to 14th Street-
Union Square. **Open** 10am-8pm Mon-
Sat; 11am-6pm Sun. **Map** p61 D2 🟢
The apothecary founded on this East
Village site in 1851 has morphed into a
major skincare brand, but the products,
in their minimal packaging, are still
good value and give great results. Lip
balms and the thick-as-custard Creme
de Corps have become cult classics.

Other Music

*15 E 4th Street, between Broadway
& Lafayette Street (1-212 477 8150).
Subway B, D, F, M to Broadway-
Lafayette Street; 6 to Bleecker Street.*
Open 11am-9pm Mon-Fri; noon-8pm
Sat; noon-7pm Sun. **Map** p60 C3 **106**
Other Music opened in the shadow of
Tower Records in the mid '90s, a
pocket of resistance to chain-store
tedium. All these years later, the
Goliath across the street is gone, but
tiny Other Music carries on. Whereas
the shop's mishmash of indie rock,
experimental music and stray slabs of
rock's past once seemed adventurous,
the curatorial foundation has proved
prescient, amid the emergence of
mixed-genre venues in the city.

St Mark's Bookshop

*31 Third Avenue, between 8th and 9th
Streets (1-212 260 7853, www.stmarks
bookshop.com). Subway N, R to 8th
Street-NYU, 6 to Astor Place.* **Open**
10am-midnight Mon-Sat; 11am-midnight
Sun. **Map** p61 D2 **107**
Students, academics and arty types
gravitate to this East Village bookseller,
which maintains strong inventories on
cultural theory, graphic design, poetry
and film, as well as numerous avant-
garde journals and zines. The fiction
section is one of the finest in the city.

The Smile

*26 Bond Street, at Lafayette Street
(1-646 329 5836, www.thesmilenyc.
com). Subway B, D, F, M at Broadway-
Lafayette Street; 6 at Bleecker Street.*
Open 8am-6pm Tue-Sun.
Map p61 D3 **108**
The artfully weathered sign, mullioned
windows and benches outside make this
mixed-use enterprise look like a cross
between a tavern and a general store. In
the rustic, stone-walled space – the
brainchild of Carlos Quirarte (formerly
of Earnest Sewn) and Matt Kliegman –
wooden shelves display disparate yet
discerningly chosen goods: scarves and
ties made of dead-stock chambray by

Brooklyn-based company Hillside;
Moscot sunglasses; hip knitting kits; toiletries by Santa Maria Novella; coffee
from New York State roastery
Plowshares; and teas by Mariage Frères
– the latter two can be supped in the
Smile's restaurant.

Strand Bookstore

*828 Broadway, at 12th Street (1-212
473 1452, www.strandbooks.com).
Subway L, N, Q, R, 4, 5, 6 to 14th
Street-Union Square.* **Open** 9.30am-
10.30pm Mon-Sat; 11am-10.30pm Sun.
Map p60 C1 **109**
Boasting 18 miles of books, the Strand
has a mammoth collection of more than
two million discount volumes, and the
store is made all the more daunting by
its chaotic, towering shelves and surly
staff. Reviewer discounts are in the
basement, while rare volumes lurk
upstairs. If you spend enough time here
you can find just about anything, from
that out-of-print Victorian book on
manners to the kitschiest of sci-fi pulp.

Voz

*W 618 E 9th Street, between Avenues
B & C (1-646 845 9618, www.voznew
york.com). Subway L to First Avenue.*
Open 2-8pm Tue-Fri. **Map** p61 E3 **110**
This shop is a pleasure to browse –
loose pages from a 1950s Webster's
dictionary are pressed and sealed into
the floors, and the stock spans fashion,
mid-century Danish and modern furniture, paintings and pottery. Owners
Alex de Laxalt and Naoko Ito believe a
woman's wardrobe should be equally
eclectic, so they've rounded up a mix of
labels, including Gary Graham,
Givenchy and Lolita Lempicka, with
vintage pieces by the likes of Yves St
Laurent and Sonia Rykiel.

Nightlife

The Cock

*29 Second Avenue, between 2nd &
3rd Streets (no phone, www.thecockbar.
com). Subway F to Lower East Side-*

Second Avenue. **Open** 11pm-4am daily. No credit cards. **Map** p61 D3 🄿

This grungy hole-in-the-wall still holds the title of New York's sleaziest gay hangout, but nowadays it's hit-and-miss. On weekends, it's a packed grind-fest, but on other nights the place is often depressingly under-populated. It's best to go very late when the cruising is at its peak.

EastVille Comedy Club

85 E 4th Street, between Bowery & Second Avenue (1-212 260 2445, www.eastvillecomedy.com). Subway F to Lower East Side-Second Avenue. **Shows** 9pm Mon-Thur; 7pm, 9pm, 11pm Fri, Sat. **Map** p61 D3 🄿

The first dedicated stand-up club in this patch, Eastville puts up much of the same club-circuit talent that populates the city's other rooms, plus a fresh crop of comics from the Downtown alt scene.

Joe's Pub

Public Theater, 425 Lafayette Street, between Astor Place & E 4th Street (1-212 539 8770, www.joespub.com). Subway N, R to 8th Street-NYU; 6 to Astor Place. **Map** p61 D3 🄿

Probably the city's premier small spot for sit-down audiences, Joe's Pub brings in impeccable musical talent of all genres and origins. While some well-established names have played here (Pete Townshend's 'From the Attic' show, for example), Joe's also lends its stage to up-and-comers (this is where Amy Winehouse made her US debut), along with drag acts and cabaret performers. A small but solid menu and deep bar selections seal the deal here – just keep an eye on those drinks prices.

Nublu

62 Avenue C, between 4th & 5th Streets (1-646 546 5206, www.nublu. net). Subway F to Lower East Side-Second Avenue. **Open** 8pm-4am daily. No credit cards. **Map** p61 E3 🄿

Nublu's prominence on the local globalist club scene has been inversely proportional to its size. A pressure cooker of creativity, the venue gave rise to the Brazilian Girls – who started jamming at one late-night session and haven't stopped yet – as well as starting New York City's romance with the northern Brazilian style *forró*. Even on weeknights, events usually start no earlier than 10pm – but if you show up early (and find the unmarked door), the bar is well stocked.

Webster Hall

125 E 11th Street, between Third & Fourth Avenues (1-212 353 1600, www.websterhall.com). Subway L to Third Avenue; N, Q, R, 4, 5, 6 to 14th Street-Union Square. **Map** p61 D2 🄿

A great-sounding alternative for bands (and fans) who've had their fill of the comparably sized Irving Plaza, Webster Hall is booked by Bowery Presents, the folks who run Bowery Ballroom and Mercury Lounge. Expect to find high-calibre indie acts (Animal Collective, Battles, the Gossip), but be sure to show up early if you want a decent view.

Arts & leisure

Anthology Film Archives

32 Second Avenue, at 2nd Street (1-212 505 5181, www.anthologyfilm archives.org). Subway F to Lower East Side-Second Avenue; 6 to Bleecker Street. No credit cards. **Map** p61 D3 🄿

This red-brick building feels a little like a fortress – and in a sense, it is one, protecting the legacy of NYC's fiercest experimenters. Anthology is committed to screening the world's most adventurous fare, from 16mm found-footage works to digital video dreams. Dedicated to the preservation, study and exhibition of independent and avant-garde film, it houses a gallery and film museum, in addition to its two screens.

NEW YORK BY AREA

Washington Square Park p92

Bowery Poetry Club

*308 Bowery, between Bleecker &
Houston Streets (1-212 614 0505,
www.bowerypoetry.com). Subway F
to Lower East Side-Second Avenue.*
No credit cards. **Map** p61 D3 ⓷
The BPC features a jam-packed programme of high-energy spoken word
events, plus hip hop, burlesque, comedy, theatre and workshops. The
Urbana Poetry Slam team leads an
open mic on Tuesday nights.

Great Jones Spa

*29 Great Jones Street, at Lafayette
Street (1-212 505 3185, www.great
jonesspa.com). Subway 6 to Astor
Place.* **Open** 9am-10pm daily.
Map p61 D3 ⓷
Based on the theory that water brings
health, Great Jones is outfitted with
a popular water lounge complete with
subterranean pools, saunas, steam
rooms and a three-and-a-half-storey
waterfall. Enjoy the serenity of
the 15,000sq ft paradise before a hair-
cut ($90 and up), or treat yourself to
a Coconut Paradise Manicure ($40).
Access to the water lounge is complimentary with services over $100;
alternatively, a three-hour pass
is available for $50. Note that the spa
is closed for maintenance some
Monday mornings.

New York Theatre Workshop

*79 E 4th Street, between Bowery
& Second Avenue (1-212 460 5475,
www.nytw.org). Subway F to Lower
East Side-Second Avenue; 6 to Astor
Place.* **Map** p61 D3 ⓷
Founded in 1979, the New York
Theatre Workshop works with emerg-
ing directors eager to take on chal-
lenging pieces. Besides plays by
world-class artists like Caryl Churchill
(Far Away, A Number) and Tony
Kushner (Homebody/Kabul), this
company also premièred Rent,
Jonathan Larson's Pulitzer Prize-
winning musical.

Performance Space 122

*150 First Avenue, at 9th Street (1-212
477 5288, www.ps122.org). Subway L
to First Avenue; 6 to Astor Place.*
Map p61 D2 ⓷
One of New York's most interesting
venues, this not-for-profit arts centre
presents experimental theatre, dance,
performance art, music, film and video.
Whoopi Goldberg, Eric Bogosian and
John Leguizamo have all developed
projects here. Australian trendsetter
Vallejo Gantner serves as artistic director, and has been working to give the
venue a more international scope.

Public Theater

*425 Lafayette Street, between Astor
Place & E 4th Street (1-212 539 8500,
Telecharge 1-212 239 6200, www.
publictheater.org). Subway N, R to 8th
Street-NYU; 6 to Astor Place.*
Map p61 D3 ⓷
The civic-minded Oskar Eustis is artistic director of this institution dedicated
to performing the work of new
American playwrights but also known
for its Shakespeare in the Park productions. The building, an Astor Place
landmark, has five stages and Joe's Pub
(see p89). It's also home to one of the
city's most dynamic troupes: Labyrinth
Theater Company, co-founded by actor
Philip Seymour Hoffman.

The Stone

*Avenue C, at 2nd Street (no phone,
www.thestonenyc.com). Subway F to
Lower East Side-Second Avenue.* No
credit cards. **Map** p61 E3 ⓷
Don't call sax star John Zorn's not-
for-profit venture a 'club'. You'll find
no food or drinks here, and no non-
sense, either: the Stone is an art space
dedicated to 'the experimental and the
avant-garde'. If you're down for some
rigorously adventurous sounds
(Anthony Coleman, Okkyung Lee,
Tony Conrad), Zorn has made it easy:
no advance sales, and all ages admitted. Bookings are left to a different
artist-cum-curator each month.

Greenwich Village

Stretching from Houston Street to 14th Street, between Broadway and Sixth Avenue, the Village has inspired bohemians for almost a century. Now that it's one of the most expensive neighbourhoods in the city, you need a lot more than a struggling artist's income to inhabit its leafy streets, but it's still a fine place for idle wandering, candlelit dining and hopping between bars and cabaret venues.

Sights & museums

Washington Square Park

Subway A, B, C, D, E, F, M to W 4th Street. **Map** p60 C3 123

The city's main burial ground until 1825, Washington Square Park has served ever since as the spiritual home, playground and meeting place for Greenwich Village. The Washington Square Arch at the northern end, was designed by Stanford White and dedicated in 1895. It marks the southern end of Fifth Avenue. The central fountain, completed in 1872, was recently shifted as part of the park's ongoing renovations to align it with the arch.

In the sixties, the park was a frequent gathering spot for the Beat poets – Allen Ginsberg gave several impromptu readings here – and it retains its vitality, thanks to the numerous street performers, NYU students, chess players, political agitators and hustlers who congregate when the weather is fine.

Eating & drinking

Blue Hill

75 Washington Place, between Sixth Avenue & Washington Square West (1-212 539 1776, www.bluehillnyc.com). Subway A, B, C, D, E, F, M to W 4th Street. Open 5.30-11pm Mon-Sat; 5.30-10pm Sun. **$$$. American. Map** p60 C3 124

More than a mere crusader for sustainability, Dan Barber is also one of the most talented cooks in town, building his menu around whatever's at its peak on his Westchester farm (home to a sibling restaurant). During fresh pea season, bright green infuses every inch of the menu, from a velvety spring pea soup to sous-vide duck breast as soft as sushi fanned over a bed of slivered sugar snap peas. Thanks to the 2009 visit from the Obamas, the restaurant's popularity is unlikely to wane any time soon.

Lupa

170 Thompson Street, between Bleecker & Houston Streets (1-212 982 5089, www.luparestaurant.com). Subway A, B, C, D, E, F, M to W 4th Street. **Open** noon-midnight daily. **$$. Italian. Map** p60 C3 125

No mere 'poor man's Babbo' (celeb-chef Mario Batali's pricier restaurant around the corner), this convivial trattoria offers communal dining, reasonably priced wines and hit-the-spot comfort foods. Come for classic Roman fare including punchy orecchiette with greens and sausage.

Minetta Tavern

113 MacDougal Street, between Bleecker & W 3rd Streets (1-212 475 3850, www.minettatavernny.com). Subway A, B, C, D, E, F, M to W 4th Street. **Open** 5.30pm-1am daily. **$$. Eclectic. Map** p60 C3 126

Thanks to restaurateur extraordinaire Keith McNally's spot-on restoration, this former literati hangout, once frequented by Hemingway and Fitzgerald, is as buzzy now as it must have been in its mid 20th-century heyday. The big-flavoured bistro fare is as much of a draw as the scene and includes classics such as roasted bone marrow, trout meunière topped with crabmeat, and an airy Grand Marnier soufflé for dessert. But the most illustrious thing on the menu is the Black Label burger. You might find the $26 price tag a little hard to swallow, but the superbly tender sandwich – essentially chopped steak in a bun smothered with caramelised onions – is worth every penny.

Vol de Nuit Bar (aka Belgian Beer Lounge)

148 W 4th Street, between Sixth Avenue & MacDougal Street (1-212 982 3388, www.voldenuitbar.com). Subway A, B, C, D, E, F, M to W 4th Street. **Open** 4pm-midnight Mon-Thur, Sun; 4pm-2.30am Fri, Sat. **Bar**. **Map** p60 C3 ⓫

Duck through an unmarked doorway on a busy stretch of West 4th Street and find yourself in a red-walled Belgian bar that serves brews exclusively from the motherland. Clusters of European grad students knock back glasses of De Konick and La Chouffe – just two of 19 beers on tap and 26 by the bottle. Moules and frites, fittingly, are the only eats available.

Shopping

Mxyplyzyk

125 Greenwich Avenue, at 13th Street (1-212 989 4300, www.mxyplyzyk.com). Subway A, C, E to 14th Street, L to Eighth Avenue. **Open** 11am-7pm Mon-Sat; noon-6pm Sun. **Map** p60 B2 ⓬

New York apartments are notoriously small, so finding home goods that do double duty is a necessity. At this shop (whose name – pronounced 'mix-ee-pliz-ick' – refers to an old Superman comic-book character), almost every practical item also functions just as well decoratively. Every inch of this 1,500-square-foot shop is lined with giftable utilitarian items packaged in hyperstylish exteriors. Though playfulness is certainly a theme, there are also organically influenced pieces, including reclaimed-wood nesting tables and grasscloth-covered lamps.

Nom de Guerre

640 Broadway, at Bleecker Street (1-212 253 2891, www.nomde guerre.net). Subway 6 to Bleecker Street.

Open noon-8pm Mon-Sat; noon-7pm Sun. **Map** p60 C3 ⓬

Fitting in nicely with its revolutionary name, this upscale streetwear label's Noho flagship store is designed to resemble a bunker; a forbidding caged metal staircase leads down to the store. A design collective founded by four New Yorkers, the understated line has a rugged, utilitarian look, encompassing upscale denim, military-inspired jackets, and classic shirts and knitwear.

Nightlife

Blue Note

131 W 3rd Street, between MacDougal Street & Sixth Avenue (1-212 475 8592, www.bluenote.net). Subway A, B, C, D, E, F, M to W 4th Street. **Map** p60 C3 ⓭

The Blue Note prides itself on being 'the jazz capital of the world'. Bona fide musical titans (Cecil Taylor, Charlie Haden) rub against hot young talents (the Bad Plus), while the close-set tables in the club get patrons rubbing up against each other. The Late Night Groove series and the Sunday brunches are the best bargain bets.

Comedy Cellar

117 MacDougal Street, between Bleecker & W 3rd Streets (1-212 254 3480, www.comedycellar.com). Subway A, B, C, D, E, F, M to W 4th Street. **Map** p60 C3 ⓭

Despite being named one of NYC's best stand-up clubs year after year, the Cellar maintains a hip, underground feel. It gets packed, but no-nonsense comics such as Colin Quinn, Jim Norton and Marina Franklin will distract you from your bachelorette-party neighbours.

Love

179 MacDougal Street, at 8th Street (1-212 477 5683, www.musicislove.net). Subway A, B, C, D, E, F, M to W 4th Street; R, W to 8th Street-NYU. **Open**

10pm-4am Thur-Sat; hrs vary Wed, Sun. **Map** p60 C3 **132**

The focus here is squarely on the music (ranging from techno and electro to deep house and hip hop). Although the main room is a sparsely furnished box, the DJ line-up is pretty impressive – the likes of the seminal Chicago house DJ Derrick Carter and Body & Soul's Joe Claussell have graced the decks – and the sound system is stunning.

(Le) Poisson Rouge

158 Bleecker Street, at Thompson Street (1-212 505 3474, www.lepoisson rouge.com). Subway A, B, C, D, E, F, M to W 4th Street. **Map** p60 C3 **133**

Located beneath the site of the legendary Village Gate – a performance space that once hosted Miles Davis and Jimi Hendrix – (Le) Poisson Rouge is reviving the corner's reputation as a musical intersection. The sleek new venue, replete with table service and a dinner menu, is a far cry from the basement where Bob Dylan wrote 'A Hard Rain's A-Gonna Fall', but what really sets it apart is the adventurous booking policy, pairing young classical artists such as pianist Simone Dinnerstein with compatible indie musicians like singer-songwriter Essie Jain. Jazz, experimental, hip hop, kids' events, comedy and even film screenings mingle on the schedule.

Sullivan Room

218 Sullivan Street, between Bleecker & W 3rd Streets (1-212 252 2151, www.sullivanroom.com). Subway A, B, C, D, E, F, M to W 4th Street. **Open** 10pm-5am Wed-Sun. **Map** p60 C3 **134**

Where's the party? It's right here in this unmarked subterranean space, which hosts some of the best deep-house, tech-house and breaks bashes the city has to offer. It's an utterly unpretentious place, but hell, all you really need are some thumpin' beats and a place to move your feet, right? Keep a special lookout for the nights hosted by special stalwarts Sleepy and Boo.

Arts & leisure

IFC Center

323 Sixth Avenue, at 3rd Street (1-212 924 7771, www.ifccenter.com). Subway A, B, C, D, E, F, M to W 4th Street. **Map** p60 B3 **135**

The long-darkened 1930s Waverly cinema was reborn in 2005 as the modern three-screen art house IFC Center, showing the latest indie hits, choice midnight cult items and foreign classics. You may occasionally rub elbows with the actors on the screen, as many introduce their work on opening night. A high-toned café provides sweets, lattes and substantials.

West Village & Meatpacking District

The area west of Sixth Avenue to the Hudson River, from 14th Street to Houston Street, has held on to much of its picturesque charm. Bistros abound along Seventh Avenue and Hudson Street and high-rent shops, including three Marc Jacobs boutiques, proliferate on this stretch of Bleecker Street. The West Village is also a long-standing gay mecca, although the young gay scene has mostly moved north to Chelsea.

The north-west corner of the West Village is known as the Meatpacking District, dating to its origins as a wholesale meat market in the 1930s. In recent years designer flagships, self-consciously hip eateries and nightclubs have moved in, and the area is the starting point for the High Line.

Sights & museums

High Line

www.thehighline.org. **Map** p102 B4 **136**

Running from Gansevoort Street in the Meatpacking District to 20th Street, the gateway to Chelsea's gallery district,

Bitter sweets

Confectionery gets tough.

Magnolia Bakery

In 1996, an indie West Village bakery kickstarted the trend for nostalgic, pastel-frosted cupcakes. After featuring in *Sex and the City* and *The Devil Wears Prada*, the success of **Magnolia Bakery** (401 Bleecker Street, at W 11th Street, 1-212 462 2572, www.magnolia bakery.com) was sealed. Fifteen years on, lines still snake out onto Bleecker Street and not only has it spawned a slew of cupcake copycats, it has opened branches on the Upper West Side and in the Rockefeller Center.

Time for a backlash against cutesy confectionery: now a handful of bakeries and chocolate shops are giving the sweet stuff a harder edge – with delicious results. A hot contender for the anti-Magnolia, nearby bakery-cum-bar **Sweet Revenge** (see p98) tops its cupcakes with spiky peaks of frosting in grown-up flavours, such as peanut butter with a ganache centre, and each one comes with a recommended beer or wine pairing. Over in the East Village, pastry chef Christina Tosi has been making waves at iconoclastic new **Momofuku Milk Bar** (see p84). Compost Cookies, Crack Pie (filled with a highly addictive butter, heavy cream and sugar concoction)… this is not your grandma's bake shop. Soft-serve ice-cream comes in unusual flavours such as 'Cereal Milk'. If you're more of a chocolate junkie, look no further than the clashing flavours at **Bespoke Chocolates** (see p86). Rising star Rachel Zoe Insler creates some of the best bonbons this side of the Bowery: sea-salted caramel coated in dark chocolate and crushed pretzels; a strawberry balsamic number with that telltale tang of vinegar; a Turkish coffee and cardamom truffle – all cater to sophisticated palates. Even more subversive, **Bond Street Chocolate** (see p87) turns out moulded dark chocolate skulls, religious icons (Jesus, Buddha) and unorthodox combinations, like corn nuts coated in milk chocolate and cocoa. Being bad has never tasted so good.

NEW YORK BY AREA

Meatpacking District p94

this slender, sinuous green strip – formerly an elevated freight train track – has been designed by landscape architects James Corner Field Operations and architects Diller Scofidio + Renfro. As well as lawns, trees and plantings, it has several interesting features along the way. Commanding an expansive river view, the 'sun deck' between 14th and 15th Streets features wooden deck chairs that can be rolled along the original tracks, plus a water feature with benches for cooling your feet. The old Nabisco factory that houses Chelsea Market received deliveries via the line; now the section cutting through the building is devoted to long-term, site-specific art. At 17th Street, steps descend into a sunken amphitheatre with a glassed-over 'window' in the steel structure overlooking the avenue. Further along, look out for the Empire State Building rising above the skyline to the east. The second phase, from 20th to 30th Streets, opened in the spring of 2011. See also box p75.

Eating & drinking

Corner Bistro
331 W 4th Street, at Jane Street (1-212 242 9502). Subway A, C, E to 14th Street; L to Eighth Avenue. **Open** 11.30am-4am Mon-Sat; noon-4am Sun. No credit cards. **Bar**. Map p60 B3 ⓲
There's only one reason to come to this legendary pub: it serves what many New Yorkers believe are the city's best burgers – and beer is just $2.50 a mug (well, that makes two reasons). The prime patties here are no frills and served on a paper plate. To get one, you may have to wait for a good hour, especially on weekend nights; if the wait is too long for a table, try to slip into a space at the bar.

Fedora
NEW *239 W 4th Street, between Charles & W 10th Streets (1-646 449 9336, www.fedoranyc.com). Subway A, B, C,*

D, E, F, M to W 4th Street; 1 to Christopher Street-Sheridan Square. **Open** 5pm-midnight daily. **$$**.
Canadian. Map p60 B3 ⓲
Restaurateur Gabriel Stulman has expanded his West Village mini-empire with this clubby French-Canadian knockout, the most chef-focused of any of his ventures. Au Pied de Cochon vet Mehdi Brunet-Benkritly produces some of the most exciting toe-to-tongue cooking in town, plying epicurean hipsters with Quebecois party food that's eccentric, excessive and fun. Feast on crispy octopus with brown-buttered sweetbreads – an inspired take on surf and turf – and a monster double-thick pork chop for two, or grab a stool at the bar for a killer steak sandwich and an old-fashioned cocktail, polished up with pecan bitter.

Gottino
NEW *52 Greenwich Avenue, between Charles & Perry Streets (1-212 633 2590, www.ilmiogottino.com/). Subway A, B, C, D, E, F, M to W 4th Street; 1 to Christopher Street-Sheridan Square.* **Open** 4pm-2am Mon-Fri; 11am-2am Sat, Sun. **Bar**. Map p60 B2 ⓲
See box p85.

Kesté Pizza & Vino
271 Bleecker Street, between Cornelia & Jones Streets (1-212 243 1500, www.kestepizzeria.com). Subway 1 to Christopher Street-Sheridan Square. **Open** noon-3.30pm, 5-11pm Mon-Sat; noon-3.30pm, 5-10pm Sun. **$**. **Pizza**. Map p60 B3 ⓲
If anyone can claim to be an expert on Neapolitan pizza, it's Kesté's Roberto Caporuscio: as president of the US branch of the Associazione Pizzaiuoli Napoletani, he's top dog for the training and certification of pizzaioli. At his intimate, 46-seat space pizzeria, it's all about the crust – blistered, salty and elastic, it could easily be eaten plain. Add fantastic toppings such as sweet-tart San

Marzano tomato sauce, milky mozzarella and fresh basil, and you have one of New York's finest pies.

Little Branch

20 Seventh Avenue South, at Leroy Street (1-212 929 4360). Subway 1 to Houston Street. **Open** 7pm-3am daily. **No credit cards**. **Bar**. **Map** p60 B3 **141**
Sasha Petraske's members-only Lower East Side bar Milk & Honey (134 Eldridge Street, between Broome & Delancey Streets, www.mlkhny.com) may require a referral, but Little Branch, his clubby, low-ceilinged Village rathskeller, retains an open-door policy. The drinks – such as a velvety smooth, mildly spiced hot buttered rum – are nigh perfect.

Pearl Oyster Bar

18 Cornelia Street, between Bleecker & W 4th Streets (1-212 691 8211, www.pearloysterbar.com). Subway A, B, C, D, E, F, M to W 4th Street. **Open** noon-2.30pm, 6-11pm Mon-Fri; 6-11pm Sat. **$$** **Seafood**. Map p60 B3 **142**
There's a good reason this convivial, no-reservations, New England-style fish joint always has a line – the food is outstanding. Signature dishes from the Pearl Oyster Bar include the lobster roll – sweet lemon-scented meat laced with mayonnaise on a butter-enriched bun – and a contemporary take on bouillabaisse: a briny lobster broth packed with mussels, cod, scallops and clams, topped with an aïoli-smothered croûton.

Rusty Knot

425 West Street, at 11th Street (1-212 645 5668). Subway 1 to Christopher Street-Sheridan Square. **Open** 4pm-4am Mon-Fri; noon-4am Sat, Sun. **Bar**. Map p60 A3 **143**
This Hudson River-hugging nautical 'dive bar' from Taavo Somer (Freemans) and Ken Friedman (the Spotted Pig) is a confusing, but successful, high-low hybrid. Faux Tiffany lamps and neon beer signs clash with the elaborate tiki cocktails (devised by Milk & Honey vet Toby Maloney), and with the foppish hordes who queue up outside the place. You'd never find the eponymous Rusty Knot – a refreshing, blender-whirred mix of rum, ice and mint – or food such as a luxe bacon and chicken liver sandwich at a grimy pub. But you would find three-buck pints of Busch and 50¢ rounds of pool. Happily, the Rusty Knot has those bases covered too.

Spotted Pig

314 W 11th Street, at Greenwich Street (1-212 620 0393, www.thespottedpig.com). Subway A, C, E to 14th Street; L to Eighth Avenue. **Open** noon-3pm, 5.30pm-2am Mon-Fri; 11am-3pm, 5.30pm-2am Sat, Sun. **$$**. **Eclectic**. Map p60 B3 **144**
With a creaky interior that recalls an ancient pub, this Anglo-Italian hybrid is still hopping – and even after opening more seating upstairs, a wait can always be expected. Some might credit the big names involved (Mario Batalil consults and April Bloomfield, of London's River Café, is in the kitchen). The burger is a must-order: a top-secret blend of ground beef grilled rare (unless otherwise specified) and covered with gobs of pungent roquefort cheese. It arrives with a tower of crispy shoestring fries tossed with rosemary. But the kitchen saves the best treat for dessert: a delectable slice of moist orange and bourbon chocolate cake.

Sweet Revenge

62 Carmine Street, between Bedford Street & Seventh Avenue (1-212 242 2240, www.sweetrevengenyc.com). Subway A, B, C, D, E, F, M to W 4th Street; 1 to Christopher Street-Sheridan Square. **Open** 8am-11pm Mon-Thur; 8am-12.30am Fri; 11am-12.30am Sat; 11am-9pm Sun. **$**. **Café/Bar**. Map p60 B3 **145**
See box p95.

Shopping

Castor & Pollux

238 W 10th Street, between Bleecker & Hudson Streets (1-212 645 6572, www.castorandpolluxstore.com). Subway A, B, C, D, E, F, M to W 4th Street; 1 to Christopher Street-Sheridan Square. **Open** noon-7pm Tue-Sat; 1-6pm Sun. **Map** p60 B3 ⓐ146

This beloved Brooklyn-born boutique unites European and New York labels in a stylish yet relaxed setting. Owner Kerrilynn Pamer sleuths out such breakout stars as Macedonian-born Risto Bimbiloski, the Louis Vuitton knitwear designer who launched his own womenswear label, and Caron Callahan, formerly of Derek Lam, whose beautifully simple line, Standard Finery, is manufactured in New York's Garment District. Unusual accessories are a constant feature at Castor & Pollux – look for the exquisitely handcrafted Reece Hudson lambskin bags by Parsons graduate Reece Solomon, and Katie Finn's delicate Elizabeth Street gold and gem jewellery.

Earnest Sewn

821 Washington Street, between Gansevoort & Little W 12th Streets (1-212 242 3414, www.earnestsewn. com). Subway A, C, E to 14th Street; L to Eighth Avenue. **Open** 11am-7pm Mon-Sat; 11am-6pm Sun. **Map** p60 A2 ⓐ147

Established by former Paper Denim & Cloth designer Scott Morrison, this culty jeans label marries vintage American style with old-school workmanship. Shirts and T-shirts for both men and women, and select accessories, are also sold in the rustic, brick-walled space.

Jeffrey New York

449 W 14th Street, between Ninth & Tenth Avenues (1-212 206 1272, www.jeffreynewyork.com). Subway A, C, E to 14th Street; L to Eighth Avenue. **Open** 10am-8pm Mon-Wed, Fri; 10am-9pm Thur; 10am-7pm Sat; 12.30-6pm Sun. **Map** p60 A2 ⓐ148

Jeffrey Kalinsky, a former Barneys shoe buyer, was a Meatpacking District pioneer when he opened his store in 1999. Designer clothing abounds here – by Yves Saint Laurent, Halston, L'Wren Scott and young British star Christopher Kane, among others. But the centrepiece is the shoe salon, featuring Manolo Blahnik, Prada and Christian Louboutin, as well as newer names to watch.

Rag & Bone

100 & 104 Christopher Street, between Bedford & Bleecker Streets (1-212 727 2990, 2999, www.rag-bone.com). Subway 1 to Christopher Street-Sheridan Square. **Open** noon-7pm daily. **Map** p60 B3 ⓐ149

Born out of its founders' frustration with mass-produced jeans, what began as a denim line in 2002 has expanded to cover clothing for both men and women, all with an emphasis on craftsmanship. The designs, in substantial, luxurious fabrics such as cashmere and tweed, nod towards tradition (riding jackets, greatcoats), while exuding an utterly contemporary vibe. This aesthetic is reflected in the brand's elegant, industrial-edged his 'n' hers stores.

Nightlife

Cielo

18 Little W 12th Street, between Ninth Avenue & Washington Street (1-212 645 5700, www.cieloclub.com). Subway A, C, E to 14th Street; L to Eighth Avenue. **Open** 10pm-4am Mon, Wed-Sat. **Map** p60 A2 ⓐ150

You'd never guess from the Heidi Montag wannabes hanging out in the neighbourhood that the attitude inside this exclusive club is close to zero – at least once you get past the bouncers. On the sunken dancefloor, hip-to-hip crowds gyrate to deep beats from top

NEW YORK BY AREA

DJs, including NYC old-schoolers Tedd Patterson and Louie Vega. Cielo, which features a crystal-clear sound system, has won a bevy of 'best club' awards – and it deserves them all.

Comix

353 W 14th Street, between Eighth & Ninth Avenues (1-212 524 2500, www.comixny.com). Subway A, C, E to 14th Street. **Map** p60 A2 **151**

Over the past few years, Comix has emerged as the club bridging the gap between the alternative and mainstream comedy worlds; its programming hovers somewhere between blockbuster spots like Carolines and the city's smaller, scrappier venues. The result is a mix of big names at the weekend and impressive up-and-comers during the week.

Henrietta Hudson

438 Hudson Street, at Morton Street (1-212 924 3347, www.henrietta hudson.com). Subway 1 to Christopher Street-Sheridan Square. **Open** 5pm-2am Mon, Tue; 4pm-4am Wed-Fri; 1pm-4am Sat, Sun. **Map** p60 B3 **152**

A much-loved lesbian nightspot, this glam lounge attracts young hottie girls from all over the New York area. Every night's a different party, with hip hop, pop and rock music and live shows among the musical pulls. Super-cool Lisa Cannistraci is in charge.

Smalls

183 W 10th Street, between Seventh Avenue South & W 4th Street (1-212 252 5091, www.smallsjazzclub.com). Subway 1 to Christopher Street-Sheridan Square. **Open** 7.30pm-4am daily. No credit cards. **Map** p60 B3 **153**

The resurrected version of this youth-friendly jazz spot offers a big concession for the grown-ups: a liquor licence and a fully stocked bar. One thing hasn't changed, though: the subterranean spot is still a place to catch the best and brightest up-and-comers, as well as the occasional moonlighting star.

Stonewall Inn

53 Christopher Street, between Seventh Avenue South & Waverly Place (1-212 488 2705, www.thestonewallinnnyc. com). Subway 1 to Christopher Street-Sheridan Square. **Open** 2pm-4am daily. **Map** p60 B3 **154**

This gay landmark is located next door to the famous original, the site of the 1969 gay rebellion against police harassment. Is it hip? No. But then you have to give the Stonewall Inn credit for being one of the few queer bars in the city that caters equally to males and females. Special nights range from dance soirées (upstairs) to bingo gatherings.

Village Vanguard

178 Seventh Avenue South, at Perry Street (1-212 255 4037, www.village vanguard.com). Subway A, C, E, 1, 2, 3 to 14th Street; L to Eighth Avenue. **Map** p60 B2 **155**

Seventy-five years old but still going strong, the Village Vanguard is one of New York's legendary jazz centres. History surrounds you: John Coltrane, Miles Davis and Bill Evans have all grooved in this hallowed hall. Big names both old and new still fill the schedule, and the 16-piece Vanguard Jazz Orchestra has been the Monday-night regular for more than 40 years.

Arts & leisure

Film Forum

209 W Houston Street, between Sixth Avenue & Varick Street (1-212 727 8110, www.filmforum.org). Subway 1 to Houston Street. **Map** p60 B4 **156**

The city's leading revival and repertory cinema, Film Forum is programmed by fest-scouring staff who take their duties as seriously as a Kurosawa samurai. The print qualities are invariably excellent, and a recent renovation included new seats, all the better to take in the hottest films from Cannes or that long-awaited Fellini retrospective.

Henrietta Hudson

Midtown

Midtown – the area roughly between 14th Street and 59th Street, from river to river – gets a bad rap. This is where most of New York works, and the throngs take over here along crowded pavements and congested streets. The area is not without attractions, however, boasting the city's most recognisable skyscrapers, including the Empire State Building, Chrysler Building and Rockefeller Center. But there's more to Midtown than iconic towers and commerce. It contains the city's most concentrated contemporary gallery district (Chelsea), its hottest gay enclaves (Chelsea and Hell's Kitchen), some of its swankiest shops (Fifth Avenue) and most of its big theatres on Broadway.

Chelsea

The corridor between 14th and 29th Streets west of Sixth Avenue emerged as the nexus of New York's queer life in the 1990s. While it's slowly being eclipsed by Hell's Kitchen to the north as a gay hotspot, it's still home to numerous bars, restaurants and shops catering to 'Chelsea boys'. The western edge of the neighbourhood is the city's major art gallery zone.

Sights & museums

Museum at FIT

Building E, Seventh Avenue, at 27th Street (1-212 217 4558, www.fitnyc. edu/museum). Subway 1 to 28th Street. **Open** noon-8pm Tue-Fri; 10am-5pm Sat. **Admission** free. **Map** p104 C3 ❶ The Fashion Institute of Technology owns one of the largest and most impressive collections of clothing, textiles and accessories in the world, including some 50,000 costumes and fabrics dating from the fifth century to the present. Overseen by fashion historian Valerie Steele, the museum showcases a selection from the permanent

Grand Central Terminal p135

collection, as well as temporary exhibitions focusing on individual designers or the role fashion plays in society.

Rubin Museum of Art

150 W 17th Street, at Seventh Avenue (1-212 620 5000, www.rmanyc.org). Subway A, C, E to 14th Street; L to Eighth Avenue; 1 to 18th Street. **Open** 11am-5pm Mon, Thur; 11am-7pm Wed; 11am-10pm Fri; 11am-6pm Sat, Sun. **Admission** $10; $5 reductions; free under-12s; free 6-10pm Fri.
Map p104 C4 ❷

Dedicated to Himalayan art, the Rubin is a very stylish museum – which falls into place when you learn the six-storey space was once occupied by famed fashion store Barneys. Rich-toned walls are classy foils for the serene statuary and intricate, multicoloured painted textiles. The second level is dedicated to What Is It? Himalayan Art, an introductory exhibit that displays selections from Donald and Shelley Rubin's collection of more than 2,000 pieces from the second century to the present day. The upper floors are devoted to temporary themed exhibitions.

Event highlights 'Gateway to Himalayan Art' (until 1 Jan 2012).

Eating & drinking

Cookshop

156 Tenth Avenue, at 20th Street (1-212 924 4440, www.cookshopny.com). Subway C, E to 23rd Street. **Open** 8-11am, 11.30am-3pm, 5.30-11.30pm Mon-Fri; 11am-3pm, 5.30-11.30pm Sat; 11am-3pm, 5.30-10pm Sun. **$$**.
American. Map p104 B4 ❸

Chef Marc Meyer and his wife/co-owner Vicki Freeman want Cookshop to be a platform for sustainable ingredients from independent farmers. True to the restaurant's mission, the ingredients are consistently top-notch, and the menu changes every day. While organic ingredients alone don't guarantee a great meal, Marc Meyer knows how to let the natural flavours speak for themselves, and Cookshop scores points for getting the house-made ice-cream to taste as good as Ben & Jerry's.

Half King

505 W 23rd Street, between Tenth & Eleventh Avenues (1-212 462 4300, www.thehalfking.com). Subway C, E to 23rd Street. **Open** 11am-4am Mon-Fri; 9am-4am Sat, Sun. **Bar.**
Map p104 B4 ❺

Don't let their blasé appearance fool you – the creative types gathered at the Half King's yellow pine bar are probably as excited as you are to catch a glimpse of the part-owner, author Sebastian Junger. While you're waiting, order one of the 14 draught beers – which include Lagunitas, IPA and a cloudy hefeweizen – or a speciality cocktail (we like the Parisian, made with Hendrick's Gin, sauvignon blanc and elderflower liquor).

Tillman's

165 W 26th Street, between Sixth & Seventh Avenues (1-212 627 8320, www.tillmansnyc.com). Subway F, 1 to 23rd Street. **Open** 5pm-2am Mon-Wed; 5pm-4am Thur, Fri; 7pm-4am Sat. **Bar. Map** p104 C3 ❻

NEW YORK BY AREA

Midtown 1

THEATER DISTRICT

A B C

See p106

Times Square
Information Cent

TKTS

Intrepid Sea, Air &
Space Museum

W 48TH ST
W 46TH ST
W 44TH ST
W 42ND ST

ELEVENTH AVE
TENTH AVE
NINTH AVE
EIGHTH AVE

Times
Square

A,C,E

N,Q,R,S,
1,2,3,7

Bry
Pa

W 40TH ST

Port Authority
Bus Terminal

Madame
Tussaud's
New York

GARMENT

DISTRICT

Javits
Center

W 38TH ST
W 36TH ST
W 34TH ST

Macy's

HERALD
SQUARE

A,C,E   1,2,3

B,D,F,N,Q,

BROADWAY

General
Post Office

Madison
Square
Garden

Penn
Station

Manhatt
Mall

W 30TH ST

WEST SIDE HWY

W 28TH ST

Chelsea
Park

Museum
at FIT

ELEVENTH AVE
TENTH AVE
NINTH AVE
EIGHTH AVE
SEVENTH AVE
SIXTH AVE

W 26TH ST

W 23RD ST

C,E

Chelsea Piers
Sports
Complex

W 22ND ST

CHELSEA

FLATIRO

DISTRIC

General Theological
Seminary of the
Episcopal Church

W 20TH ST

W 18TH ST

High Line

W 16TH ST

W 14TH ST

A,C,E,L   1,2,3   F,L

W 13TH ST

MEATPACKING
DISTRICT

LITTLE W 12TH ST

GANSEVOORT ST

HORATIO ST

JANE ST

W 12TH ST

GREENWICH AVE

WAVERLY PL

W 4T

WEST
VILLAGE

SIXTH AVE

D

E

F

See p107

E 48TH ST

E 46TH ST

Japan Society

1

Grand Central Terminal

101
105

Chrysler Building

100

United Nations Headquarters

102

E 44TH ST

E 42ND ST

S,4,5,6,7

107

104

7

M

TUDOR CITY PL

QUEENS-MIDTOWN TUNNEL

84

NY Public Library

E 40TH ST

Scandinavia House: The Nordic Center in America

E 38TH ST

2

Morgan Library

40

E 36TH ST

E 34TH ST

East River

Empire State Building

84

6

M

E 32ND ST

3

42

9

47

E 30TH ST

29

N,R

E 28TH ST

E 28TH ST

6

M

21

Museum of Sex

46

MT CARMEL PL

FIRST AVE

0   300 m

0   300 yds

© Copyright Time Out Group 2011

22

Madison Square

27

E 26TH ST

SECOND AVE

THIRD AVE

LEXINGTON AVE

PARK AVE SOUTH

MADISON AVE

E 24TH ST

Manhattan Marina

33

N,R

M

20

45

M

6

E 23RD ST

GRAMERCY PARK

ASSER LEVY PL

FRANKLIN D ROOSEVELT DR

70

4

69

Flatiron Building

37

E 22ND ST

Peter Cooper Village

Theodore Roosevelt Birthplace

43

Gramercy Park

National Arts Club

BROADWAY

32

24

41

IRVING PL

E 18TH ST

26

RUTHERFORD PL

NATHAN D PERLMAN PL

E 20TH ST

Stuyvesant Town

4

31

FIFTH AVE

32

36

E 16TH ST

44

Stuyvesant Square

Sights & museums

Eating & drinking

Union Square

L,N,Q,R,M
4,5,6

M

L

M

L

Shopping

Nightlife

Arts & leisure

5

13TH ST

12TH ST

E 12TH ST

AVE

AVE

11TH ST

DOWNTOWN
(pp56-101)

FOURTH AVE

E 11TH ST

10TH ST

St Mark's Church in-the-Bowery

E 10TH ST

Grace Church

UNIVERSITY PL

Time Out Shortlist | **New York 2012** 105

9TH ST

Midtown 2

A B C

W 72ND ST
B,C

Strawberry Fields

W 70TH ST

HENRY HUDSON PKWY

FREEDOM PL

WEST END AVE

AMSTERDAM AVE

COLUMBUS AVE

CENTRAL PARK WEST

WEST DRIVE

W 68TH ST

Sheep Meadow

W 66TH ST

BROADWAY

W 66TH ST

65TH ST TRANSVERSE

W 64TH ST

RIVERSIDE BLVD

Lincoln Center

Heckscher Playground

W 62ND ST

W 60TH ST
A,B,C,D

Columbus Circle

Time Warner Center

Museum of Arts & Design 93

W 58TH ST

Hearst Tower

W 57TH ST

Carnegie Hall N,Q,R 77

W 56TH ST

7

W 54TH ST

92 AVE

De Witt Clinton Park

HELL'S KITCHEN

Official N Informatio Center

B,D,E

W 52ND ST

78

TWELFTH AVE

ELEVENTH AVE

TENTH AVE

NINTH AVE

SEVENTH AVE

60

73

B,D,

W 50TH ST

C,E

1

N,R

69

64

99
98
97
96
95
94
92
90
88

Intrepid Sea, Air & Space Museum

86 56

W 48TH ST

THEATER DISTRICT

76

Times Square Information Cen

W 46TH ST 71

61

67

63 72 70

EIGHTH AVE

56

TKTS

84

65

59

68

75

81

Times Square

83 53

82

A,C,E

57

N,Q,R,S 1,2,3,7

81

W 42ND ST

80

Port Authority Bus Terminal

66

LINCOLN TUNNEL

W 40TH ST

Madame Tussaud's New York

SEVENTH AVE

BROA

78

W 38TH ST

GARMENT DISTRICT

76

Javits Center

W 36TH ST

Macy's 50

See p104 ▼

W 34TH ST
A,C,E
1,2,3

D **E** **F**

E 72ND ST

Naumburg
Bandshell

Asia Society
and Museum

The Frick
Collection

E 70TH ST

❶ Sights & museums
❶ Eating & drinking
❶ Shopping
❶ Nightlife
❶ Arts & leisure

1

E 68TH ST

6

Balto

China
Institute

E 66TH ST

Tisch Children's
Zoo

Delacorte
Musical Clock

E 64TH ST

Rockefeller
University

The
Dairy

F

Zoo

E 62ND ST

Trump
Wollman
Rink

**UPTOWN
(pp137-160)**

E 60TH ST

TRAMWAY

Scholars'
Gate

N,R

N,R

2

**QUEENSBORO
(59TH ST)BRIDGE**

Grand Army
Plaza

4,5,6

E 58TH ST

99

94   95

Trump Tower

E 57TH ST

E 56TH ST

100 96

E 54TH ST

103

Museum of
Modern Art

American
Folk Art
Museum

83 86 91

E,M

E 52ND ST

98 Paley Center
for Media

E,M

MIDTOWN

Radio City
Music Hall

St Patrick's Cathedral

E 50TH ST

98

6

89

90

Rockefeller
Center

NBC

Christie's

E 48TH ST

97

Japan Society

E 46TH ST

3

102

**United Nations
Headquarters**

Grand Central
Terminal

E 44TH ST

Chrysler
Building

B,D,F,M

101
105

7

100

107

4

Bryant
Park

87

S,4,5,6,7

E 42ND ST

NY Public
Library

E 40TH ST

Scandinavia House:
The Nordic Center
in America

E 38TH ST

0

300 m

40

Morgan
Library

E 36TH ST

0

300 yds

© Copyright Time Out Group 2011

5

ERALD
UARE

D,F,N,Q,R

Empire State
Building

6

See
p105

E 34TH ST

Sepia images of jazz, funk and soul legends line the walls at this warm, earth-toned cocktail emporium. Waitresses glide amid crescent-shaped leather booths, and you'll likely hear Coltrane oozing from the speakers. Given the old-fashioned aesthetic, a classic cocktail is the way to go: try a well-crafted negroni or a bracing dark & stormy (dark rum, ginger beer and lime juice).

Shopping

Antiques Garage

112 W 25th Street, between Sixth & Seventh Avenues (1-212 243 5343, www.annexmarkets.com). Subway F to 23rd Street. **Open** *9am-5pm Sat, Sun. No credit cards.* **Map** p104 C3 **7**
Designers (and the occasional celebrity) hunt regularly at this flea market held in a vacant parking garage. Specialities include old prints, vintage clothing and household paraphernalia. The weekend outdoor Hell's Kitchen Flea Market (39th Street, between Ninth & Tenth Avenues), run by the same people, features a mix of vintage clothing and textiles, furniture and miscellaneous bric-a-brac.

Billy's Bakery

184 Ninth Avenue, between 21st & 22nd Streets (1-212 647 9956, www.billys bakerynyc.com). Subway C, E to 23rd Street. **Open** *8.30am-11pm Mon-Thur; 8.30am-midnight Fri, Sat; 9am-10pm Sun.* **Map** p104 B4 **8**
Amid super-sweet retro delights such as coconut cream pie, cupcakes and Famous Chocolate Icebox Cake, you'll find friendly service in a setting that will remind you of grandma's kitchen – or at least, it will if your grandmother was Betty Crocker.

Loehmann's

101 Seventh Avenue, at 16th Street (1-212 352 0856, www.loehmanns.com). Subway A, C, E to 14th Street; L to Eighth Avenue; 1 to 18th Street. **Open** *9am-9pm Mon-Sat; 11am-7pm Sun.* **Map** p104 C5 **9**

You'll find five floors of major mark-downs on current and off-season clothes at this venerable discount emporium. Make a beeline upstairs to the Back Room for big names such as Prada and Armani. There are also accessories, fragances and housewares.

Mantiques Modern

146 W 22nd Street, between Sixth & Seventh Avenues (1-212 206 1494, www.mantiquesmodern.com). Subway 1 to 23rd Street. **Open** *10.30am-6.30pm Mon-Fri; 11am-7pm Sat, Sun.* **Map** p104 C4 **10**
Specialising in industrial and modernist furnishings and art from the 1880s to the 1980s, Mantiques Modern is a fantastic repository of beautiful and bizarre items, from kinetic sculptures and early-20th-century wooden artists' mannequins to a Russian World War II telescope and a rattlesnake frozen in a slab of Lucite. Pieces by famous designers such as Hermès sit side by side with natural curiosities, and skulls (in metal or Lucite), crabs, animal horns and robots are all recurring themes.

Printed Matter

195 Tenth Avenue, between 21st & 22nd Streets (1-212 925 0325, www. printedmatter.org). Subway C, E to 23rd Street. **Open** *11am-6pm Tue, Wed; 11am-7pm Thur-Sat.* **Map** p104 B4 **11**
This non-profit organisation, which operates a public reading room as well as a shop, is exclusively devoted to artists' books, from David Shrigley's deceptively naive illustrations to provocative photographic self-portraits by Matthias Herrmann. Works by unknown and emerging artists share shelf space with those of veterans such as Edward Ruscha.

Nightlife

The Eagle

554 W 28th Street, between Tenth & Eleventh Avenues (1-646 473 1866, www.eaglenyc.com). Subway C, E to

23rd Street. **Open** 10pm-4am Tue-Sat;
5pm-4am Sun. **No credit cards. Bar.**
Map p104 A3 🄬

You don't have to be a kinky leather
daddy to enjoy this manly outpost, but
it definitely doesn't hurt. Surprisingly
spic-and-span, this fetish bar is home
to an array of beer blasts, foot-worship
fêtes and leather soirées, plus simple
pool playing and cruising nights. In
summer, it hosts rooftop barbecues.

G Lounge

*225 W 19th Street, between Seventh
& Eighth Avenues (1-212 929 1085,
www.glounge.com). Subway 1 to 18th
Street.* **Open** 4pm-4am daily. No credit
cards. **Map** p104 C4 🄭

The neighbourhood's original slick boy
lounge – a rather moodily lit cave with
a cool brick-and-glass arched entrance –
wouldn't look out of place in an upscale
boutique hotel. It's a favourite after-
work cocktail spot, where an excellent
roster of DJs stays on top of the mood.

Highline Ballroom

*431 W 16th Street, between Ninth
& Tenth Avenues (1-212 414 5994,
www.highlineballroom.com). Subway
A, C, E to 14th Street; L to Eighth
Avenue.* **Map** p104 B5 🄮

This West Side club is LA-slick and
bland, in a corporate sense. But it still
has a lot to recommend it: the sound is
top-of-the-heap and sightlines are pretty
good. The bookings are also impressive,
whether a club appearance from the
Arctic Monkeys or the drag performer
Justin Bond. Perhaps coolest of all is a
weekly residency by the Roots, who
swing by after *Late Night with Jimmy
Fallon* tapings in the mood to jam – and
often accompanied by big-name guests.

Upright Citizens Brigade Theatre

*307 W 26th Street, between Eighth
& Ninth Avenues (1-212 366 9176,
www.ucbtheatre.com). Subway C, E
to 23rd Street; 1 to 28th Street.*
No credit cards. **Map** p104 B3 🄯

The UCB, which migrated from Chicago
in the 1990s, has been the most visible
catalyst in New York's current alternative comedy boom. The improv troupes
and sketch groups anchored here are the
best in the city. Stars of *Saturday Night
Live* and writers for late-night talk
shows gather on Sunday nights to wow
crowds in the long-running *ASSSSCAT
3000*. Other premier teams include the
Stepfathers (Fridays), Reuben Williams
and Death by Roo Roo (both on
Saturdays). If you can, get to your show
early so you can choose a good seat – the
venue has challenging sightlines.

Event highlights ASSSSCAT 3000
(7.30pm, 9.30pm Sun).

Arts & leisure

Atlantic Theater Company

*336 W 20th Street, between Eighth &
Ninth Avenues (Telecharge 1-212 239
6200, www.atlantictheater.org). Subway
C, E to 23rd Street.* **Map** p105 B4 🄰

Created in 1985 as an offshoot of acting
workshops led by playwright David
Mamet and actor William H Macy, the
dynamic Atlantic Theater Company
has presented dozens of new plays,
including Martin McDonagh's *The
Lieutenant of Inishmore* and Duncan
Sheik and Steven Sater's *Spring
Awakening*. Both productions trans-
ferred to Broadway.

Chelsea Piers

*Piers 59-62, W 17th to 23rd Streets,
at Eleventh Avenue (1-212 336 6666,
www.chelseapiers.com). Subway C, E to
23rd Street.* **Open** times vary; phone or
check website for details.
Map p104 A4 🄱

Chelsea Piers is still the most impressive
all-in-one athletic facility in New York.
Between the ice rink (Pier 61, 1-212 336
6100), the bowling alley (between Piers
59 & 60, 1-212 835 2695), the driving
range (Pier 59, 1-212 336 6400) and scads
of other choices, there's definitely something for everyone here. The Field
House (Pier 62, 1-212 336 6500) has a

Flatiron Building

climbing wall, a gymnastics centre, batting cages and basketball courts. At the Sports Center Health Club (Pier 60, 1-212 336 6000), you'll find a gym complete with comprehensive weight deck and cardiovascular machines, plus classes covering everything from boxing to triathlon training.

Joyce Theater

175 Eighth Avenue, at 19th Street (1-212 242 0800, www.joyce.org). Subway A, C, E to 14th Street; 1 to 18th Street; L to Eighth Avenue. **Map** p104 B4 ⓭
This intimate space houses one of the finest theatres – we're talking about sightlines – in town. Companies and choreographers that present work here, among them Ballet Hispanico, Pilobolus Dance Theater and Doug Varone, tend to be somewhat traditional. The Joyce also hosts dance throughout much of the year – Pilobolus is a summer staple. At the Joyce Soho, emerging companies present work most weekends.

The Kitchen

512 W 19th Street, between Tenth & Eleventh Avenues (1-212 255 5793, www.thekitchen.org). Subway A, C, E to 14th Street; L to Eighth Avenue. **Map** p104 B4 ⓮
The Kitchen, led by Debra Singer, offers some of the best experimental dance around – inventive, provocative and rigorous. Some of the artists who have presented work here are the finest in New York: Sarah Michelson, who also curates artists, Dean Moss, Jon Kinzel, Ann Liv Young and Jodi Melnick.

Flatiron District & Union Square

Taking its name from the distinctive wedge-shaped **Flatiron Building**, this district extends from 14th to 29th Streets, between Sixth and Lexington Avenues. The former commercial district became more residential in the 1980s as buyers were drawn to its early 20th-century industrial architecture and 19th-century brownstones; clusters of restaurants and shops followed.

Sights & museums

Flatiron Building

175 Fifth Avenue, between 22nd & 23rd Streets. Subway N, R, 6 to 23rd Street. **Map** p105 D4 ⓴
One of New York's most celebrated structures, the Flatiron Building was the world's first steel-frame skyscraper when it was completed in 1902. The 22-storey Beaux Arts edifice is clad in white limestone and terracotta, but it's the unique triangular shape as well as its singular position at the crossing of Fifth Avenue and Broadway that draws the stares of sightseers and natives alike.

Madison Square Park

23rd to 26th Streets, between Fifth & Madison Avenues (www.madison squarepark.org). Subway N, R, 6 to 23rd Street. **Map** p105 D3/D4 ㉑
Madison Square Park, which first opened in 1847, is one of the most elegant spaces in New York, surrounded by some of the city's most fabled buildings. The world's tallest skyscraper from 1909 to 1913, the Metropolitan Life Tower at 1 Madison Avenue was designed to resemble the Campanile in Venice's Piazza San Marco, whose reconstruction (after a collapse in 1902) Met Life had funded. The Appellate Division Courthouse at 27 Madison Avenue is one of the finest Beaux-Arts buildings in New York. The park itself hosts summer concerts, literary readings and kids' events. The undoubted star of the initiative is Mad Sq Art, a year-round 'gallery without walls', featuring installations from big-name artists such as Sol LeWitt and William Wegman.

Museum of Sex

233 Fifth Avenue, at 27th Street (1-212 689 6337, www.museumofsex.com). Subway N (weekends only), R, 6 to 28th

Street. **Open** 10am-8pm Mon-Thur, Sun; 10am-9pm Fri, Sat. **Admission** $16.75; $15.25 reductions. **Map** p105 D3 ㉒

Situated in the former Tenderloin district, which bumped-and-grinded with dance halls and brothels in the 1800s, MoSex explores the subject within a cultural context. On the ground floor, 'Action!', which screens around 220 clips from more than 150 years of sex on film, includes explicit scenes from such (literally) seminal porn flicks as *Deep Throat*. Upstairs, highlights of the permanent collection range from the tastefully erotic to the outlandish. The gift shop is stocked with books and arty sex toys.

Eating & drinking

230 Fifth

230 Fifth Avenue, between 26th & 27th Streets (1-212 725 4300, www. 230-fifth.com). Subway N, R to 28th Street. **Open** 4pm-4am daily.

Cocktail bar. **Map** p105 D3 ㉓

The 14,000-sq-ft roof garden dazzles with truly spectacular views, including a close-up of the Empire State Building, but the glitzy indoor lounge – with its ceiling-height windows, wraparound sofas and bold lighting – shouldn't be overlooked. While the sprawling outdoor space gets mobbed on sultry nights, it's less crowded in the cooler months when heaters, fleece robes and hot ciders make it a winter hotspot.

ABC Kitchen

NEW *ABC Carpet & Home, 35 E 18th Street, between Broadway and Park Avenue South (1-212 475 5829, www.abckitchennyc.com). Subway L, N, Q, R, 4, 5, 6 to 14th Street-Union Square.* **Open** noon-2.30pm, 5.30-10.30pm Mon-Thur; noon-2.30pm, 5.30-11pm Fri; 11am-2.30pm, 5.30-11.30pm Sat; 11am-2.30pm, 5.30-10.30pm Sun.

$$ Eclectic. **Map** p105 D4 ㉔

The haute green cooking at Jean-Georges Vongerichten's artfully decorated restaurant is based on the most gorgeous ingredients from up and down the East Coast. The local, seasonal bounty finds its way into dishes like a clam pizza, topped with pristine littlenecks, Thai chillies, sweet onions, garlic, lemon and herbs. Larger plates include a roasted chicken bathed in a vinegary glaze with wilted escarole and butter-sopped potato purée. Desserts, meanwhile, include a dazzling brown-butter tart with toasted hazelnuts and chocolate ganache. ABC delivers one message overall: Food that's good for the planet needn't be any less opulent, flavourful or stunning to look at.

Breslin Bar & Dining Room

Ace Hotel, 20 W 29th Street, at Broadway (1-212 679 1939). Subway B, D, F, M, N, Q, R to 34th Street-Herald Square. **Open** 7am-midnight daily. **$$$**. **Eclectic**. **Map** p105 D3 ㉕

The third project from restaurant savant Ken Friedman and Anglo chef April Bloomfield, the Breslin breaks gluttonous new ground. Expect a war at this no-reservations hotspot – quell your appetite at the bar with an order of scrumpets (fried strips of lamb belly). The overall ethos could be described as late-period Henry VIII: groaning boards of house-made terrines feature thick slices of guinea hen, rabbit and pork. The pig's foot for two – half a leg, really – could feed the full Tudor court. Amped-up classic desserts, such as sticky-toffee pudding, would befit a Dickensian Christmas feast.

Casa Mono/Bar Jamón

Casa Mono: *52 Irving Place, at 17th Street.* Bar Jamón: *125 E 17th Street, at Irving Place (1-212 253 2773, www.casamononyc.com). Subway L to Third Avenue; N, Q, R, 4, 5, 6 to 14th Street-Union Square.* **Open** *Casa Mono* noon-midnight daily. *Bar Jamón* 5pm-2am Mon-Fri; noon-2am Sat, Sun. **$-$$**.

Spanish. **Map** p105 E4 ㉖

Offal-loving consulting chef Mario Batali and protégé Andy Nusser go where many standard Manhattan tapas restaurants fear to tread: cocks' combs

Top tables – with beds

Many of the best new restaurants have hotels attached.

Breslin Bar & Dining Room

Time Out New York's 2010 Eat Out Awards revealed a surprising trend: not one, but three of the winning restaurants are in hotels. The antithesis of stodgy tourist traps or gilded expense-account dens, these are genuine hotspots with standout food, Downtown pedigrees and an energetic casual atmosphere.

Ken Friedman and chef April Bloomfield, the team behind glitzy gastropub the Spotted Pig, have mounted a double threat at Midtown's Ace Hotel, with the **Breslin Bar & Dining Room** (see left), and the **John Dory Oyster Bar** (see p114). Both are packed nightly as much for the scene as their excellent food.

Another white-hot destination is **Locanda Verde** (see p69) at Tribeca's Greenwich Hotel, from chef Andrew Carmellini and part-owner Robert De Niro. The rustic, wood-beamed dining room is boisterous (as is the bar), prices are reasonable, and the lusty Italian cuisine approachable yet impeccable (don't skip desserts

by the talented pastry chef Karen DeMasco). Master restaurateur Danny Meyer also tackled Italian, teaming up with hotelier Ian Schrager at the Gramercy Park Hotel. The result is **Maialino** (see p118), a Roman-style establishment with a salumi station, house-made pastries and breads, a top-notch wine list and a menu of the Eternal City's classics (spaghetti carbonara, roasted suckling pig, fried artichokes). If it's tough to get a table in the dining room, pop into the casual enoteca up front for a glass of wine and nibbles.

But the most unexpected move off the hotel lobby – and to Midtown – is by quintessential East Village chef and culinary bad boy David Chang, who debuted his first Vietnamese-inspired eatery, **Má Pêche** (see p136), in the Chambers Hotel, bringing his signature spare aesthetic (wooden communal dining tables), a branch of his unorthodox bakery, Momofuku Milkbar – and a Downtown vibe.

with ceps, pigs' feet with caper aïoli, and sweetbreads dusted with almond flour and fried. There are some equally intriguing options for non-organ lovers, which might include fried duck egg, a delicately flavoured breakfast-meets-dinner dish topping a mound of sautéed fingerling potatoes and salt-cured tuna loin. For a cheaper option, head to the attached Bar Jamón, which serves a more casual menu of Ibérico hams, *bocaditos* and Spanish cheeses.

Eleven Madison Park

11 Madison Avenue, at 24th Street (1-212 889 0905, www.elevenmadison park.com). **Subway** *N, R, 6 to 23rd Street.* **Open** noon-2pm, 5.30-10pm Mon-Thur; noon-2pm, 5.30-10.30pm Fri; 5.30-10.30pm Sat. **$$$**. **American**. Map p105 D4 ㉗
Eat Out Award-winning chef Daniel Humm mans the kitchen at Danny Meyer's vast art deco jewel. His lofty intentions are best expressed in a three- or four-course tasting menu: A starter of *la ratte* potatoes features Hawaiian prawns and delicate rings of calamares spiked with lemon, and an entrée of Muscovy duck gets a floral note from lavender-honey glaze. In a classic Meyer show of hospitality, you'll head out with a quartet of delectable petits fours.

Flatiron Lounge

37 W 19th Street, between Fifth & Sixth Avenues (1-212 727 7741, www.flatiron lounge.com). **Subway** *F, N, R to 23rd Street.* **Open** 5pm-2am Mon-Wed, Sun; 5pm-3am Thur; 5pm-4am Fri, Sat. **Cocktail Bar**. Map p105 D4 ㉘
Red leather booths, mahogany tables and globe-shaped lamps amp up the vintage vibe at this art deco space. Co-owner Julie Reiner's notable mixology skills have made the bar a destination, and her Beijing Punch (jasmine-infused vodka and white peach purée) is not to be missed.

John Dory Oyster Bar

NEW *1196 Broadway, at 29th Street (1-212 792 9000, www.thejohndory.com).* *Subway N, R to 28th Street.* **Open** noon-2am Mon-Sat. **$$$**. **American**. Map p105 D3 ㉙
April Bloomfield and Ken Friedman's original Meatpacking District's John Dory was an ambitious, pricey endeavour, but its reincarnation in the Ace Hotel is an understated knockout. Tall stools face a raw bar stocked with East and West Coast oysters, all expertly handled and impeccably sourced. True to form, the rest of Bloomfield's tapas-style seafood dishes are intensely flavoured. Chilled lobster tastes larger than life, its sweet flesh slicked in an herbaceous tomalley vinaigrette. Meanwhile, warm dishes take their cues mostly from the garlic-and-olive-oil belt – meaty octopus doused in aïoli, plus miniature mussels stuffed with boisterous mortadella meatballs. Though the utilitarian sweets aren't worth sticking around for, the savoury food here merits the inevitable wait for a table.

Raines Law Room

48 W 17th Street, between Fifth & Sixth Avenues (no phone). *Subway F to 14th Street; L to Sixth Avenue.* **Open** 5pm-2am Mon-Thur; 5pm-3am Fri; 7pm-3am Sat; 8pm-2am Sun. **Cocktail bar**. Map p105 D4 ㉚
There's no bar to belly up to at this louche lounge. In deference to its name (which refers to an 1896 law designed to curb liquour consumption), drinks are prepared in a half-hidden room at the back of the plush, upholstered space. The cocktail list includes classics like the manhattan and negroni, and variations thereof.

Rye House

11 W 17th Street, between Fifth & Sixth Avenues (1-212 255 7260, www.ryehousenyc.com). *Subway F to 14th Street; L to Sixth Avenue.* **Open** noon-2am Mon-Fri; 11am-4pm, 5pm-2am Sat, Sun. **Cocktail bar**. Map p105 D4 ㉛
As the name suggests, American spirits are the emphasis at this dark, sultry bar.

Along with a selection of bourbons and ryes, there are gins, vodkas and rums, all distilled in the States. Top-notch mixed drinks include chai-infused rye, and the Creole daiquiri, which combines New Orleans rum with chorizo-flavoured mescal (it's a bit like sipping a taco, in a good way). While the focus is clearly on drinking, there's excellent upscale pub grub; we liked the fiery fried buffalo sweetbreads.

Shopping

ABC Carpet & Home

888 Broadway, at 19th Street (1-212 473 3000, www.abchome.com). Subway L, N, Q, R, 4, 5, 6 to 14th Street-Union Square. **Open** 10am-7pm Mon-Sat; 11am-6.30pm Sun. **Map** p105 D4 ❸❷
Most of ABC's 35,000-strong carpet range is housed in the store across the street at No.881 – except the rarest rugs, which reside on the sixth floor of the main store. Browse everything from organic soap to hand-beaded lamp-shades on the ground floor. Furniture, on the upper floors, spans every style, from European minimalism to antique oriental and mid-century modern.

Eataly

[NEW] *200 Fifth Avenue, between 23rd & 24th Streets (1-212 229 2560, www.eataly.com). Subway F, M, N and R to 23rd Street.* **Open** 7am-11pm daily. **Map** p105 D4 ❸❸
This massive food and drink complex, from Mario Batali and Joe and Lidia Bastianich, sprawls across 42,500 square feet in the Flatiron District. A spin-off of an operation by the same name just outside of Turin, the store's retail maze and six full-service restaurants include a rotisserie with the city's best flame-roasted chickens, an awe-inspiring display of hard-to-find produce (plus an in-house 'vegetable butcher') and the meatcentric white-tablecloth joint Il Manzo, which serves a gorgeous tartare of Montana-raised Piedmontese-breed beef.

Idlewild

12 W 19th Street, between Fifth & Sixth Avenues (1-212 414 8888, www.idlewildbooks.com). Subway F to 14th Street; L to Sixth Avenue. **Open** 11.30am-8pm Mon-Fri; noon-7pm Sat, Sun. **Map** p105 D4 ❸❹
Opened by a former United Nations press officer, Idlewild stocks travel guides to more than 100 countries and all 50 states, which are grouped with related works of fiction and non-fiction. Fun fact: Idlewild was the original name for JFK Airport before it was renamed to honour the assassinated president.

Showplace Antique & Design Center

40 W 25th Street, between Fifth & Sixth Avenues (1-212 633 6063, www.nyshowplace.com). Subway F to 23rd Street. **Open** 10am-6pm Mon-Sat; 8.30am-5.30pm Sun. **Map** p104 C3 ❸❺
Set over four expansive floors, this indoor market houses more than 200 high-quality dealers selling everything from vintage designer wear to Greek and Roman antiquities. Among the highlights are Joe Sundlie Vintedge's colourful, on-trend vintage pieces from Lanvin and Alaïa on the ground floor and Mood Indigo – arguably the best source in the city for collectible bar accessories and dinnerware. The Bakelite jewellery and table accessories, and Fiestaware, are dazzling.

Union Square Greenmarket

From 16th to 17th Streets, between Union Square East & Union Square West (1-212 788 7476, www.grownyc.org/unionsquaregreenmarket). Subway L, N, Q, R, 4, 5, 6 to 14th Street-Union Square. **Open** 8am-6pm Mon, Wed, Fri, Sat. **Map** p105 D4 ❸❻
There are more than fifty open-air Greenmarkets throughout the city run by the non-profit GrowNYC organisation. At this, the largest and best known, small producers of cheese, herbs, fruits and vegetables hawk their goods directly to the public.

Vintage Thrift Shop

268 Third Avenue, between 22nd & 23rd Streets (1-212 871 0777, www.vintagethriftshop.org). Subway 6 to 23rd Street. **Open** 10.30am-8pm Mon-Sat; 11am-7pm Sun **Map** p105 E4 ㊲
There's a rotating mix of astoundingly well-preserved designer and nonvintage clothing here, as well as one-of-a-kind housewares, shoes and accessories. We've found vintage Yves Saint Laurent blouses for $12, striped skinny ties for $6 and a pair of classic Salvatore Ferragamo pumps with bows on them for $10. Pretty much everything is a find, but you still get that thrill-of-the-hunt feeling.

Nightlife

Metropolitan Room

34 W 22nd Street, between Fifth & Sixth Avenues (1-212 206 0440, www.metropolitanroom.com). Subway F, R to 23rd Street. **Map** p105 D4 ㊳
The Met Room has established itself as the must-go venue for high-level nightclub singing that won't bust your wallet. Regular performers range from rising musical-theatre stars to established cabaret acts (including Baby Jane Dexter and English songstress Barb Jungr), plus legends such as Tammy Grimes, Julie Wilson and Annie Ross.

Splash

50 W 17th Street, between Fifth & Sixth Avenues (1-212 691 0073, www.splash bar.com). Subway F to 14th Street; L to Sixth Avenue. **Open** 4pm-4am daily. No credit cards. **Map** p104 C4 ㊴
This NYC queer institution offers 10,000sq ft of dance and lounge space, plus the famous onstage showers, where hunky go-go boys get wet and wild. The super-muscular bartenders here seem bigger than ever, and nationally known DJs still rock the house, local drag celebs give good face, and in-house VJs flash hypnotic snippets of classic musicals spliced with video visuals.

Gramercy Park & Murray Hill

A key to Gramercy Park, the gated square at the southern end of Lexington Avenue (between 20th & 21st Streets), is the preserve of residents of the surrounding homes (and members of a couple of venerable private clubs). Murray Hill spans 30th to 40th Streets, between Third and Fifth Avenues. Townhouses of the rich and powerful were once clustered around Madison and Park Avenues, but these days, only a few streets retain their former elegance and the area is mainly populated by upwardly mobiles fresh out of university.

Sights & museums

Morgan Library & Museum

225 Madison Avenue, at 36th Street (1-212 685 0008, www.themorgan.org). Subway 6 to 33rd Street. **Open** 10.30am-5pm Tue-Thur; 10.30am-9pm Fri; 10am-6pm Sat; 11am-6pm Sun. **Admission** $15; free-$10 reductions. **Map** p105 D2/p105 D5 ㊵
This Madison Avenue institution began as the private library of financier J Pierpont Morgan. It houses first-rate works on paper, including drawings by Michelangelo, Rembrandt and Picasso; a copy of *Frankenstein* annotated by Mary Shelley; manuscripts by Steinbeck, Twain and Wilde; sheet music handwritten by Beethoven and Mozart; and an original edition of Dickens' *A Christmas Carol* that's displayed every Yuletide.
Event highlights Charles Dickens at 200 (23 Sept 2011-12 Feb 2012).

Eating & drinking

71 Irving Place Coffee & Tea Bar

71 Irving Place, between 18th & 19th Streets (1-212 995 5252,

Broadway's Arachnophobia

Spider-Man: Hero with 1,000 Previews.

Broadway producers have long craved a pre-opening night buzz, but the noise surrounding *Spider-Man: Turn off the Dark* before the rise of the first curtain has already turned the musical into a pop-cultural sensation. Costing over $65 million (thus far), the musical is the most expensive in Broadway history, earning the dubious distinction of having the longest preview run (it is expected to have had close to 200 by the time it opens). The delays and several accidents during rehearsal have spun talk of a *Spider-Man* 'curse'.

Given the runaway success of the *Spider-Man* film trilogy as well as music and lyrics by U2's The Edge and Bono, expectations have been high for a massive hit. Respected director Julie Taymor (*The Lion King*) was hired to oversee the ambitious production, which was marked by elaborate aerial stunts involving actors (and stuntmen) swinging from 'webs' above the stage and audience. Because the highly technical stunts were designed for the

Foxwoods Theatre, *Spider-Man* had no out-of-town previews to iron out its kinks before the first preview in November 2010.

The disasters began that night, when an actress was struck on the head by some equipment offstage, suffering concussion. Several weeks later, the cord to a safety harness broke during a stuntman's performance and he fell 30 feet, sustaining multiple injuries. Two other stunt doubles were hurt during rehearsals, and one preview performance was marred when the Green Goblin's flight over the audience was abruptly halted because his steering mechanism failed, leaving him dangling in mid-air. As these hapless previews continued, the actual opening night was pushed back six times. Eventually, Taymor left citing 'artistic differences', *Spider-Man* took some time off for retooling and the show finally opened in June 2011. After all that, critics didn't deem it a flop, nor did they see a show that lived up to the hype and budget.

www.irvingfarm.com). *Subway L, N, Q,*
R, 4, 5, 6 to 14th Street-Union Square.
Open 7am-11pm Mon-Fri; 8am-11pm
Sat. **$**. **Café**. **Map** p105 D4 🟠
Irving Farm's beans are roasted in a
100-year-old carriage house in the
Hudson Valley; fittingly, its Gramercy
Park café, in a stately brownstone, also
has a quaint, rustic edge. Breakfast
(granola, oatmeal, waffles, bagels),
sandwiches and salads accompany the
superior-quality java.

Artisanal

2 Park Avenue, at 32nd Street (1-212
725 8585, www.artisanalbistro.com).
Subway 6 to 33rd Street. **Open** 11.45am-
11pm Mon-Sat; 11am-10pm Sun. **$$**.
French. **Map** p105 D3 🟠
As New York's bistros veer towards
uniformity, Terrance Brennan's high-
ceilinged deco gem makes its mark
with an all-out homage to fromage.
Skip the appetisers and open with fon-
due, which comes in three varieties.
Familiar bistro fare awaits, with such
dishes as steak frites and a delectable
glazed Scottish salmon, but the curd
gets the last word with the cheese and
wine pairings. These selections of three
cheeses – chosen by region, style or
theme (for example, each one produced
in a monastery) – are matched with
three wines (or beers or even sakés) for
a sumptuous and intriguing finale.

Maialino

Gramercy Park Hotel, 2 Lexington
Avenue, at 21st Street (1-212 777
2410). Subway 6 to 23rd Street.
Open 7.30am-10.30pm Mon-Thur;
7.30am-11pm Fri; 10am-11pm Sat;
10am-10.30pm Sun. **$$**. **Italian**.
Map p105 D4 🟠
Danny Meyer's first full-fledged foray
into Italian cuisine is a dedicated homage to the neighbourhood trattoria.
Salumi and bakery stations between the
front bar and the wood-beamed dining
room – hog jowls and sausages dangling
near shelves stacked with crusty loaves
of bread – mimic a market off the

Appian Way. Chef Nick Anderer's menu
offers exceptional facsimiles of dishes
specific to Rome: carbonara, braised
tripe and suckling pig, among others.

Nightlife

Fillmore New York at Irving Plaza

17 Irving Place, at 15th Street (1-212
777 6800, www.livenation.com). Subway
L, N, Q, R, 4, 5, 6 to 14th Street-Union
Square. **Map** p105 D5 🟠
Just east of Union Square, this mid-sized
rock venue has served as a Democratic
Party lecture hall, a Yiddish theatre and
a burlesque house (Gypsy Rose Lee
made an appearance). New York rock
fans still know it as simply 'Irving
Plaza'; it received the 'Fillmore' addition
in 2007 and was inaugurated with a Lily
Allen show. Regardless, it's a great
place to see big stars keeping a low pro-
file (Jeff Beck, Devo and Lenny Kravitz)
and medium heavies on their way up.

Gramercy Theatre

127 E 23rd Street, between Park
& Lexington Avenues (1-212 777
6800). Subway R, 6 to 23rd Street.
Map p105 D4 🟠
The Gramercy Theatre – formerly
known as the Blender Bar at Gramercy
Theatre – looks exactly like what it is,
a run-down former movie theatre; yet
it has a decent sound system and good
sightlines. Patrons can lounge in raised
seats on the top level or get closer to the
stage. Bookings have included such
Baby Boom underdogs as Loudon
Wainwright III and Todd Rundgren,
and the occasional hip hop show (Kool
Keith, Asher Roth), but tilt towards
musty, 1990s-flavoured rock bands.

Rodeo Bar & Grill

375 Third Avenue, at 27th Street (1-212
683 6500, www.rodeobar.com). Subway
6 to 28th Street. **Map** p105 E3 🟠
The unpretentious, if sometimes rau-
cous crowd, roadhouse atmosphere and
absence of a cover charge help make the

Rodeo the city's best roots club, with a steady stream of rockabilly, country and related sounds. Kick back with a beer from the bar – an old, hollowed-out bus sitting in the middle of the room.

Shopping

Cheap Jack's

303 Fifth Avenue, at 31st Street (1-212 777 9564, www.cheapjacks.com). Subway B, D, F, M, N, Q, R to 34th Street-Herald Square. **Open** 11am-8pm Mon-Sat; noon-7pm Sun. **Map** p105 D3 ④⑦

Some people pass this Cheap Jack's store off as too 'costumey', but you just need to know how to buy here. Avoid the fringed suede vests (too '70s) and poofy prom dresses (too '80s) and you can land plenty of interesting pieces. Racks of separates that won't clean you out are just what your wardrobe has been wanting.

Herald Square & Garment District

Seventh Avenue is the main drag of the Garment District (roughly from 34th to 40th Streets, between Broadway & Eighth Avenue), where designers feed America's multibillion-dollar clothing industry. The world's largest store, Macy's, looms over Herald Square (at the junction of Broadway and Sixth Avenue). To the east, the spas, restaurants and karaoke bars of Koreatown line 32nd Street, between Fifth and Sixth Avenues.

Eating & drinking

Keens Steakhouse

72 W 36th Street, between Fifth & Sixth Avenues (1-212 947 3646, www.keens.com). Subway B, D, F, M, N, Q, R to 34th Street-Herald Square. **Open** 11.45am-10.30pm Mon-Fri; 5-10.30pm Sat; 5-9pm Sun. **$$**. **Steakhouse**. **Map** p104 C2 ④⑧

The ceiling and walls are hung with pipes, some from such long-ago Keens regulars as Babe Ruth, J.P. Morgan and Teddy Roosevelt. Even in these non-smoking days, you can catch a whiff of the restaurant's 120-plus years of history. Beveled-glass doors, two working fireplaces and a forest's worth of dark wood suggest a time when "Diamond Jim" Brady piled his table with bushels of oysters, slabs of seared beef and troughs of ale. The menu still lists a three-inch-thick mutton chop (imagine a saddle of lamb but with more punch) and desserts such as key lime pie. Sirloin and porterhouse (for two or three) hold their own against any steak in the city.

Mandoo Bar

2 W 32nd Street, between Fifth Avenue & Broadway (1-212 279 3075). Subway B, D, F, M, N, Q, R to 34th Street-Herald Square. **Open** 11am-11pm daily. **$**. **Korean**. **Map** p105 D3 ④⑨

If the staff painstakingly filling and crimping dough squares in the front window don't give it away, we will – this wood-wrapped industrial-style spot elevates *mandoo* (Korean dumplings) above mere appetiser status. Six varieties of the tasty morsels are filled with such delights as subtly piquant kimchi, juicy pork, succulent shrimp and vegetables. Try them miniaturised, as in the 'baby mandoo', swimming in a soothing beef broth or atop springy, soupy ramen noodles.

New York Kom Tang Kalbi House

32 W 32nd Street, between Fifth Avenue & Broadway (1-212 947 8482). Subway B, D, F, M, N, Q, R to 34th Street-Herald Square. **Open** 24hrs Mon-Sat. **$$**. **Korean**. **Map** p105 D3 ⑤⓪

Tender *kalbi* (barbecued short ribs) are indeed the stars here; their signature smoky flavour comes from being cooked over *soot bul* (wood chips). The oldest Korean restaurant in the city also makes crisp, seafood-laden *haemool pajun* (pancakes); sweet, juicy *yuk hwe* (raw beef salad); and garlicky *bulgogi*. *Kom tang*, or 'bear soup', is a milky beef broth that's deep and soothing.

Shopping

B&H

420 Ninth Avenue, at 34th Street (1-212 444 5040, www.bhphotovideo.com). Subway A, C, E to 34th Street-Penn Station. **Open** *9am-7pm Mon-Thur; 9am-1pm Fri; 10am-6pm Sun.* **Map** *p104 B2* ⑤1
In this huge, busy store, goods are transported from the stock room via an overhead conveyor belt. B&H is the ultimate one-stop shop for all your photographic, video and audio needs. Note that, due to the largely Orthodox Jewish staff, the store is closed on Saturdays.

Macy's

151 W 34th Street, between Broadway & Seventh Avenue (1-212 695 4400, www.macys.com). Subway B, D, F, M, N, Q, R to 34th Street-Herald Square; 1, 2, 3 to 34th Street-Penn Station. **Open** *10am-9.30pm Mon-Sat; 11am-8.30pm Sun.* **Map** *p104 C2/p106 C5* ⑤2
It may not be as glamorous as New York's other famous retailers, but for sheer breadth of stock, the 34th Street behemoth is hard to beat. You won't find exalted labels here, though; mid-priced fashion and designers' diffusion lines for all ages are its bread and butter, along with all the big beauty names. Among the largely mainstream refreshment options is a Ben & Jerry's outpost. There's also a branch of the Metropolitan Museum of Art gift store.

Arts & leisure

Juvenex

5th Floor, 25 W 32nd Street, between Fifth Avenue & Broadway (1-646 733 1330, www.juvenexspa.com). Subway B, D, F, M, N, Q, R to 34th Street-Herald Square. **Open** *24hrs daily.* **Map** *p105 D3* ⑤3

This bustling K-town relaxation hub may be slightly rough around the edges (frayed towels, dingy sandals), but we embrace it for its bathhouse-meets-Epcot feel (igloo saunas, tiled 'soaking ponds' and a slatted bridge), and 24hr availability (women only before 5pm). A basic Purification Program – including soak and sauna, face, body and hair cleansing and a salt scrub – is great value at $115.

Madison Square Garden

Seventh Avenue, between 31st & 33rd Streets, Garment District (1-212 465 6741, www.thegarden.com). Subway A, C, E, 1, 2, 3 to 34th Street-Penn Station. **Map** *p104 C3* ⑤4
Some of music's biggest acts – Jay-Z, U2, Neil Young, Lady Gaga among others – come out to play at the self-styled 'world's most famous arena', where basketball's Knicks and hockey's Rangers also ply their trades. Whether you'll actually be able to get a look at them depends on your seat number or the quality of your binoculars. The arena is far too vast for a rich concert experience, ugly and a little bit musty, but it remains part of the fabric of New York and begrudgingly beloved.

Theater District & Hell's Kitchen

Times Square is the gateway to the Theater District, the zone roughly between 41st Street and 53rd Street, from Sixth Avenue to Ninth Avenue. Thirty-eight of the opulent show houses here – those with more than 500 seats – are designated as being part of Broadway (plus the Vivian Beaumont Theater, uptown at Lincoln Center; p154). Just west of Times Square is Hell's Kitchen, which maintained a crime-ridden, tough veneer well into the 1970s. Today, it's emerging as the city's new queer mecca. Pricey Restaurant Row (46th Street, between Eighth

Times Square p122

& Ninth Avenues) caters to theatregoers, but Ninth Avenue itself, with its cornucopia of ethnic eateries, is a better bet.

Sights & museums

Circle Line Cruises

Pier 83, 42nd Street, at the Hudson River (1-212 563 3200, www.circleline 42.com). Subway A, C, E to 42nd Street-Port Authority. **Tickets** *$36; $23-$31 reductions.* **Map** p104 A1/p106 A4 ⑮

Circle Line's famed three-hour guided circumnavigation of Manhattan Island is a fantastic way to get your bearings and see many of the city's sights as you pass under its iconic bridges. Themed tours include an evening 'Harbor Lights' sailing and an autumn foliage ride to Bear Mountain in the Hudson Valley. If you don't have time for the full round trip, there's a two-hour 'Liberty' tour that takes you around Downtown to the Brooklyn Bridge and back.

Intrepid Sea, Air & Space Museum

USS Intrepid, Pier 86, Twelfth Avenue & 46th Street (1-877 957 7447, www. intrepidmuseum.org). Subway A, C, E to 42nd Street-Port Authority, then M42 bus to Twelfth Avenue or 15min walk. **Open** *Apr-Oct 10am-5pm Mon-Fri; 10am-6pm Sat, Sun. Nov-Mar 10am-5pm Tue-Sun.* **Admission** *$22; free-$18 reductions.* **Map** p104 A1/p106 A4 ⑯

Commissioned in 1943, this 27,000-ton, 898ft aircraft carrier survived torpedoes and kamikaze attacks in World War II, served during Vietnam and the Cuban Missile Crisis, and recovered two space capsules for NASA. It was decommissioned in 1974, then resurrected as an educational institution. On its flight deck and portside aircraft elevator are top-notch examples of American military might, including the US Navy F-14 Tomcat (from *Top Gun*), an A-12 Blackbird spy plane and a fully restored Army AH-1G Cobra gunship helicopter. In the spring of 2011, the museum

became home to the Enterprise (OV-101), the first Space Shuttle Orbiter, which was recently retired.

Times Square

From 42nd to 47th Streets, between Broadway & Seventh Avenue. Subway N, Q, R, S, 1, 2, 3, 7 to 42nd Street-Times Square. **Map** p104 C1/p106 C4 ㊹

Times Square's evolution from a traffic-choked fleshpot to a tourist-friendly theme park has accelerated in the past year. Not only has the 'crossroads of the world' gained an elevated viewing platform atop the new TKTS discount booth, but in summer 2009 Mayor Bloomberg designated stretches of Broadway, including the area from 47th to 42nd Streets, as pedestrian zones.

Originally called Longacre Square, Times Square was renamed after the *New York Times* moved here in the early 1900s. The first electrified billboard graced the district in 1904. The same year, the inaugural New Year's Eve party in Times Square doubled as the *Times*' housewarming party in its new HQ. More than 300,000 still gather here to watch a mirrorball descend every 31 December. The paper left the building only a decade after it arrived. However, it retained ownership of its old headquarters until the 1960s, and erected the world's first scrolling electric news 'zipper' in 1928. The readout, now sponsored by Dow Jones, has trumpeted breaking stories from the stock-market crash of 1929 to the election of the country's first black president in 2008.

TKTS

Father Duffy Square, Broadway & 47th Street (www.tdf.org). Subway N, Q, R, S, 1, 2, 3, 7 to 42nd Street-Times Square. **Open** *Evening tickets 3-8pm Mon, Wed-Sat; 2-8pm Tue; 3-7pm Sun. Same-day matinée tickets 10am-2pm Wed, Sat; 11am-3pm Sun.* **Map** p104 C1/p106 C4 ㊽

At this architecturally striking new base, you can get tickets on the day of the performance for as much as 50% off face value. Although there's often a queue when it opens for business, this has usually dispersed one to two hours later, so it's worth trying your luck an hour or two before the show. The Downtown and Brooklyn branches (see website for details) are much less busy and open earlier (so you can secure your tickets on the morning of the show); they also sell matinée tickets the day before a show. Never buy tickets from anyone who approaches you in the queue as they may have been obtained illegally.

Eating & drinking

5 Napkin Burger

630 Ninth Avenue, at 45th Street (1-212 757 2277, www.5napkinburger. com). Subway A, C, E to 42nd Street- Port Authority. **Open** 11.30am- midnight daily. **$. American.** **Map** p104 B1/p106 B4 ⓢ

With glossy tiled walls and light fix- tures dangling from the ceiling, this casual yet stylish joint appeals to fami- lies, friends and after-work revellers. The menu is broader than the name sug- gests, spanning sushi, substantial meal- size salads and an eclectic selection of cooked main dishes, but our advice is to stick to what the place does best: the burger is a delicious ten-ounce handful that's topped with sweet caramelised onions, gruyère cheese and rosemary- infused aïoli, served with superb fries.

Ardesia

NEW *510 W52nd Street, between Tenth & Eleventh Avenues (1-212 247 9191, www.ardesia-ny.com). Subway C, E to 50th Street.* **Open** 5pm-midnight Mon, Tue; 5pm-2am Wed-Fri; noon-2am Sat; noon-midnight Sun. **$. Bar.** **Map** p106 B3 ⓦ

Le Bernardin vet Mandy Oser's iron- and-marble gem offers superior wines in an extremely relaxed setting. The 75- strong collection of international bot- tles is a smart balance of Old and New World options that pair beautifully with the eclectic small plates. Our

grüner veltliner – a dry, oaky white from the Knoll winery in Wachau, Austria – had enough backbone to stand up to a duck *banh mi* layered with house-made pâté and duck pro- sciutto. A blended red from Spain's Cellar Can Blau, meanwhile, was a spicy, velvety match for coriander-rich homemade mortadella.

Pony Bar

637 Tenth Avenue, at 45th Street (1- 212 586 2707, www.theponybar.com). Subway A, C, E to 50th Street. **Open** 3pm-4am Mon-Fri; noon-4am Sat, Sun. **Bar. Map** p106 B4 ⓖ

Hell's Kitchen has long been a dead zone for civilised bars, but this sunny paean to American microbrews is an oasis. There are 20 beers on tap and two cask ales artfully listed on sign- boards according to provenance and potency. The thoughtful selections include Dogfish Head's peachy Berliner Weisse-style Festina Pêche and Victory's Bags Packed Porter, a toasty treat rich with coffee and choco- late. The low prices (all beers served cost $5) and expert curation suggest that the drought may finally be easing.

Virgil's Real BBQ

152 W44th Street, between Sixth Avenue & Broadway (1-212 921 9494, www.virgilsbbq.com). Subway B, D, F, M , 7 to 42nd Street-Bryant Park. **Open** 11.30am-11pm Mon; 11.30am-midnight Tue-Fri; 11am-midnight Sat; 11am-11pm Sun. **$. Barbecue. Map** p106 C4 ⓖ

As befits its Times Square location, perennially crowded Virgil's is the Epcot Center of barbecue: Paper place- mats present a map of the country's barbecue-producing regions and their specialities, from Texas beef brisket to Memphis pork ribs to vinegary Carolina pulled pork – all of which are on the menu, along with oddities like Oklahoma State Fair corndogs, served with a jalapeño 'mustard.' The dessert selection is a schizophrenic sugar rush, with peanut butter pie sharing a dessert sampler plate with key lime pie and fluffy banana pudding, among others. The Memphis pork ribs – dry-rubbed and slow-smoked, like the rest of Virgil's meats, with a mix of hickory, oak and fruit woods – are but a hair's-breadth from being too tender.

Shopping

Amy's Bread

672 Ninth Avenue, between 46th & 47th Streets (1-212 977 2670, www.amys bread.com). Subway C, E to 50th Street; N, R to 49th Street. **Open** 7.30am-11pm Mon-Fri; 8am-11pm Sat; 9am-6pm Sun. **Map** p104 B1/p106 B4 ⑥③

Whether you want sweet (double chocolate pecan Chubbie cookies) or savoury (hefty French sourdough boules), Amy's never disappoints. Snacks such as the grilled cheese sandwich (made with New York State cheddar) are also served.

Colony Records

Brill Building, 1619 Broadway, at 49th Street (1-212 265 2050, www.colony music.com). Subway N, R to 49th Street; 1 to 50th Street. **Open** 9am-1am Mon-Sat; 10am-midnight Sun. **Map** p106 C4 ⑥④

Push the musical-note door handles to enter a portal to Times Square's past; Colony, a longtime resident of the rockin' Brill Building, was founded in 1948. In addition to sheet music (the selection covers everything from an AC/DC songbook to hot Broadway musicals such as *Billy Elliot*), CDs and vinyl, there are glass cases full of era-spanning ephemera. Get a whiff of the King with Elvis 'Teddy Bear' perfume from the '50s ($500) or pay tribute to the original superwaif in a pair of cream lace tights 'inspired by Twiggy' ($50).

Domus

413 W 44th Street, between Ninth & Tenth Avenues, Hell's Kitchen (1-212 581 8099, www.domusnewyork.com). Subway A, C, E to 42nd Street-Port Authority. **Open** noon-8pm Tue-Sat; noon-6pm Sun. **Map** p106 C4 ⑥⑤

Scouring the globe for unusual design products is nothing new, but owners Luisa Cerutti and Nicki Lindheimer take the concept a step further; each year they visit a far-flung part of the world to forge links with and support co-operatives and individual craftspeople. The beautiful results reflect a fine attention to detail and a sense of place. With their vivid colours and swirling abstract patterns, baskets woven from telephone wire by South African Zulu tribespeople ($29-$335) would look fantastic in a modern apartment. A great place to find reasonably priced gifts, from handmade Afghan soaps ($8.25) to Italian throws (from $69), plus cushions, glassware, toys and much more.

Grast

NEW *Subway concourse, 625 Eighth Avenue, unit 17 between 41st and 42nd Sts (1-212 244 4468). Subway N, Q, R, S, 1, 2, 3, 7 to 42nd Street-Times Square.* **Open** 10am-8pm daily. **Map** p106 C4 ⑥⑥

If you think tourist-filled Times Square is an unlikely spot for a hip boutique, then the subway concourse beneath the hub is the last spot you'd expect to find one. But that's exactly where Merwin Andrade has decided to open this sleek sliver of a store, hidden in the mezzanine of the 42nd St–Port Authority station. Grast makes commuting much more pleasant with its giftable gear, including Urbanears rainbow-bright headphones ($40-$60), chunky Baby-G Glide watches ($90) and collectible Japanese toys from Medicom ($5-$350). Don't miss the store's ultra-rare set of knee-high Beatles Kubrick figurines, whose $2,500 price tag might necessitate taking the subway for the rest of your life.

Nightlife

Bartini

642 Tenth Avenue, between 45th & 46th Streets (1-917 388 2897). Subway

Triumph of the Willem

A new MoMA retrospective takes a look at an NYC great.

'It's not so much that I'm an American', observed Willem de Kooning (1904-1997). 'I'm a New Yorker.' Few immigrant artists were as influential to the city's art scene as the Dutch-born abstract expressionist, who moved to New York in 1926. The painter spent his initial years in the city working as a decorator, painting on the side and sharing a studio with Arshile Gorky during the 1930s. Over the following decade, the prolific de Kooning developed his own style, influenced by the surrealists and Picasso and characterised by abstract, biomorphic figures painted with an intense use of colour ('one day, I'd like to get all the colours in the world into one single painting' he once vowed).

In 1948, he had his first solo show at the Charles Egan Gallery. Three years later, his work was included in Leo Castelli's seminal 9th Street Art Exhibition. This landmark show proved to be the coming-out party for the New York School, a group of abstract expressionists popular in the 1950s that included de Kooning, Gorky and Mark Rothko, among others. De Kooning, who signed a famous 1950 open letter to the Met protesting the august museum's lack of interest in 'advanced art', became a major figure in the movement.

The new exhibit of de Kooning's paintings at MoMA (see p130) is the first major museum retrospective devoted to the scope of his seven-decade career, highlighted by his urban abstractions of the 1950s and the figurative paintings of the following decade. The show brings together more than 200 of his works (including sculptures, drawings and prints). Among the highlights to look for are his *Pink Angels* (1945), *Excavation* (1950), the third of his famous 'Woman series' (1950-53), and his rarely seen 17-sq-ft *Labyrinth* (1946).

A, C, E to 42nd Street-Port Authority.
Open 4pm-4am daily. **Map** p106 B4 **67**
The newest spot in the neighbourhood, in the former Tenth Ave Lounge space, is a study in white – white bar, white bar stools, white trim on grey walls. It's all rather lovely and clean, until you down one too many pretty cocktails, which is a cinch to do here. (Try the vitamin-infused vodka for help with your hangover.)

Birdland

315 W 44th Street, between Eighth & Ninth Avenues (1-212 581 3080, www.birdlandjazz.com). Subway A, C, E to 42nd Street-Port Authority. **Open** 5pm-1am daily. **Map** p104 B1/p106 C4 **68**
Its name is synonymous with jazz (Kurt Elling, Jim Hall), but Midtown's Birdland is also a prime cabaret destination (Christine Andreas, Christine Ebersole), and the bookings in both fields are excellent. The Chico O'Farrill Afro-Cuban Jazz Orchestra owns Sundays, and David Ostwald's Louis Armstrong Centennial Band hits on Wednesdays; Mondays see cabaret's waggish Jim Caruso's Cast Party.

Carolines on Broadway

1626 Broadway, between 49th & 50th Streets (1-212 757 4100, www.carolines.com). Subway N, R to 49th Street; 1 to 50th Street. **Map** p106 C3 **69**
This New York City institution's long-term relationships with national comedy headliners, sitcom stars and cable-special pros ensure that its stage always features marquee names. Although a majority of the bookings skew towards mainstream appetites, the club also makes time for undisputedly darker fare such as Louis CK.

Don't Tell Mama

343 W 46th Street, between Eighth & Ninth Avenues (1-212 757 0788, www.donttellmamanyc.com). Subway A, C, E to 42nd Street-Port Authority. **Open** *Piano bar* 9pm-4am daily. **Map** p104 B1/p106 C4 **70**

Showbiz pros and piano bar buffs adore this dank but homey Theater District stalwart, where acts range from the strictly amateur to potential stars of tomorrow. The nightly line-up at Don't Tell Mama may include pop, jazz and musical theatre singers, as well as female impersonators, comedians and musical revues.

Pacha

618 W 46th Street, between Eleventh & Twelfth Avenues (1-212 209 7500, www.pachanyc.com). Subway C, E to 50th Street. **Open** 10pm-8am Fri, Sat. **Map** p104 A1/p106 A4 **71**
The worldwide glam-club chain Pacha hit the US market in 2005 with this swanky joint helmed by superstar spinner Erick Morillo. The spot attracts heavyweights ranging from local hero Danny Tenaglia to big-time visiting jocks such as Jeff Mills and Josh Wink, but like most big clubs, it pays to check the line-up in advance if you're into underground beats.

Ritz

369 W 46th Street, between Eighth & Ninth Avenues (1-212 333 4177). Subway A, C, E to 42nd Street-Port Authority. **Open** 4pm-4am daily. **Map** p106 B4 **72**
Although it's in the heart of the Theater District, this small, homey gay bar has a neighbourhood vibe. It's perfect for a pre- or post-Broadway cocktail; late nights bring special performances and theme parties.

Therapy

348 W 52nd Street, between Eighth & Ninth Avenues (1-212 397 1700, www. therapy-nyc.com). Subway C, E to 50th Street. **Open** 5pm-2am Mon-Wed, Sun; 5pm-4am Thur-Sat. **Map** p106 C3 **73**
This minimalist, dramatic two-level gay hotspot offers up comedy and musical performances, some clever cocktails (including the Freudian Sip) and a crowd of gorgeous guys. You'll find good food and a cosy fireplace to boot.

Arts & leisure

The Addams Family

Lunt-Fontanne Theatre, 205 W 46th Street, between Broadway & Eighth Avenue (Ticketmaster 1-800 982 2787, www.ticketmaster.com). Subway N, Q, R, S, 1, 2, 3, 7 to 42nd Street-Times Square. **Map** p106 C4 ⓐ

Inspired by Charles Addams's macabre cartoons, this musical features clever songs and swoony visuals – yet the whole never soars to the heights we expect of a bona fide hit. Although the production could be edgier and more grotesque, Nathan Lane, Bebe Neuwirth and a generally strong ensemble land their jokes and numbers with aplomb.

Billy Elliot

Imperial Theatre, 249 W 45th Street, between Broadway & Eighth Avenue (Telecharge 1-212 239 6200, www.billy elliotbroadway.com). Subway A, C, E to 42nd Street-Port Authority. **Map** p106 C4 ⓑ

A London import, based on the 2000 movie about an English mining-town boy who dreams of being a ballet dancer, *Billy Elliot* is one of the most passionate and exhilarating shows to land on Broadway in years. Stephen Daldry's superb direction pulls together spectacular dancing, working-class drama, plus plenty of heart and grit, into an electrifying whole.

Book of Mormon

NEW *Eugene O'Neill Theatre, 230 W 49th Street, between Broadway & Eighth Avenue (1-212 239 6200, www.bookofmormonbroadway.com). Subway A, C, E, to 42nd Street-Port Authoirty; N, Q, R, S, 1, 2, 3, 7 to 42nd Street-Times Square.* **Map** p106 C4 ⓒ

If theatre is your religion, and the Broadway musical your particular sect, it's time to rejoice. This gleefully obscene and subversive satire is one of the funniest shows to grace the Great White Way since *The Producers* and *Urinetown*. Writers Trey Parker and Matt Stone of South Park, along with composer Robert Lopez (Avenue Q), find the perfect blend of sweet and nasty for this tale of mismatched Mormon proselytizers in Uganda.

Carnegie Hall

154 W 57th Street, at Seventh Avenue (1-212 247 7800, www.carnegiehall.org). Subway N, Q, R to 57th Street. **Map** p106 C3 ⓓ

Artistic director Clive Gillinson continues to put his stamp on Carnegie Hall. The stars still shine the most brightly in the Isaac Stern Auditorium – but it's the spunky upstart Zankel Hall that has generated the most buzz, offering an eclectic mix of classical, contemporary, jazz, pop and world music.

Jersey Boys

August Wilson Theatre, 245 W 52nd Street, between Broadway & Eighth Avenue (Telecharge 1-212 239 6200, www.jerseyboysinfo.com/broadway). Subway C, E, 1 to 50th Street. **Map** p106 C3 ⓔ

This nostalgic behind-the-music tale presents the Four Seasons' energetic 1960s tunes, including classics 'Walk Like a Man' and 'Big Girls Don't Cry,' as they were meant to be performed. A dynamic cast ensures that Marshall Brickman and Rick Elice's script comes across as canny instead of canned.

New York City Center

131 W 55th Street, between Sixth & Seventh Avenues (1-212 581 7907, www.nycitycenter.org). Subway B, D, E to Seventh Avenue; F, N, Q, R to 57th Street. **Map** p106 C3 ⓕ

Before Lincoln Center changed the city's cultural geography, this was the home of American Ballet Theatre, the Joffrey Ballet and the New York City Ballet. City Center's lavish decor is golden – as are the companies that pass through here. Regulars include the Alvin Ailey American Dance Theater and the Paul Taylor Dance Company. In the autumn, the popular Fall for Dance Festival has tickets to mixed bills for just $10.

14 Street
Union Square Station
Ⓛ Ⓝ Ⓠ Ⓡ Ⓦ Ⓐ Ⓑ Ⓒ

♿ Elev to Ⓛ Ⓝ Ⓠ Ⓡ Ⓦ at
NE corner 14 St & 4 Av

Union Square p111

Union Square
Greenmarket p115

Playwrights Horizons

416 W 42nd Street, between Ninth & Tenth Avenues, Theater District (Ticket Central 1-212 279 4200, www.playwrightshorizons.org). Subway A, C, E to 42nd Street-Port Authority. **Map** p106 B4 ⑳

More than 300 important contemporary plays have premiered here, among them dramas such as *Driving Miss Daisy* and *The Heidi Chronicles* and musicals such as Stephen Sondheim's *Assassins* and *Sunday in the Park with George*. Recent seasons have included works by Craig Lucas and an acclaimed musical version of the cult film *Grey Gardens*.

Rock of Ages

Helen Hayes Theatre, 240 W44th Street, between Broadway & Eighth Avenue (1-8212 239 6200, www. rockofagesmusical.com). Subway A, C, E to 42nd Street-Port Authority; N, Q, R, S, 1, 2, 3, 7 to 42nd Street-Times Square. **Map** p106 C4 ㉛

Even if you never grew a mullet or banged your head at a Quiet Riot concert, this insanely fun mixtape musical will hit your retro sweet spot. A parade of pop and metal ballads fits beautifully with Chris D'Arienzo's self-mocking book. It's *Urinetown* for the I Love the '80s crowd.

Signature Theatre Company

555 W 42nd Street, between Tenth & Eleventh Avenues (1-212 244 7529, www.signaturetheatre.org). Subway A, C, E to 42nd Street-Port Authority. **Map** p106 B4 ㉜

This award-winning company focuses on the works of a single playwright each season. Signature has delved into the oeuvres of Edward Albee, August Wilson, John Guare, Paula Vogel and Tony Kushner. A smart corporate sponsorship deal helps keep ticket prices remarkably low. In 2012, the company will move to a new Frank Gehry-designed complex that will include theatres, studios, a café and a bookstore.

Fifth Avenue & around

The stretch of Fifth Avenue between Rockefeller Center and Central Park South showcases retail palaces bearing names that were famous long before the concept of branding was developed. Bracketed by Saks Fifth Avenue (49th to 50th Streets) and Bergdorf Goodman, tenants include Gucci, Prada and Tiffany & Co, plus the usual global mall suspects. A number of landmarks and first-rate museums are on, or in the vicinity of, the strip.

Sights & museums

American Folk Art Museum

45 W 53rd Street, between Fifth & Sixth Avenues (1-212 265 1040, www.folkart museum.org). Subway E, to Fifth Avenue-53rd Street. **Open** 10.30am-5.30pm Tue-Thur, Sat, Sun; 10.30am-7.30pm Fri. **Admission** $12; free-$8 reductions. **Map** p107 D3 ㉝

MoMA's next-door neighbour celebrates 'outsider' art, along with traditional crafts such as pottery, quilting, woodwork and jewellery design. The museum holds the world's largest assemblage of works and ephemera collected by the posthumously famous self-taught artist and author Henry Darger.

Empire State Building

350 Fifth Avenue, between 33rd & 34th Streets (1-212 736 3100, www.esbnyc. com). Subway B, D, F, M, N, Q, R to 34th Street-Herald Square. **Open** 8am-2am daily (last elevator at 1.15am). **Admission** *86th floor* $20; free-$18 reductions. *102nd floor* add $15. **Map** p105 D2 ㉞

Financed by General Motors executive John J Raskob at the height of New York's skyscraper race, the Empire State sprang up in a mere 14 months, weeks ahead of schedule and $5 million under budget. Since its opening in 1931, it's been immortalised in countless photos and films, from the original *King Kong* to *Sleepless in Seattle*. Following the destruction of the World Trade Center in 2001, the 1,250ft tower resumed its title as New York's tallest building; the nocturnal colour scheme of the tower lights often honours holidays, charities or special events.

The enclosed observatory on the 102nd floor is the city's highest lookout point, but the panoramic deck on the 86th floor, 1,050ft above the street, is roomier. From here, you can enjoy views of all five boroughs and five neighbouring states (when the skies are clear); at sunset, you can glimpse an elongated urban shadow cast from Manhattan all the way across to Queens.

International Center of Photography

1133 Sixth Avenue, at 43rd Street (1-212 857 0000, www.icp.org). Subway B, D, F, M, 7 to 42nd Street-Bryant Park; N, Q, R, S, 1, 2, 3, 7 to 42nd Street-Times Square. **Open** 10am-6pm Tue-Thur, Sat, Sun; 10am-8pm Fri. **Admission** $12; free-$8 reductions. **Map** p107 D4 ⑤

Since 1974, the ICP has served as a pre-eminent library, school and museum devoted to the photographic image. Photojournalism remains a vital facet of the centre's programme, which also includes contemporary photos and video. Recent shows in the two-floor exhibition space have focused on the work of W Eugene Smith, Richard Avedon and Eugène Atget.

Event highlights Roman Vishniac reerospective (begins May 2012).

Museum of Modern Art

11 W 53rd Street, between Fifth & Sixth Avenues (1-212 708 9400, www.moma.org). Subway E, M to Fifth Avenue-53rd Street. **Open** 10.30am-5.30pm Mon, Wed, Thur, Sat, Sun; 10.30am-8pm Fri. **Admission** (incl admission to film programmes & MoMA-P.S.1) $20; free-$16 reductions; free 4-8pm Fri. **Map** p107 D3 ⑧

After a two-year redesign by Japanese architect Yoshio Taniguchi, MoMA reopened in 2004 with almost double the space to display some of the most impressive artworks from the 19th-21st centuries. The museum's permanent collection is divided into seven curatorial departments: Architecture and Design, Drawings, Film, Media, Painting and Sculpture, Photography, and Prints and Illustrated Books. Among the highlights are Picasso's *Les Demoiselles d'Avignon*, Dali's *The Persistence of Memory* and Van Gogh's *The Starry Night* as well as masterpieces by Giacometti, Hopper, Matisse, Monet, O'Keefe, Pollock, Rothko, Warhol and others. Outside, the Philip Johnson-designed Abby Aldrich Rockefeller Sculpture Garden contains works by Calder, Rodin and Moore. There's also a destination restaurant: the Modern, which overlooks the garden.

Event highlights Diego Rivera: Murals for the Museum of Modern Art (13 Nov 2011-27 Feb 2012); Cindy Sherman (26 Feb 2012-11 Jun 2012); and De Kooning: A Retrospective (18 Sept 2011-9 Jan 2012). See box p125.

New York Public Library

455 Fifth Avenue, at 42nd Street (1-212 930 0830, www.nypl.org). Subway B, D, F, M, 7 to 42nd Street-Bryant Park. **Open** 10am-6pm Mon, Thur-Sat; 10am-8pm Tue, Wed; 1-5pm Sun. **Admission** free. **Map** p105 D1/p105 D5 ⑰

See box, right.

Paley Center for Media

25 W 52nd Street, between Fifth & Sixth Avenues (1-212 621 6600, www.paley center.org). Subway B, D, F, M to 47th-50th Streets-Rockefeller Center; E, M to Fifth Avenue-53rd Street. **Open** noon-6pm Wed, Fri-Sun; noon-8pm Thur. **Admission** $10; $5-$8 reductions. No credit cards. **Map** p107 D3 ⑱

A nirvana for TV addicts and pop-culture junkies, the Paley Center houses an immense archive of more than 100,000 radio and TV shows. Head to the fourth-

Higher Learning

The New York Public Library turns 100

Guarded by the marble lions *Patience* and *Fortitude*, the main branch of the New York Public Library presents an imposing Beaux-Arts façade that almost belies its mission as a facilitator of learning. Designed by Carrère and Hastings, the library was the largest marble edifice in the US upon its completion in 1911. In 2008, it was renamed in honour of philanthropist Stephen A. Schwarzman, yet Gothamites still know it as the New York Public Library. (The entire NYPL system has 87 branches, spread out over Manhattan, the Bronx and Staten Island). Free hour-long tours (11am and 2pm Mon-Sat; 2pm Sun) are a terrific means of getting to know the collections.

The highlight is the enormous Rose Main Reading Room. At 78' wide x 297' long x 51' 2" high, it is almost as large as a football field and divides into two large halls. Their 42 oak tables can seat as many as 16 readers each, and it is not surprising to see most of them full, particularly on weekends. Some 88 miles of bookshelf space lurk below the reading room in eight levels of stacks; another 40 miles of shelving was recently added under Bryant Park just behind the library. Patrons first visit the Bill Blass Public Catalog to find the call numbers of the books they desire then present call slips to staff in the Reading Room, where the books are brought.

The specialist collections at the main branch include the Map Division, containing some 431,000 maps and 16,000 atlases; the Rare Books Division, boasting Walt Whitman's personal copies of the first (1855) and third (1860) editions of *Leaves of Grass*; and the Children's Center, home to the original Winnie-the-Pooh, Eeyore, Piglet and Tigger toys that Christopher Robin Milne played with. And when you're done with them, you can always play with *Patience* and *Fortitude* on the steps outside.

floor library to search the system for your favourite episode of *Star Trek* or *Seinfeld*, then walk down one flight to your assigned console. (The radio listening room operates in the same fashion.)

Rockefeller Center

From 48th to 51st Streets, between Fifth & Sixth Avenues (NBC tours 1-212 664 3700/7174, Top of the Rock 1-877 692 7625, www.rockefellercenter.com). Subway B, D, F, M to 47th-50th Streets-Rockefeller Center. **Open** 7am-11pm daily. *Rockefeller Center Tours* hourly (except 2pm) 10am-5pm Mon-Sat; 10am-4pm Sun. *NBC Studio tours* 8.30am-5.30pm Mon-Thur; 8.30am-6.30pm Fri, Sat; 9.15am-4.30pm Sun *Observation deck* 8am-midnight daily (last entry 11pm). **Admission** *Rockefeller Center tours* $15; (under-6s not admitted). *NBC Studio tours* $20; $17 reductions (under-6s not admitted). *Observation deck* $22; $20 reductions. **Map** p107 D3/D4 ⑥⑨

Constructed under the aegis of industrialist John D Rockefeller in the 1930s, this art deco city-within-a-city is inhabited by NBC, Simon & Schuster, McGraw-Hill and other media giants, as well as Radio City Music Hall, Christie's auction house, and an underground shopping arcade. Guided tours of the entire complex are available daily, and there's a separate NBC Studio tour too.

The buildings and grounds are embellished with works by several well-known artists; look out for Isamu Noguchi's stainless-steel relief, *News*, above the entrance to 50 Rockefeller Plaza, and José Maria Sert's mural *American Progress* in the lobby of 30 Rockefeller Plaza. But the most breathtaking sights are those seen from the 70th-floor Top of the Rock observation deck. In the cold-weather months, the Plaza's sunken courtyard transforms into an ice skating rink.

St Patrick's Cathedral

Fifth Avenue, between 50th & 51st Streets (1-212 753 2261, www.saint patrickscathedral.org). Subway B, D,
F, M to 47th-50th Streets-Rockefeller Center; E, M to Fifth Avenue-53rd Street.* **Open** 7am-8.30pm daily. **Admission** free. **Map** p107 D3 ⑨⓪

The largest Catholic church in the US, St Patrick's was built 1858-79. The Gothic-style façade features intricate white-marble spires, but just as impressive is the interior, including the Louis Tiffany-designed altar, solid bronze baldachin, and the rose window by stained-glass master Charles Connick.

Eating & drinking

Bar Room at the Modern

9 W 53rd Street, between Fifth & Sixth Avenues (1-212 333 1220, www.the modernnyc.com). Subway E to Fifth Avenue-53rd Street. **Open** 11.30am-3pm, 5-10.30pm Mon-Thur; 11.30am-3pm, 5-11pm Fri, Sat; 11.30am-3pm, 5-9.30pm Sun. **$$.** **American creative.** **Map** p107 D3 ⑨①

Those who can't afford to drop a pay cheque at award-winning chef Gabriel Kreuther's formal MoMA dining room, the Modern, should drop into the equally stunning and less pricey Bar Room at the front. The Alsatian-inspired menu is constructed of 30 small and medium-sized plates that can be mixed and shared. Desserts come courtesy of pastry chef Marc Aumont, and the wine list is extensive to say the least.

Carnegie Deli

854 Seventh Avenue, at 55th Street (1-212 757 2245, www.carnegiedeli. com). Subway B, D, E to Seventh Avenue; N, Q, R to 57th Street. **Open** 6.30am-4am daily. **$.** No credit cards. **American. Map** p106 C3 ⑨②

If the Carnegie Deli didn't invent schmaltz, it has certainly perfected it. All of the gargantuan sandwiches have punning names: Bacon Whoopee (BLT with chicken salad), Carnegie Haul (pastrami, tongue and salami). A waiter sings the deli's virtues in a corny video loop, and more than 600 celebrity glossies crowd the walls. This sexagenarian legend is a time capsule of the bygone Borscht Belt-era, when shtick could make up for cramped quarters, surly waiters and shabby tables. But when you're craving a deli classic, you can't do much better than the Carnegie's obscenely stuffed pastrami and corned beef sandwiches on rye.

Marea

240 Central Park South, between Seventh Avenue & Broadway (1-212 582 51000, www.marea-nyc. com). Subway A, B, C, D, 1 to 59th Street-Columbus Circle. **Open** noon-2.30pm, 5.30-11pm Mon-Thur; noon-2.30pm, 5-11.30pm Fri; 5-11.30pm Sat; 5-10.30pm Sun. **$$$**.
Italian/Seafood. Map p106 C2 🕄

Chef Michael White's shrine to the Italian coastline seems torn between its high and low ambitions. You might find lofty items such as an unorthodox starter of cool lobster with creamy burrata, while basic platters of raw oysters seem better suited to a fish shack. Seafood-focused pastas are the meal's highlight: we loved the *sedanini* (like ridgeless rigatoni) in a smoky cod-chowder sauce with potatoes and speck. But the desserts – such as a chocolate-hazelnut Kit Kat – confirm a split identity that a little editing could easily fix.

Shopping

Bergdorf Goodman

754 Fifth Avenue, at 57th Street (1-212 753 7300, www.bergdorfgoodman.com). Subway E to Fifth Avenue-53rd Street; N, R to Fifth Avenue-59th Street. **Open** 10am-8pm Mon-Fri; 10am-7pm Sat; noon-6pm Sun. **Map** p107 D3 🕘

Synonymous with understated luxury, Bergdorf's is known for its designer clothes (the fifth floor is dedicated to younger, trend-driven labels) and accessories – seek out the wonderful vintage-jewellery cache on the ground floor. The men's store is across the street at 745 Fifth Avenue.

FAO Schwarz

767 Fifth Avenue, at 58th Street (1-212 644 9400, www.fao.com). Subway N, R to Lexington Avenue-59th Street; 4, 5, 6 to 59th Street. **Open** 10am-7pm Mon-Thur; 10am-8pm Fri, Sat; 11am-6pm Sun. **Map** p107 D2 🕄

Although it's now owned by Toys 'R' Us, this emporium is still the ultimate NYC toy box. Children will marvel at the giant stuffed animals and Lego figures, and there are lots of fun opportunities to create custom playthings at the Madame Alexander Doll Factory, Styled by Me Barbie area and Muppet Whatnot Workshop.

Henri Bendel

712 Fifth Avenue, at 56th Street (1-212 247 1100, www.henribendel.com). Subway E to Fifth Avenue-53rd Street; N, R to Fifth Avenue-59th Street. **Open** 10am-8pm Mon-Sat; noon-7pm Sun. **Map** p107 D3 🕄

While the merchandise (a mix of high-end and diffusion designer clothes, accessories and big-brand cosmetics) and prices are comparable to those of other upscale stores, the goods at Bendel's somehow seem more desirable in this opulent atmosphere – and those darling brown-striped shopping bags don't hurt, either.

Nightlife

Oak Room

Algonquin Hotel, 59 W 44th Street, between Fifth & Sixth Avenues (1-212 840 6800, reservations 1-212 419 9331, www.algonquinhotel.com). Subway B, D, F , M, 7 to 42nd Street-Bryant Park. **Map** p107 D4 🕄

This banquette-lined room is the perfect place in which to enjoy cabaret eminences such as Karen Akers, Jack Jones and Andrea Marcovicci, plus rising stars such as the ethereal Maude Maggart and the jazz singer Paula West. The pianist and bebop icon Barbara Carroll plays a luminous brunch show on many Sundays.

Chrysler Building

Radio City Music Hall

*1260 Sixth Avenue, at 50th Street
(1-212 247 4777, www.radiocity.com).
Subway B, D, F, M to 47th-50th
Streets-Rockefeller Center.*
Map p107 D3 ❾❽

Few rooms scream 'New York City!'
more than this gilded hall, which has
recently drawn Ne-Yo, Leonard Cohen
and Yeah Yeah Yeahs as headliners. The
greatest challenge for any performer is
not to be upstaged by the awe-inspiring
art deco surrounds. On the other hand,
those same surroundings lend historic
heft to even the flimsiest showing.
Event highlights Christmas
Spectacular (11 Nov 2011-2 Jan 2012).

Arts & leisure

Caudalie Vinothérapie Spa

*4th Floor, 1 W 58th Street, at Fifth
Avenue (1-212 265 3182, www.
caudalie-usa.com).* **Open** noon-6pm
Mon; 11am-7pm Tue, Wed; 11am-8pm
Thur, Fri; 10am-7pm Sat; 11am-6pm
Sun. **Map** p107 D2 ❾❾

The first Vinothérapie outpost in the
US, this original spa harnesses the
antioxidant power of grapes and vine
leaves. The 8,000sq ft facility in the
Plaza offers such treatments as a Red
Vine bath ($75) in one of its cherry-
wood 'barrel' tubs.

Midtown East

Shopping, dining and entertainment
options wane east of Fifth Avenue in
the 40s and 50s. However, this area
is home to a number of landmarks.
What the area lacks in street-level
attractions it makes up for with an
array of world-class architecture.

Sights & museums

Chrysler Building

*405 Lexington Avenue, between 42nd
& 43rd Streets. Subway S, 4, 5, 6, 7
to 42nd Street-Grand Central.*
Map p105 E1/p107 E4 ❿⓪

Completed in 1930 by architect William
Van Alen, the gleaming Chrysler
Building is a pinnacle of art deco architecture, paying homage to the automo-
bile with vast radiator-cap eagles in lieu
of traditional gargoyles and a brickwork
relief sculpture of racing cars complete
with chrome hubcaps. During the famed
three-way race for New York's tallest
building, a needle-sharp stainless-steel
spire was added to the blueprint to
make it taller than 40 Wall Street, under
construction at the same time – but the
Chrysler Building was soon outdone by
the Empire State Building.

Grand Central Terminal

*From 42nd to 44th Streets, between
Lexington & Vanderbilt Avenues
(tours 1-212 340 2347, www.grand
centralterminal.com). Subway S, 4, 5,
6, 7 to 42nd Street-Grand Central.*
Map p105 D1/p107 D4 ❿❶

Each day, the world's most famous
terminal sees more than 750,000
people shuffle through its Beaux Arts
threshold. After its 1998 renovation, the
terminal metamorphosed from a mere
transport hub into a destination in
itself, with decent shopping and first-
rate drinking and dining options such
as the Campbell Apartment lounge
(located off the West Balcony, 1-212 953
0409) and the Grand Central Oyster Bar
& Restaurant (see p136). Don't forget to
look up when you're inside the station's
80,000 sq ft main concourse. French
painter Paul Helleu's astronomical
mural depicts the Mediterranean sky
complete with 2,500 stars (some of
which are illuminated).

United Nations Headquarters

*Visitors' Entrance: First Avenue, at 46th
Street (tours 1-212 963 8687, http://
visit.un.org). Subway S, 4, 5, 6, 7 to 42nd
Street-Grand Central.* **Tours** 9.45am-
4.45pm Mon-Fri; 10am-4.15pm Sat, Sun
(escorted audio tours only). **Admission**
$16; $9-$11 reductions (under-5s not
admitted). **Map** p105 F1/p107 ❿❷

The UN's Secretariat building, designed by Le Corbusier, is off-limits, and the Security Council Chamber is under renovation until 2013, but tours discuss the history of the UN and its architecture, visit the General Assembly Hall, and highlight art and objects given by member nations. One of the best-known works, the stained-glass window by Marc Chagall memorialising Secretary-General Dag Hammarskjöld, is on view. Visitors can sup from the international buffet in the Delegates Dining Room (1-212 963 7626), which is open to the public 11.30am-2.30pm Mon-Fri (advance reservations are required).

Eating & drinking

Bill's Gay Nineties

57 E 54th Street, between Madison & Park Avenues (1-212 355 0243). Subway E to Fifth Avenue-53rd Street. **Open** 11.30am-1am Mon-Fri; 5pm-2am Sat. **Bar. Map** p107 D3 ⓳
The pseudo speakeasies beloved by today's cocktail set have nothing on Bill's – a real Prohibition throwback. Down a small flight of stairs in an ancient brownstone you'll find this low-ceilinged gem, lined with photos of Ziegfeld girls, boxers and thoroughbreds. Rye manhattans go down smooth, and the piano can be heard most nights.

Convivio

45 Tudor City Place, at 43rd Street (1-212 599 5045, www.convivionyc.com). Subway S, 4, 5, 6, 7 to 42nd St-Grand Central. **Open** noon-2.15pm, 5.30-10.15pm Mon-Thur; noon-2.15pm, 5-11.15pm Fri; 5.30-11.30pm Sat; 5-9.30pm Sun. **$$$.**
Italian. Map p105 E1/p107 F4 ⓴
At this tucked-away spot in peaceful residential microcosm Tudor City, the emphasis is squarely on southern Italy. Antipasti might include country bread slathered with chicken liver mousse, while the pastas – saffron gnocchetti with crabmeat, sea urchin, chilli flakes, scallion and garlic, for example – are hauntingly good.

Grand Central Oyster Bar & Restaurant

Grand Central Terminal, Lower Concourse, 42nd Street, at Park Avenue (1-212 490 6650, www.oysterbarny.com). Subway S, 4, 5, 6, 7 to 42nd Street-Grand Central. **Open** 11.30am-9.30pm Mon-Fri; noon-9.30pm Sat. **$$.**
Seafood. Map p105 D1/p107 D4 ⓮
At the legendary nonagenarian Grand Central Oyster Bar, located in the epic and gorgeous hub that shares its name, the surly countermen at the mile-long bar (the best seats in the house) are part of the charm. Avoid the more complicated fish concoctions and play it safe with a reliably awe-inspiring platter of iced, just-shucked oysters – there can be a whopping three-dozen varieties to choose from at any given time.

Má Pêche

Chambers Hotel, 15 W 56th Street, between Fifth & Sixth Avenues (212 757 5878, www.momofuku.com). Subway E to Fifth Avenue-53rd Street; F to 57th Street. **Open** 7am-11pm daily. **$$. Vietnamese. Map** p107 D3 ⓰
See box p113.

Sushi Yasuda

204 E 43rd Street, between Second and Third Avenues (212 972 1001, www.sushiyasuda.com). Subway S, 4, 5, 6, 7 to 42nd St-Grand Central.. **Open** noon-2.15pm, 6-10.15pm Mon-Fri; 6-10.15pm Sat. **$$.**
Japanese Map p105 E1/p107 E4 ⓱
Seeing the sushi master practice in this bamboo-embellished space is the culinary equivalent of observing Buddhist monks at prayer. Counter seating, where you can witness – and chat up – the chefs, is the only way to go. Prime your palate with a miso soup and segue into the raw stuff: petals of buttery fluke; rich eel; dessert-sweet egg custard; nearly translucent discs of sliced scallop over neat cubes of milky sushi rice. Still craving a California roll? Move along.

Frick Collection p143

Uptown

In the 19th century, the area above 59th Street was a bucolic getaway for locals living at the southern tip of the island. Today, much of this locale maintains an air of serenity, thanks largely to Central Park and the presence of a number of New York's premier cultural institutions.

Central Park

Ever since landscaper Frederick Law Olmsted and architect Calvert Vaux's vision of an urban 'greensward' was realised in 1873, the first man-made public park in the US has been a haven for New Yorkers of every stripe. Despite its 843 acres, Central Park (framed by 59th Street, Central Park West, 110th Street and Fifth Avenue) is very easy to negotiate. We have included its main features below, but for an in-depth walking tour covering its highlights, see 'Garden Variety' on p49-51.

As well as a wide variety of landscapes, from open meadows to woodland, the park offers numerous child-friendly attractions and activities, from the **Central Park Zoo** (830 Fifth Avenue, between 63rd & 66th Streets, 1-212 439 6500, www.centralparkzoo.org; Apr-Sept 10am-5.30pm daily, Nov-Mar 10am-4.30pm daily; $12, free-$9 reductions) to marionette shows in the quaint **Swedish Cottage** (west side, at 81st Street). Stop by the **Dairy** visitor centre (midpark at 65th Street, 1-212 794 6564, www.centralparknyc.org) for information on activities and events. In winter, ice-skaters lace up at the picturesque **Trump Wollman Rink** (midpark at 62nd Street, 1-212 439 6900, www.wollmanskatingrink.com). A short stroll to about 64th Street brings you to the **Friedsam Memorial Carousel** (closed weekdays in

Uptown 1

A **B** **C**

See p140

1

W 102ND ST

W 100TH ST

W 98TH ST

COLUMBUS AVE

The Pool

99TH ST TRANSVE

W 96TH ST 1,2,3 Ⓜ B,C Ⓜ

Symphony
Space ⓵⓪

W 94TH ST

WEST END AVE BROADWAY AMSTERDAM AVE

W 92ND ST

HENRY J BROWNE BLVD W 90TH ST

Central Pa

WEST DRIVE

The Reserv

2

Soldiers' & Sailors'
Monument ▪

W 88TH ST

**UPPER
WEST SIDE**
㉕

1 Ⓜ W 86TH ST B,C Ⓜ

㉙

86TH ST TRANSV

Great Lawn

W 84TH ST

W 82ND ST

B,C Ⓜ

Delacorte
Theater

3

㊱
㉝ W 80TH ST ㉜
W 79TH ST 1 Ⓜ
W 78TH ST

㉛

**American Museum
of Natural History**
㉒⓪

Luce Nature
Observatory

79TH ST TRANSVE

Belve
Cas

RIVERSIDE DR

W 76TH ST

㉓

**New-York
Historical Society**

The
Ramble

Lo
Boa

㊲ ㉞
W 74TH ST

The Lake

Bow
Bridge

VERDI
SQUARE

1,2,3 Ⓜ

The Dakota ▪
W 72ND ST Ⓜ
B,C Ⓜ

Strawberry
Fields

Bethe
Terra

4

HENRY HUDSON PKWY FREEDOM PL WEST END AVE

W 70TH ST

W 68TH ST

AMSTERDAM AVE BROADWAY COLUMBUS AVE CENTRAL PARK WEST

W 66TH ST 1 Ⓜ W 66TH ST

WEST DRIVE

Sheep
Meadow

85TH ST TRANSVERSE R

Heckscher
Playground
▪

The [
Dairy

W 64TH ST

㊴

**Lincoln
Center** W 62ND ST

RIVERSIDE BLVD

Trum
Wollm
Rink

A,B,C,D
1 Ⓜ

W 60TH ST

5

99
98

W 58TH ST

Time
Warner
Center

㉔㉖
㉚
㉟㊳

Columbus
Circle

㉒

N,Q,R
Ⓜ

Museum of Arts
& Design

Carnegi

W 57TH ST

D **E** **F**

FIFTH AVE
MADISON AVE
PARK AVE
LEXINGTON AVE
THIRD AVE
SECOND AVE
FIRST AVE

E 100TH ST

See p141

① Sights & museums
① Eating & drinking
① Shopping
① Nightlife
① Arts & leisure

1

E 98TH ST

E 96TH ST Ⓜ 6

E 94TH ST

FRANKLIN D ROOSEVELT DR

EAST DRIVE

E 92ND ST

3 Jewish Museum

E 90TH ST

1 Cooper-Hewitt National Design Museum

9 Solomon R Guggenheim Museum

E 88TH ST

Neue Galerie
8 13

YORKVILLE

□ Gracie Mansion

2

E 86TH ST Ⓜ 4,5,6

EAST END AVE

Carl Schurz Park

E 84TH ST

15

UPPER EAST SIDE

E 82ND ST

4

Metropolitan Museum of Art

E 80TH ST

E 79TH ST

3

E 78TH ST

18 **12**

6 Ⓜ

E 76TH ST

John Jay Park

11

rvatory ater

Whitney Museum **10** of American Art

E 74TH ST

mburg dshell

19

E 72ND ST

Roosevelt Island

2

The Frick Collection

Asia Society and Museum

E 70TH ST

E 68TH ST

Ⓜ 6

Rockefeller University

4

lto

China Institute

E 66TH ST

Tisch Children's Zoo

PARK AVE
LEXINGTON AVE
THIRD AVE
SECOND AVE
FIRST AVE

FRANKLIN D ROOSEVELT DR

Delacorte Musical Clock
14

E 64TH ST

Zoo

E 62ND ST

Ⓜ F

0   300 m

0   300 yds

© Copyright Time Out Group 2011

holars' Gate

16

Ⓜ
N,R

N,R

E 60TH ST

YORK AVE

5

Grand Army Plaza

17 Bloomingdale's

4,5,6 Ⓜ

TRAMWAY

QUEENSBORO (59TH ST) BRIDGE

E 58TH ST

□ Trump Tower

E 57TH ST

Time Out Shortlist | New York 2012 **139**

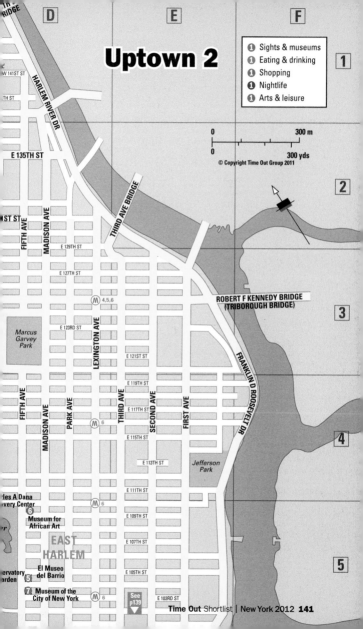

Uptown 2

D   **E**   **F**

1
1 Sights & museums
1 Eating & drinking
1 Shopping
1 Nightlife
1 Arts & leisure

2
© Copyright Time Out Group 2011

3

4

5

HARLEM RIVER DR

W 141ST ST

TH ST

E 135TH ST

ST ST

THIRD AVE BRIDGE

FIFTH AVE

MADISON AVE

E 129TH ST

E 127TH ST

Ⓜ 4,5,6

E 123RD ST

LEXINGTON AVE

E 121ST ST

E 119TH ST

Marcus
Garvey
Park

FIFTH AVE

MADISON AVE

PARK AVE

THIRD AVE

SECOND AVE

FIRST AVE

E 117TH ST

Ⓜ 6

E 115TH ST

E 113TH ST

Jefferson
Park

E 111TH ST

E 109TH ST

les A Dana
very Center

Ⓜ 6

6 Museum for
African Art

**EAST
HARLEM**

E 107TH ST

El Museo
del Barrio

E 105TH ST

ervatory
arden

5

7 Museum of the
City of New York

Ⓜ 6

E 103RD ST

See
p139
▼

ROBERT F KENNEDY BRIDGE
(TRIBOROUGH BRIDGE)

FRANKLIN D ROOSEVELT DR

0   300 m
0   300 yds

winter), a bargain at $2.50 a ride. Come summer, kites, Frisbees and soccer balls seem to fly every which way across **Sheep Meadow**, the designated quiet zone that begins at 66th Street. Sheep did indeed graze here until 1934, but they've since been replaced by sunbathers. East of Sheep Meadow, between 66th and 72nd Streets, is the elm-lined promenade, the **Mall**, where in-line skaters congregate. And just east of the Mall's Naumburg Bandshell is Rumsey Playfield – site of the annual **Central Park SummerStage** (see p41) series, an eclectic roster of free and benefit concerts.

One of the most popular meeting places in the park is north of the Mall: the grand **Bethesda Fountain & Terrace**, near the midpoint of the 72nd Street Transverse Road. *Angel of the Waters*, the sculpture in the centre of the fountain, was created by Emma Stebbins, the first woman to be granted a major public art commission in New York. Be sure to admire the Minton-tiled ceiling of the ornate passageway that connects the plaza around the fountain to the Mall.

To the west of the fountain, near the W 72nd Street entrance, sits **Strawberry Fields**, a section of the park that memorialises John Lennon, who lived in the nearby Dakota Building. It features a mosaic of the word 'imagine' and more than 160 species of flowers and plants from all over the world. Just north of the Bethesda Fountain is the **Loeb Boathouse** (midpark, at 75th Street). From here, you can take a rowboat or gondola out on the lake, which is crossed by the elegant Bow Bridge. The Loeb houses the **Central Park Boathouse Restaurant** (Central Park Lake, park entrance on Fifth Avenue,

at 72nd Street, 1-212 517 2233, www.thecentralparkboathouse.com, closed dinner Sat & Sun Nov-Mar), which commands a great view of the lake, and has a popular outdoor bar.

Further north is **Belvedere Castle**, a restored Victorian structure that sits atop the park's second-highest peak. Besides offering excellent views, it also houses the **Henry Luce Nature Observatory**. The nearby Delacorte Theater hosts **Shakespeare in the Park** (see p41). And further north still sits the **Great Lawn** (midpark, between 79th & 85th Streets), a sprawling stretch of grass that serves as a rallying point for political protests, sports fields and a concert spot; the Metropolitan Opera and the New York Philharmonic perform here during the summer.

In the mid 1990s, the **Jacqueline Kennedy Onassis Reservoir** (midpark, between 85th & 96th Streets) was renamed in honour of the late first lady, who used to jog around it. Whether you prefer a running or walking pace, the path affords great views of the surrounding skyscrapers, especially at the northern end, looking south.

Upper East Side

Although Manhattan's super-rich now live all over town, the air of old money is most pronounced on the Upper East Side. Along Fifth, Madison and Park Avenues, from 61st to 81st Streets, you'll see the great old mansions, many of which are now foreign consulates. Philanthropic gestures made by the moneyed classes over the past 130-odd years have helped create an impressive cluster of art collections, museums and cultural institutions. Indeed, Fifth Avenue from 82nd to 110th Streets is known as Museum Mile because it's lined with half a dozen celebrated institutions.

Sights & museums

Cooper-Hewitt, National Design Museum

2 E 91st Street, at Fifth Avenue (1-212 849 8400, www.cooperhewitt.org). Subway 4, 5, 6 to 86th Street. **Open** 10am-5pm Mon-Thur; 10am-6pm Fri-Sun. **Admission** $15; free-$10 reductions. **Map** p139 D2 **❶**
Founded in 1897 by the Hewitt sisters, granddaughters of industrialist Peter Cooper, the only museum in the US solely dedicated to design (both historic and modern) has been part of the Smithsonian since the 1960s. In 1976, it took up residence in the former home of steel magnate Andrew Carnegie: it's worth a look for the impressive mansion as much as for the roster of temporary exhibitions, which include an always-interesting series in which pieces are selected from the permanent collection by a prominent artist or designer. The museum's gift shop is stocked with international design objects (some very affordable) as well as the appropriate books. While the Carnegie Mansion is currently closed for a massive renovation, scheduled for completion in 2013, the museum will be presenting several off-site exhibitions during that period.
Event highlights Design with the Other 90%: CITIES (15 Oct 2011-9 Jan 2012) will be on display at the United Nations.

Frick Collection

1 E 70th Street, between Fifth & Madison Avenues (1-212 288 0700, www.frick.org). Subway 6 to 68th Street-Hunter College. **Open** 10am-6pm Tue-Sat; 11am-5pm Sun. **Admission** $18; $5-$12 reductions; under-10s not admitted. Pay what you wish 11am-1pm Sun. **Map** p139 D4 **❷**

Industrialist, robber baron and collector Henry Clay Frick commissioned this opulent mansion with a view to leaving his legacy to the public. Designed by Thomas Hastings of Carrère & Hastings and built in 1914, the building was inspired by 18th-century British and French architecture.
In an effort to preserve the feel of a private residence, labelling is minimal, but you can opt for a free audio guide or pay $2 for a booklet. Works spanning the 14th to the 19th centuries include masterpieces by Rembrandt, Vermeer, Whistler, Monet and Bellini, exquisite period furniture, porcelain and other decorative objects. The interior fountain court is a serene spot in which to rest your feet.
Event highlights Picasso's Drawings, 1890 to 1921: Reinventing Tradition (4 Oct 2011-8 Jan 2012).

Jewish Museum

1109 Fifth Avenue, at 92nd Street (1-212 423 3200, www.thejewishmuseum. org). Subway 4, 5 to 86th Street; 6 to 96th Street. **Open** 11am-5.45pm Mon, Tue, Sat, Sun; 11am-8pm Thur; 11am-4pm Fri. Closed on Jewish holidays. **Admission** $12; free-$10 reductions; free Sat. **Map** p139 D2 **❸**
The former home of the financier, collector and Jewish leader Felix Warburg, the Jewish Museum's magnificent French Gothic-style mansion is still gleaming following an exterior spruce-up for its 100th birthday in 2008. Inside, those with an interest in Jewish culture will find a far-reaching collection of more than 28,000 works of art, artefacts and media installations, which are all arranged thematically in a two-floor permanent exhibition: 'Culture and Continuity: The Jewish Journey'. This traces the evolution of Judaism from antiquity to the present day. The excellent temporary shows appeal to a broad audience.
Event highlights The Snowy Day and the Art of Ezra Jack Keats (9 Sept 2011-29 Jan 2012).

NEW YORK BY AREA

Metropolitan Museum of Art

1000 Fifth Avenue, at 82nd Street (1-212 535 7710, www.metmuseum.org). Subway 4, 5, 6 to 86th Street. **Open** 9.30am-5.30pm Tue-Thur, Sun; 9.30am-9pm Fri, Sat. **Admission** suggested donation (incl same-day admission to the Cloisters) $20; free-$15 reductions. **Map** p139 D3 ④

Occupying 13 acres of Central Park, the Metropolitan Museum of Art, which opened in 1880, is impressive in terms both of quality and scale. Added in 1895 by McKim Mead and White, the neoclassical façade is daunting, but the museum is surprisingly easy to negotiate, particularly if you come early on a weekday and avoid the crowds.

In the ground floor's north wing sit the collection of Egyptian art and the glass-walled atrium housing the Temple of Dendur, moved en masse from its original Nile-side setting and now overlooking a reflective pool. Antiquity is also well represented on the southern wing of the ground floor by the halls housing Greek and Roman art, which reopened in 2007 after receiving an elegant makeover. Turning west brings you to the Arts of Africa, Oceania and the Americas collection; it was donated by Nelson Rockefeller as a memorial to his son Michael, who disappeared while visiting New Guinea in 1961.

A wider-ranging bequest, the two-storey Robert Lehman Wing, is at the western end of the floor. This eclectic collection is housed in a re-creation of the Lehman family townhouse and features works by Botticelli, Bellini, Ingres and Rembrandt, among others.

Rounding out the ground-floor highlights is the American Wing on the north-west corner. The museum's grand, conservatory-style Engelhard Court reopened in 2009 as part of the wing's revamp. Now more a sculpture court than an interior garden, the light-filled space is flanked by the façade of Wall Street's Branch Bank of the United States (saved when the building was torn down in 1915) and a stunning loggia designed by Louis Comfort Tiffany for his Long Island estate.

Upstairs, the 19th-century European galleries contain some of the Met's most popular works – in particular the two-room Monet holdings and a colony of Van Goghs that includes his oft-reproduced *Irises*.

At the northern wing of the floor, you'll find the sprawling collection of Asian art; be sure to check out the ceiling of the Jain Meeting Hall in the South-east Asian gallery. If you're still on your feet, give them a deserved rest in the Astor Court, a tranquil re-creation of a Ming Dynasty garden, or head up to the Iris & B Gerald Cantor Roof Garden (late May-late Oct). For the Cloisters, which houses the Met's medieval art collection, see p159.

Event highlights Stieglitz and His Artists: Matisse to O'Keeffe (13 Oct 2011-2 Jan 2012); Infinite Jest: Caricature and Satire from Leonardo to Levine (13 Sept 2011-4 Mar 2012); Story-Telling in Japanese Painting (19 Nov 2011-6 May 2012).

El Museo del Barrio

1230 Fifth Avenue, between 104th & 105th Streets (1-212 831 7272, www.elmuseo.org). Subway 6 to 103rd Street. **Open** 11am-6pm Tue-Sat; 1-5pm-Sun. **Admission** suggested $9; free-$5 reductions. **Map** p141 D5 ⑤

Located near the top of Museum Mile in Spanish Harlem (aka El Barrio), El Museo del Barrio is dedicated to the art and culture of Puerto Ricans and Latin Americans in the US. The recently redesigned spaces within the 1921 Beaux Arts building provide a contemporary showcase for the diversity and vibrancy of Hispanic art, allowing more room for rotating installations from the museum's 6,500-piece holdings – from pre-Columbian artefacts to contemporary installations – as well as around three temporary shows a year.

Reframing history

The New-York Historical Society gets an upgrade.

New-York Historical Society p152

As befitting an institution whose name retains an archaic hyphenisation, the New-York Historical Society lays claim to being the city's oldest museum. Founded in 1804, it moved around for much of the 19th century, settling on digs in the East Village in 1857 before moving into its current home in 1908, a Beaux-Arts building that was enlarged in 1938.

On 11 November 2011, the society is reopening after a $65 million renovation by the architectural firm of Platt Byard Dovell White. The redesign applies as much glass as the Landmarks Preservation Commission would allow to the building's stone façade in an effort to suggest transparency and, thus, accessibility. To that end, the windows adjacent to the main entrance have been lengthened into actual doorways, while a new glass passage has been constructed perpendicular to the entrance that permits immediate views into the great hall.

The great hall itself has been revamped so that digital screens mounted on its columns display a continuous slide show of the collection's highlights. The west sides of those columns also feature interactive touch-screens describing themes relating to American history and New York. Most intriguingly, the floor of the hall will also include 12 'porthole floorcases' exhibiting objects uncovered by amateur archaeologists below ground in the city. The hall will also feature a permanent 'Here Is New York' exhibition devoted to 9/11, including a door from the first fire engine that reached Ground Zero.

In addition, the museum's auditorium has been expanded to include 420 seats and a new mezzanine level.

A new restaurant, serving Venetian food, is also due to open by the 77th Street entrance, run by the Starr Restaurants and decorated with articles from the collection. That hyphen isn't going anywhere, however.

Lenox Lounge p160

Event highlights Caribbean: Crossroads of the World (Feb 2012-July 2012); El Museo's Bienal: The (S) Files 2011 (until 8 Jan 2012).

Museum for African Art

1280 Fifth Avenue, between 109th & 110th Streets (1-646 486 7050, www.africanart.org). Subway 6 to 110th Street. **Map** p141 D5 **6**
See box, p157.

Museum of the City of New York

1220 Fifth Avenue, between 103rd & 104th Streets (1-212 534 1672, www.mcny.org). Subway 6 to 103rd Street. **Open** 10am-5pm Tue-Sun. **Admission** suggested donation $10; free-$6 reductions; $20 family. **Map** p141 D5 **7**

A great introduction to New York, this institution contains a wealth of city history. *Timescapes*, a 25-minute multimedia film that tells NYC's story from 1624 to the present, is shown free with admission every half-hour. A spacious new gallery opened in late 2008 to allow more space for five to seven temporary exhibitions each year, which spotlight the city from different angles.

The permanent collection includes exhibits devoted to the city's maritime heritage and interiors: six rooms, among them an original 1906 Park Avenue drawing room sumptuously decorated in the style of the Sala Della Zodiaco in the Ducal Palace, Mantua, chart New York living spaces from 1680 to 1906. But the undoubted jewel is the amazing Stettheimer Dollhouse: it was created in the '20s by Carrie Stettheimer, whose artist friends reinterpreted their masterpieces in miniature to hang on the walls. Look closely and you'll even spy a tiny version of Marcel Duchamp's famous *Nude Descending a Staircase*.

Neue Galerie

1048 Fifth Avenue, at 86th Street (1-212 628 6200, www.neuegalerie.org). Subway 4, 5, 6 to 86th Street.

Open 11am-6pm Mon, Thur-Sun; 11am-8pm 1st Fri of mth. **Admission** $15; $10 reductions. Under-16s must be accompanied by an adult; under-12s not admitted. **Map** p139 D2 **8**

This elegant gallery is devoted to late 19th- and early 20th-century German and Austrian fine and decorative arts. The creation of the late art dealer Serge Sabarsky and cosmetics mogul Ronald S Lauder, it has the largest concentration of works by Gustav Klimt and Egon Schiele outside Vienna.

Solomon R Guggenheim Museum

1071 Fifth Avenue, at 89th Street (1-212 423 3500, www.guggenheim.org). Subway 4, 5, 6 to 86th Street. **Open** 10am-5.45pm Mon-Wed, Fri, Sun; 10am-7.45pm Sat. **Admission** $18; free-$15 reductions; pay what you wish 5.45-7.15pm Fri. **Map** p139 D2 **9**

The Guggenheim is as famous for its landmark building – designed by Frank Lloyd Wright and restored for its 50th birthday in 2009 – as it is for its impressive collection and daring temporary shows. The museum owns Peggy Guggenheim's trove of Cubist, Surrealist and Abstract Expressionist works, along with the Panza di Biumo Collection of American Minimalist and Conceptual art from the 1960s and '70s. As well as works by Manet, Picasso, Chagall and Bourgeois, it includes the largest collection of Kandinskys in the US. Back in 1992, the addition of a ten-storey tower provided space for a sculpture gallery (with park views), an auditorium and a café.

Event highlights The Harmony of Silence: Kandinsky's *Painting with White Border* (21 Oct 2011-15 Jan 2012); Maurizio Cattelan: All (4 Nov 2011-22 Jan 2012).

Whitney Museum of American Art

945 Madison Avenue, at 75th Street (1-212 570 3600, www.whitney.org). Subway 6 to 77th Street. **Open**

NEW YORK BY AREA

11am-6pm Wed, Thur, Sat, Sun; 1-9pm Fri. **Admission** $18; free-$12 reductions; pay what you wish 6-9pm Fri.
Map p139 D3 ⑩

Like the Guggenheim, the Whitney is set apart by its unique architecture: it's a Marcel Breuer-designed granite cube with an all-seeing upper-storey 'eye' window. When sculptor and art patron Gertrude Vanderbilt Whitney opened the museum in 1931, she dedicated it to living American artists. Today, the Whitney holds 18,000 pieces by around 2,700 artists, including Alexander Calder, Willem de Kooning, Edward Hopper (the museum owns his entire collection), Jasper Johns, Louise Nevelson, Georgia O'Keeffe and Claes Oldenburg.

Still, its reputation rests primarily on its temporary shows – particularly the Whitney Biennial, the exhibition that everyone loves to hate. Launched in 1932 and held in even-numbered years, the Biennial is the most prestigious and controversial assessment of contemporary art in America.

In May 2011, ground was finally broken on the Whitney's new 200,000 sqaure-foot downtown satellite museum. Designed by Renzo Piano and located between the High Line and the Hudson River Park in the Meatpacking District, it is expected to be completed in 2015.

Event highlights March 2012 sees the arrival of the latest Whitney Biennial (until May 2012).

Eating & drinking

Bar Pleiades

The Surrey, 20 E 76th Street, between Fifth & Madison Avenues (1-212 772 2600, www.danielnyc.com). Subway 6 to 77th Street. **Open** noon-midnight daily. **Bar**. Map p139 D3 ⑪

Designed as a nod to Coco Chanel, Daniel Boulud's bar – across the hotel lobby from Café Boulud – is framed in black lacquered panels that recall an elegant make-up compact. The luxe

setting and moneyed crowd might seem a little stiff, but the drinks are so exquisitely executed, you won't mind sharing your banquette with a suit – try La Terre, an earthy, complex blend of red vermouth, Aperol, grapefruit juice and house-infused beet gin. All of this refinement will cost you: canapés (made at Café Boulud next door) are $28 for four people, and cocktails average out at $18.

Bemelmans Bar

The Carlyle, 35 E 76th Street, at Madison Avenue (1-212 744 1600, www. thecarlyle.com). **Open** noon-1am Mon-Thur, Sun; noon-1.30am Fri, Sat. **Bar**. Map p139 D3 ⑫

The Plaza may be Eloise, but the Carlyle has its own children's book connection – the wonderful 1947 murals of Central Park by *Madeline* creator Ludwig Bemelmans in this, the quintessential classy New York bar. A jazz trio adds to the atmosphere most nights (a cover charge of $10-$25 applies from 9.30pm, when it takes up residence).

Café Sabarsky

Neue Galerie, 1048 Fifth Avenue, at 86th Street (1-212 288 0665, www.neuegalerie.org/cafes/sabarsky Subway 4, 5, 6 to 86th Street. **Open** 9am-6pm Mon, Wed; 9am-9pm, Thur, Fri-Sun. **$$ Café**. Map p139 D2 ⑬

Purveyor of indulgent pastries and whipped-cream-topped *einspänner* coffee for Neue Galerie patrons by day, this Kurt Gutenbrunner outfit with marble tabletops, high ceilings and booths peering onto Fifth Avenue becomes an upscale restaurant four nights a week. Appetizers are most adventurous – the creaminess of the *spaetzle* is a perfect base for sweet corn, tarragon and wild mushrooms, while the *palatshinken* crepes get a buzz from the horseradish crème fraiche. Main course specials like the Wiener Rostbraten in a mustard sauce, pan-seared cod or the Wiener Schnitzel tartly garnished with lingonberries are all capable yet ultimately feel like the calm before the Sturm und Drang of dessert. Try the Klimt torte, which masterfully alternates layers of hazelnut cake with chocolate.

Daniel

60 E 65th Street, between Madison & Park Avenues (1-212 288 0033, www.danielnyc.com). Subway F to Lexington Avenue-63rd Street; 6 to 68th Street-Hunter College. **Open** 5.30-11pm Mon-Sat. **$$$$. French.** **Map** p139 D5 **⑭**

The revolving door off Park Avenue and the elegant, Adam Tihany-designed interior announce it: this is fine dining. The cuisine at Daniel Boulud's flagship is rooted in French technique with *au courant* flourishes like fusion elements and an emphasis on local produce. Though the seasonally changing menu always includes a few signature dishes – Boulud's black truffle and scallops in puff pastry, introduced in 1987, remains a classic – it's the chef's new creations that keep the food as fresh as the decor. **Other locations** Café Boulud, 20 E 76th Street, between Fifth & Madison Avenues (1-212 772 2600).

Lexington Candy Shop

1226 Lexington Avenue, at 83rd Street (1-212 288 0057, www.lexingtoncandyshop.net). Subway 4, 5, 6 to 86th Street. **Open** 7am-7pm Mon-Sat; 8am-6pm Sun. **$. American. Map** p139 D3 **⑮**

You won't see much candy for sale at Lexington Candy Shop. Instead, you'll find a wonderfully preserved retro diner (it was founded in 1925), its long counter lined with chatty locals on their lunch hours, tucking into burgers and chocolate malts. If you come for breakfast, order the doorstop slabs of french toast.

Shopping

Madison Avenue, between 57th and 86th Streets, is packed with international designer names:

Gucci, Prada, Chloé, Donna Karan, Tom Ford, multiple Ralph Lauren outposts and many more.

Barneys New York

660 Madison Avenue, at 61st Street (1-212 826 8900, www.barneys.com). Subway N, R to Fifth Avenue-59th Street; 4, 5, 6 to 59th Street. **Open** 10am-8pm Mon-Fri; 10am-7pm Sat; 11am-6pm Sun. **Map** p139 D5 **⑯**

Barneys has a reputation for spotlighting less-ubiquitous designer labels than other upmarket department stores, and has its own quirky-classic line. Its funky Co-op boutiques (see website for locations) carry threads from up-and-comers and the latest hot denim lines. Every February and August, the Chelsea Co-op hosts the Barneys Warehouse Sale, when prices are slashed by 50-80 per cent.

Bloomingdale's

1000 Third Avenue, at 59th Street (1-212 705 2000, www.bloomingdales.com). Subway N, R to Lexington Avenue-59th Street; 4, 5, 6 to 59th Street. **Open** 10am-8.30pm Mon-Fri; 10am-7pm Sat; 11am-7pm Sun. **Map** p139 D5/E5 **⑰**

Ranking among the city's top tourist attractions, Bloomie's is a gigantic, glitzy department store stocked with everything from bags to beauty products, home furnishings to designer duds. The beauty hall, complete with an outpost of globe-spanning apothecary Space NK and a Bumble & Bumble dry-styling bar, recently got a glam makeover. The hipper, compact Soho outpost concentrates on young fashion, denim and cosmetics.

Lisa Perry

NEW *976 Madison Avenue, between 76th & 77th Streets (1-212 431 7467, www.lisaperrystyle.com). Subway 6 to 77th Street.* **Open** 10am-7pm Mon-Sat; 11am-6pm most Sun. **Map** p139 D3 **⑱**

You don't have to be a flower child to appreciate Lisa Perry's vivid, '60s-inspired shift dresses, retro home goods and bright baubles. The FIT graduate's new 4,000-square-foot concept store carries her full collection, so you'll find Technicolor duffel bags and flower-print throw pillows as well as a range of clothing and accessories. Customers can also browse a rotating selection of Perry's rare vintage pieces from the likes of Pierre Cardin, André Courrèges, Emilio Pucci, Rudi Gernreich and more.

Sigerson Morrison

NEW *19 E 71st Street, between Fifth & Madison Avenues (1-212 734 2100, www.sigersonmorrison.com). Subway 6 to 68th Street.* **Open** 10am-6pm Mon-Sat. **Map** p139 D4 ⑲

Kari Sigerson and Miranda Morrison's footwear brand may have a Downtown vibe, but their latest venture is a concept store (which doubles as an art gallery) on the upmarket Upper East Side. Alongside the sleek – often 1960s or '70s-inspired – boots and pixie-like flats (from around $350) you'll find accessories such as bags and gloves, plus goods from SM-approved vendors, such as Maria Beaulieu's coral-inspired earrings or the intoxicating 06130 French perfumes.

Upper West Side

The gateway to the Upper West Side is Columbus Circle, where Broadway meets 59th Street, Eighth Avenue, Central Park South and Central Park West – a rare roundabout in a city that is largely made up of right angles. The cosmopolitan neighbourhood's seat of culture is **Lincoln Center**, a complex of concert halls and auditoriums that's home to the New York Philharmonic, the New York City Ballet, the Metropolitan Opera and various other notable arts organisations.

Further uptown, Morningside Heights, between 110th and 125th Streets, from Morningside Park to the Hudson, is dominated by Columbia University. The sinuous Riverside Park, designed by Central Park's Frederick Law Olmsted, starts at 72nd Street and ends at 158th Street, between Riverside Drive and the Hudson River; in the 1990s, work began to develop the abandoned Penn Central Railyard between 59th and 72nd Streets into Riverside Park South, now a peaceful city retreat with a pier and undulating waterside paths.

Sights & museums

American Museum of Natural History/Rose Center for Earth & Space

Central Park West, at 79th Street (1-212 769 5100, www.amnh.org). Subway B, C to 81st Street-Museum of Natural History. **Open** 10am-5.45pm daily. **Admission** suggested donation $16; free-$12 reductions. **Map** p138 C3 ⑳

Home to the largest and arguably most fabulous collection of dinosaur fossils in the world, the American Museum of Natural History's fourth-floor dino halls have been blowing minds for decades. The thrills begin when you cross the threshold of the Theodore Roosevelt Rotunda, where you're confronted with a towering barosaurus rearing high on its hind legs to protect its young from an attacking allosaurus – an impressive welcome to the largest museum of its kind in the world. Roughly 80% of the bones on display were dug out of the ground by Indiana Jones types. But during the museum's mid 1990s renovation, several specimens were remodelled to incorporate discoveries made during the intervening years. The tyrannosaurus rex, for instance, was once believed to have walked upright, *Godzilla*-style; it now stalks prey with its head lowered and tail raised parallel to the ground.

The rest of the museum is equally dramatic. The Hall of Human Origins, which opened in 2007, houses a fine display of our old cousins, the Neanderthals. The Hall of Biodiversity examines world ecosystems and environmental preservation, and a life-size model of a blue whale hangs from the cavernous ceiling of the Hall of Ocean Life. In the Hall of Meteorites, the space's focal point is Ahnighito, the largest iron meteor on display anywhere in the world, weighing in at 34 tons.

The spectacular $210 million Rose Center for Earth & Space – dazzling at night – is a giant silvery globe where you can discover the universe via 3-D shows in the Hayden Planetarium and light shows in the Big Bang Theater. An IMAX theatre screens larger-than-life nature programmes, and the roster of temporary exhibitions is thought-provoking for all ages.

Event highlights The World's Largest Dinosaurs (until 2 Jan 2012).

Cathedral Church of St John the Divine

1047 Amsterdam Avenue, at 112th Street (1-212 316 7540, www. stjohndivine.org). Subway B, C, 1 to 110th Street-Cathedral Parkway. **Open** 7.30am-6pm Mon-Sat; 7am-7pm Sun. **Admission** suggested donation $5; $2-$4 reductions. **Map** p140 B4 ㉑
Construction on this massive house of worship, affectionately nicknamed 'St John the Unfinished', began in 1892 in Romanesque style, was put on hold for a Gothic Revival redesign in 1911, then ground to a halt in 1941, when the US entered World War II. It resumed in earnest in 1979, but a fire in 2001 that destroyed the church's gift shop and damaged two 17th-century Italian tapestries further delayed completion. It's still missing a tower and a north transept, among other things, but the nave has been restored and the entire interior reopened and rededicated. No further work is planned… for now.

In addition to Sunday services, the cathedral hosts concerts and tours. It bills itself as a place for all people –

and it certainly means it. Annual events include both winter and summer solstice celebrations, the Blessing of the Animals during the Feast of St Francis, which draws pets and their people from all over the city, and even an annual Blessing of the Bicycles every spring.

Museum of Arts & Design

2 Columbus Circle, at Broadway (1-212 299 7777, www.madmuseum.org). Subway A, B, C, D, 1 to 59th Street-Columbus Circle. **Open** 11am-6pm Tue, Wed, Fri-Sun; 11am-9pm Thur. **Admission** $15; free-$12 reductions; pay what you wish 6-9pm Thur.
Map p138 C5 ㉒
This institution brings together contemporary objects created in a wide range of media – including clay, glass, wood, metal and cloth – with a strong focus on materials and process. And the museum recently crafted itself a new home. Originally designed in 1964 by Radio City Music Hall architect Edward Durell Stone to house the Gallery of Modern Art, 2 Columbus Circle was a windowless monolith that had sat empty since 1998. After an 18-month overhaul (with a price tag topping $90 million), the ten-storey building now has four floors of exhibition galleries, including the Tiffany & Co Foundation Jewelry Gallery. Curators are able to display more of the 2,000-piece permanent collection, including porcelain ware by Cindy Sherman, stained glass by Judith Schaechter, basalt ceramics by James Turrell and Robert Arneson's mural *Alice House Wall.*

In addition to checking out temporary shows, you can also watch resident artists create works in studios on the sixth floor, while the ninth-floor bistro has views over the park.

Event highlights Crafting Modernism: Mid-Century American Art & Design (11 Oct 2011-15 Jan 2012); Picasso to Koons: Artist as Jeweler (20 Sept 2011-8 Jan 2012).

New-York Historical Society

170 Central Park West, between 76th & 77th Streets (1-212 873 3400, www. nyhistory.org). Subway B, C to 81st Street-Museum of Natural History. **Open** 10am-6pm Tue-Thur, Sat; 10am-8pm Fri; 11am-5.45pm Sun. **Admission** $12; free-$9 reductions; free 6-8pm Fri. **Map** p138 C3 ㉓

After an extensive renovation (see p145), New York's oldest museum reopens in November 2011. (Until then, visits to the permenant collection are by appointment only.) Highlights in the vast Henry Luce III Center for the Study of American Culture include George Washington's Valley Forge camp cot, a complete series of the extant watercolours from Audubon's *Birds of America* and the world's largest collection of Tiffany lamps.

Eating & drinking

A Voce Columbus

3rd Floor, 10 Columbus Circle, at Broadway (1-212 823 2523, www. avocerestaurant.com). Subway A, B, C, D, 1 to 59th Street-Columbus Circle. **Open** 11.30am-2.30pm, 5-10pm Mon-Wed; 11.30am-2.30pm, 5-11.30pm Thur, Fri; 11am-3pm, 5-11.30pm Sat; 11am-3pm, 5-10pm Sun. **$$. Italian.** **Map** p138 C5 ㉔

Want views over Columbus Circle and the park without paying Per Se (see p153) prices? A Voce's sleek new Uptown outpost also has a solid menu and impeccable service. Brick-flattened chicken, infused with roasted garlic, lemon and dried Calabrian chillies and served with Tuscan kale, white beans and potatoes, is a comfort-food triumph. Owner Marlon Abela's art collection, including a massive Frank Stella mixed-media piece, is a feast for the eyes.

Barney Greengrass

541 Amsterdam Avenue, between 86th & 87th Streets (1-212 724 4707, www.barneygreengrass.com). Subway
B, C, 1 to 86th Street. **Open** 8.30am-4pm Tue-Fri; 8.30am-5pm Sat, Sun. **$. No credit cards. American.** **Map** p138 B2 ㉕

Despite decor that Jewish mothers might call 'schmutzy', this legendary deli is a madhouse at breakfast and brunch. Egg platters come with the usual choice of smoked fish (such as sturgeon or Nova Scotia salmon). Prices are on the high side, but portions are large, and that goes for the sandwiches too. Or try the less costly dishes: matzoball soup or cold pink borscht.

Bouchon Bakery

3rd Floor, Time Warner Center, 10 Columbus Circle, at Broadway (1-212 823 9366, www.bouchonbakery.com). Subway A, B, C, D, 1 to 59th Street-Columbus Circle. **Open** 11.30am-9pm Mon-Sat; 11.30am-7pm Sun. **$-$$.** **Café. Map** p138 C5 ㉖

The appeal is obvious: sample Thomas Keller's food for a fraction of the cost of a meal at Per Se. The reality is that you will have to eat in an open café setting in the middle of a mall, under a giant Samsung sign, and choose from a limited selection of sandwiches, salads, quiches and spreadable delights (pâté, foie gras and so on). That said, this is a great place for lunch. The sandwiches are impeccably plated, although portions can be small.

Ding Dong Lounge

929 Columbus Avenue, between 105th & 106th Street (Duke Ellington Boulevard) (1-212 663 2600, www. dingdonglounge.com). Subway B, C to 103rd Street. **Open** 4pm-4am daily. **Bar. Map** p140 B5 ㉗

Goth chandeliers and kick-ass music mark this dark dive as punk – with broadened horizons. The taps, dispensing Stella Artois, Guinness and Bass, are sawn-off guitar necks, and the walls are covered with vintage concert posters (from Dylan to the Damned). The affable local clientele and mood-lit conversation nooks make it surprisingly accessible (even without a working knowledge of Dee Dee Ramone).

Hungarian Pastry Shop

1030 Amsterdam Avenue, between 110th & 111th Street. Subway 1 to 110th Street-Cathedral Parkway. **Open** 7.30am-11.30pm Mon-Fri; 8.30am-11.30pm Sat; 8.30am-10.30pm Sun. **$**. **Café**. **Map** p140 B4 ㉙

So many theses have been dreamed up, procrastinated over or tossed aside in the almost five decades of the Hungarian Pastry Shop's existence that the Columbia University neighbourhood institution merits its own dissertation. In truth, the dim lighting and rickety chairs are not really conducive to grappling with Gramsci or demystifying Delillo, and you're better off placing your order at the counter – give your name and they'll bring it to you when it's ready – and settling in for a coffee-fuelled schmooze with a flaneur. The java itself is strong enough to make up for the erratic array of pastries, and the Euro feel is enhanced by the view of St John the Divine cathedral from outdoor tables.

Ouest

2315 Broadway, at 84th Street (1-212 580 8700, www.ouestny.com). Subway 1 to 86th Street. **Open** 5-10.30pm Mon-Thur; 5-11.30pm Fri, Sat; 5-9.30 Sun. **$$**. **American**. **Map** p138 B3 ㉙

Ouest still stands out as much as it did when chef-owner Tom Valenti opened it in 2001. The *frisée aux lardons* with generous slices of buttery house-cured sturgeon wrapped around a poached egg plus candy-like piece of bacon is one of the best dishes in New York; and Valenti's signature braised short ribs with beets and horseradish *spaetzle* remains nonpareil – the slow-cooked beef, nearly caramelized, is grilled before being served, imparting a smokiness that compounds the meat's richness, all of which is cut nicely by the spicy dumplings.

It's a rare place that can both please crowds and wow elitists – but Ouest is that place.

Per Se

Fourth Floor, Ten Columbus Circle, at Broadway (1-212 823 9335, www.perse ny.com). Subway A, B, C, D, 1 to 59th Street-Columbus Circle. **Open** 5.30-10pm Mon-Thur; 11.30am-1.30pm, 5.30-10pm Fri-Sun. **$$$**. **French**. **Map** p138 C5 ㉚

Expectations are high at Per Se – and that goes both ways. You are expected to come when they'll have you – you might be put on standby for four nights, only to win a 10pm Tuesday spot – and fork over $150 a head if you cancel. You're expected to wear the right clothes, pay a non-negotiable service charge, and pretend you aren't eating in a shopping mall. The restaurant, in turn, is expected to deliver one hell of a tasting menu for $250 ($280 if you want foie gras). And it does. Dish after dish is flawless and delicious, if not altogether surprising, beginning with Thomas Keller's signature salmon tartare cone and luxe oysters-and-caviar starter. In the end, it's all worth every penny (as long as someone else is paying). The à la carte option in the lounge, meanwhile, offers miserly portions at high prices, making it even more of a splurge than the celebrated tasting menu available in the formal dining room.

Shake Shack

366 Columbus Avenue, at 77th Street (1-646 747 8770, www.shakeshack nyc.com). Subway 1 to 79th Street. **Open** 10.45am-11pm daily. **$**. **American**. **Map** p138 B3 ㉛

The spacious offspring of Danny Meyer's wildly popular Madison Square Park concession stand, Shake Shack gets several local critics' votes for New York's best burger. Sirloin and brisket are ground daily for the prime patties, and the franks are served Chicago-style on poppy seed buns with a 'salad' of toppings and a dash of celery salt. Frozen-custard shakes hit the spot, and there's beer and wine if you want something stronger.

Shopping

Allan & Suzi

416 Amsterdam Avenue, at 80th Street (1-212 724 7445, www.allanandsuzi.net). Subway 1 to 79th Street. **Open** 12.30-7pm Mon-Sat; noon-6pm Sun.
Map p138 B3 ㉜
Models and celebs drop off worn-once Gaultiers, Muglers, Pradas and Manolos here. The platform shoe collection is flashback-inducing and incomparable, as is the selection of vintage jewellery.

H&H Bagels

2239 Broadway, at 80th Street (1-212 595 8000, www.hhbagels.com). Subway 1 to 79th Street. **Open** 24hrs daily.
Map p138 B3 ㉝
For a taste of the real, old-fashioned (boiled and baked) thing, head straight to H&H, which lays claim to being the city's largest bagel purveyor.

Levain Bakery

167 W 74th Street, between Columbus & Amsterdam Avenues (1-212 874 6080, www.levainbakery.com). Subway 1 to 79th Street. **Open** 8am-7pm Mon-Sat; 9am-7pm Sun. **Map** p138 B3 ㉞
Forget the Big Apple – a Big Cookie is much tastier. Levain's are a full 6oz, and the massive mounds stay gooey in the middle. The lush, brownie-like double-chocolate variety, made with extra-dark French cocoa and semi-sweet chocolate chips, is a truly decadent treat.

Shops at Columbus Circle

Time Warner Center, 10 Columbus Circle, at 59th Street (1-212 823 6300, www.shopsatcolumbuscircle.com). Subway A, B, C, D, 1 to 59th Street-Columbus Circle. **Open** 10am-9pm Mon-Sat; 11am-7pm Sun (hrs vary for some shops, bars and restaurants). **Map** p138 C5 ㉟

Classier than your average mall, the retail contingent of the 2.8 million-sq-ft Time Warner Center features upscale stores such as Coach and Cole Haan for accessories and shoes, Bose home entertainment, the fancy kitchenware purveyor Williams-Sonoma and True Religion jeans, as well as shopping centre staples J Crew, Aveda, and organic grocer Whole Foods. Some of the city's top restaurants (including Thomas Keller's gourmet destination Per Se and his café Bouchon Bakery) have made it a dining destination that transcends the stigma of eating at the mall.

Zabar's

2245 Broadway, at 80th Street (1-212 787 2000, www.zabars.com). Subway 1 to 79th Street. **Open** 8am-7.30pm Mon-Fri; 8am-8pm Sat; 9am-6pm Sun.
Map p138 B3 ㊱
Zabar's is more than just a market – it's a New York City landmark. It began in 1934 as a tiny storefront specialising in Jewish 'appetising' delicacies and has gradually expanded to take over half a block of prime Upper West Side real estate. What never ceases to surprise, however, is its reasonable prices, even for high-end foods. Besides the famous smoked fish and rafts of delicacies, Zabar's has fabulous bread, cheese, olives and coffee and an entire floor dedicated to homewares.

Nightlife

Beacon Theatre

2124 Broadway, at 74th Street (1-212 465 6500, www.beacontheatrenyc.com). Subway 1, 2, 3 to 72nd Street.
Map p138 B3 ㊲
This spacious former vaudeville theatre, resplendent after a recent renovation, hosts a variety of popular acts, from 'Weird Al' Yankovic to ZZ Top. While the vastness can be daunting to performers and audience alike, the gilded interior and Uptown location make you feel as though you're having a real night out on the town.

Jazz at Lincoln Center

*Frederick P Rose Hall, Broadway, at 60th
Street (1-212 258 9800, www.jalc.org).
Subway A, B, C, D, 1 to 59th Street-
Columbus Circle.* **Map** p138 C5 ③

The jazz arm of Lincoln Center is several blocks away from the main campus (below), situated high atop the
Time Warner Center. It features three
separate rooms: the Rose Theater is a
traditional mid-size space, but the
crown jewels are the Allen Room and
the smaller Dizzy's Club Coca-Cola,
which feel like a Hollywood cinematog-
rapher's vision of a Manhattan jazz
club. Some of the best players in the
business regularly grace the spot,
among them Wynton Marsalis, who is
also Jazz at Lincoln Center's famed
artistic director.

Arts & leisure

Lincoln Center

*Columbus Avenue, at 65th Street
(1-212 546 2656, www.lincolncenter.org).
Subway 1 to 66th Street-Lincoln Center.*
Map p138 B5 ③

Built in the early 1960s, this massive
complex is the nexus of Manhattan's
performing arts scene, and a recent
revamp of its campus has left it
sparkling.

The main entry point for Lincoln
Center is at Columbus Avenue, at 65th
Street, but the venues that follow are
spread out across the square of blocks
from 62nd to 66th Streets, between
Amsterdam and Columbus Avenues.
The Julliard School and the Fiorello H
LaGuardia High School for Music &
Art and Performing Arts are also
based here. For event highlights, see
pp36-44 Calendar.
Alice Tully Hall 1-212 875 5050.
Alice Tully lives again after a recent
renovation that turned the cosy home
of the Chamber Music Society of
Lincoln Center (1-212 875 5788) into a
world-class theatre. A new contemporary foyer with an elegant (if pricey)
café is immediately striking, but, more

importantly, the revamp also brought
dramatic acoustical improvements.
Avery Fisher Hall 1-212 875 5030.
This handsome, comfortable 2,738-seat
hall is the headquarters of the New
York Philharmonic (1-212 875 5656,
www.nyphilharmonic.org), the country's oldest symphony orchestra
(founded in 1842) and one of its finest,
led by musical director Alan Gilbert.
The sound, which ranges from good to
atrocious depending on whom you ask,
stands to be improved (although the
timing of this hasn't been confirmed).
Inexpensive early-evening 'rush hour'
concerts and weekday-morning open
rehearsals are presented several times
per season. The Great Performers
series features top international
soloists and ensembles.
**David H Koch Theater 1-212 870
5570.**
As well as the New York City Ballet,
the recently renovated and rechristened David H Koch Theater is home
to the New York City Opera (www.nyc-
opera.com). The company has long
tried to overcome its second-best reputation by being both ambitious and
defiantly populist: rising American
singers often take their first bows here
and productions are still consistently
young and sexy under new director
George Steel. Following a lengthy clo-
sure for the revamp in 2009, the NYCO
has returned to the space with its
vastly improved acoustics.
**Lincoln Center Theater 1-212 239
6200, www.lct.org.**
The majestic and prestigious Lincoln
Center Theater complex has a pair of
amphitheatre-style drama venues. The
Broadway house, the 1,138-seat Vivian
Beaumont Theater, is home to star-
studded and elegant major productions. (When the Beaumont is tied up
in long runs, LCT presents its larger
works at available Times Square theatres.) Downstairs from the Beaumont
is the 338-seat Mitzi E Newhouse
Theater, an Off Broadway space
devoted to new work by the upper

layer of American playwrights. In an effort to shake off its reputation for stodginess, in 2008, Lincoln Center launched LCT3, which presents the work of emerging playwrights and directors at the Duke (229 W 42nd Street, between Seventh and Eighth Avenues). All tickets are $20; see the LCT website for details. Construction on a devoted space atop the Vivian Beaumont Theater is slated for completion in 2012.

Metropolitan Opera House 1-212 362 6000, www.metopera.org.

The grandest of the Lincoln Center buildings, the Met is a spectacular place to see and hear opera. It hosts the Metropolitan Opera from September to May, with major visiting companies appearing in summer. Opera's biggest stars appear here regularly, and artistic director James Levine has turned the orchestra into a true symphonic force. Audiences are knowledgeable and fiercely devoted, with subscriptions remaining in families for generations.

The Met had already started becoming more inclusive before current impresario Peter Gelb took the reins in 2006. Now, the company is placing a priority on creating novel theatrical experiences with visionary directors (Bartlett Sher, Richard Eyre, Patrice Chéreau) and assembling a new company of physically graceful, telegenic stars (Anna Netrebko, Danielle de Niese, Jonas Kaufmann, Erwin Schrott). Its high-definition movie-theatre broadcasts continue to reign supreme outside the opera house.

Although most tickets are expensive, 200 prime seats (50 of which are reserved for over-65s) for all performances from Monday to Thursday are sold for a mere $20 apiece two hours before the curtain.

Walter Reade Theater 1-212 875 5601, www.filmlinc.com.

The complex's cinema is the home of the Film Society of Lincoln Center, founded in 1969 to promote contemporary film. The FSLC now also hosts the prestigious New York Film Festival (p37) and other festivals throughout the year. Programmes are usually thematic with an international perspective.

Symphony Space

2537 Broadway, at 95th Street (1-212 864 5400, www.symphonyspace.org). Subway 1, 2, 3 to 96th Street.
Map p138 B1 ⓴

Despite the name, programming at Symphony Space is anything but orchestra-centric: recent seasons have featured sax quartets, Indian classical music, a capella ensembles and HD opera simulcasts from Europe. Annual Wall to Wall marathons (usually in spring) serve up a full day of music free of charge, all focused on a particular composer. Members of the New York Philharmonic are regular guests here in more intimate chamber concerts.

Harlem & beyond

Extending north from the top of Central Park at 110th Street as far as 155th Street, Harlem is the cultural capital of black America – the legacy of the Harlem Renaissance. By the 1920s, it had become the country's most populous African-American community, attracting some of black America's greatest artists: writers such as Langston Hughes and musicians like Duke Ellington and Louis Armstrong. West Harlem, between Fifth and St Nicholas Avenues, is the Harlem of popular imagination, and 125th Street is its lifeline. The area around the landmarked Mount Morris Historic District (from 119th to 124th Streets, between Malcolm X Boulevard/Lenox Avenue & Mount Morris Park West) continues to gentrify, and new boutiques, restaurants and cafés dot the double-wide Malcolm X Boulevard. Further uptown, Strivers' Row, from 138th to 139th

Home at last

The Museum for African Art's new digs on Museum Mile.

Museum for African Art p147

The Museum for African Art has certainly led a nomadic existence since its inception in 1984. It began life in an Upper East Side townhouse, moved in 1992 to a small space in Soho and decamped to Long Island City in 2002. After closing its doors in 2005, it began casting about for a larger, more permanent home, breaking ground in 2007 on a new $95 million museum on Fifth Avenue, right on the cusp of Harlem.

In October 2011, the Museum for African Art will become the first addition to Museum Mile since the Solomon R Guggenheim was completed in 1959. The space, designed by Robert AM Stern Architects, will give the Museum for African Art 75,000 square feet (6,968 square metres) and four floors (one below ground) of a 19-storey residential tower.

A glass atrium guides visitors into a soaring lobby with 45-foot (14-metre) high walls. In addition to a smaller exhibition space, the lobby contains a shop, a restaurant, a 245-seat theatre and a multimedia education centre. Upstairs, the first floor is given over to three rotating exhibition galleries. The MfAA's inaugural shows are 'El Anatsui: When Last I Wrote to You About Africa', a retrospective of some 60 works by the Ghanian-born artist, who uses found materials to create large wall sculptures; 'Grass Roots: African Origins of an American Art', which traces the influence of West African basket-making on the American South's adoption of that art form; and 'New Premises: Three Decades at the Museum for African Art', a two-part show that will explore the evolution of the Museum of African Art using works from the permanent collection.

Plans are also afoot for the MfAA's Mandela Center for Memory and Dialogue, dedicated to programmes examining humanitarian issues and social justice. In addition to stretching Museum Mile northward, the new MfAA has also broadened its artistic and cultural scope.

Apollo Theater p160

Streets, between Adam Clayton Powell Jr Boulevard (Seventh Avenue) and Frederick Douglass Boulevard (Eighth Avenue), was developed in 1891. East of Fifth Avenue is East Harlem, better known to its primarily Puerto Rican residents as El Barrio. (For El Museo del Barrio, see p144.)

From 155th Street to Dyckman (200th) Street is Washington Heights, which contains a handful of attractions and, at the tip of Manhattan, pretty Fort Tryon Park.

Sights & museums

The Cloisters

Fort Tryon Park, Fort Washington Avenue, at Margaret Corbin Plaza (1-212 923 3700, www.metmuseum.org). Subway A to 190th Street, then M4 bus or follow Margaret Corbin Drive north to the museum. **Open** *Mar-Oct* 9.30am-5.15pm Tue-Sun. *Nov-Feb* 9.30am-4.45pm Tue-Sun. **Admission** suggested donation (incl same-day admission to Metropolitan Museum of Art) $20; free-$15 reductions.

Set in a lovely park overlooking the Hudson River, the Cloisters houses the Met's medieval art and architecture collections. A path winds through the peaceful grounds to a castle that was built a mere 71 years ago using pieces from five medieval French cloisters. The collection itself is a trove of Romanesque, Gothic and Baroque treasures brought from Europe and then assembled together in a manner that manages not to clash. Be sure to check out the Unicorn Tapestries, the 12th-century Fuentidueña Chapel and the *Annunciation Triptych* by Robert Campin.

Studio Museum in Harlem

144 W 125th Street, between Malcolm X Boulevard (Lenox Avenue) & Adam Clayton Powell Jr Boulevard (Seventh Avenue) (1-212 864 4500, www.studiomuseum.org). Subway 2, 3 to 125th Street. **Open** noon-8pm Thur-Fri, 10am-6pm Sat; noon-6pm Sun. **Admission** suggested donation $7; free-$3 reductions; free Sun. No credit cards. **Map** p140 C3 ㊶

The first black fine arts museum in the country when it opened in 1968, the Studio Museum has become one of the jewels in the crown of the art scene of the African diaspora. Under the leadership of director and chief curator Thelma Golden, this vibrant institution, housed in a stripped down, three-level space, presents shows in a variety of media by black artists from around the world.

Eating & drinking

Amy Ruth's

113 W 116th Street, between Malcolm X Boulevard (Lenox Avenue) & Adam Clayton Powell Jr Boulevard (Seventh Avenue) (1-212 280 8779, www.amyruthsharlem.com). Subway 2, 3 to 116th Street. **Open** 11.30am-11pm Mon; 8.30am-11pm Tue-Thur, Sun; 24hrs Fri, Sat. **$**. **American regional**. **Map** p140 C4 ㊷

This no-reservations spot, perpetually packed, is the place for soul food. Delicately fried okra is delivered without a hint of slime, and the mac and cheese is gooey inside and crunchy-brown on top. Dishes take their names from notable African-Americans; be patriotic and vote for the President Barack Obama (fried, smothered, baked or barbecued chicken).

Red Rooster

NEW *310 Malcolm X Boulevard, between 125th & 126th Streets (1-212 792 9001, www.redroosterharlem.com). Subway 2, 3 to 125th Street.* **Open** 11.30am-3pm, 5.30-10.30 Mon-Wed; 11.30am-3pm, 5.30-11.30 Thur, Fri; 10am-4pm, 5.30-11.30pm Sat; 10am-4pm, 5-10pm Sun. **$$**. **Eclectic Map** p140 C3 ㊸

With its hobnobbing bar scrum, potent cocktails and lively jazz, this buzzy eatery serves as a worthy clubhouse for the new Harlem. Superstar chef Marcus Samuelsson is at his most populist here, drawing on a 'We Are the World' mix of Southern-fried, East African, Scandinavian and French flavours to feed the lively crowd. Harlem politicos mix at the teardrop bar with downtown fashionistas, everyone happily swilling fine cocktails and gorging on rib-sticking food: chicken-liver-enriched dirty rice topped with plump barbecued shrimp, homey desserts, and crispy fried chicken with hot sauce, mace gravy and a smoky spice shake. It all adds up to a place that, for reasons apparent as soon as you cross its threshold, has earned its status as a local hub.

Shrine Bar

2271 Adam Clayton Powell Jr Boulevard (Seventh Avenue), between 134th & 135th Streets (1-212 690 7807, www.shrinenyc.com). Subway B, C, 2, 3 to 135th Street. **Open** 4pm-4am daily. **Bar**. **Map** p140 C2 ㊹

Playfully adapting a sign left over from previous tenants (the Black United Foundation), the Shrine deems itself a "Black United Fun Plaza." The interior is tricked out with African art and vintage album covers (the actual vinyl adorns the ceiling). Harlemites and downtowners pack the Shrine for nightly concerts, which might feature indie rock, jazz, reggae or DJ sets. The cocktail menu aspires to similar diversity: drinks range from a smooth mango mojito to signature tipples like a snappy Afro Trip (a lime and ginger concoction enhanced by Jamaican or Brazilian rum), and a sweet vodka-and-Bailey's-driven Muslim Jew.

Shopping

Hue-Man Bookstore & Café

2319 Frederick Douglass Boulevard (Eighth Avenue), between 124th & 125th Streets (1-212 665 7400, www.hueman bookstore.com). Subway A, B, C, D to 125th Street. **Open** 10am-8pm Mon-Sat; 11am-7pm Sun. **Map** p140 C3 ㊺

Focusing on African-American non-fiction and fiction, this superstore-sized Harlem indie also stocks bestsellers and general interest books. It hosts readings, as well as in-store appearances by authors such as Chris Abani and Marlon James.

Nightlife

Apollo Theater

253 W 125th Street, between Adam Clayton Powell Jr Boulevard (Seventh Avenue) & Frederick Douglass Boulevard (Eighth Avenue) (1-212 531 5300, www.apollotheater.org). Subway A, B, C, D, 1 to 125th Street. **Map** p140 C3 ㊻

Visitors may think they know this venerable theatre from TV's *Showtime at the Apollo*. But as the saying goes, the small screen adds about ten pounds: the city's home of R&B and soul music is actually quite cosy. One of the Apollo's first Amateur Nights was won in 1934 by a 17-year-old Ella Fitzgerald (she took home $25), and the legendary Bessie Smith wowed the crowds with a New Year's Eve concert in 1935. Two years later, Count Basie and his Orchestra had his Apollo debut, featuring a young (and very stage-frightened) Billie Holliday. The Apollo continues to mix veteran talents such as Dianne Reeves with younger artists such as John Legend.

Lenox Lounge

288 Malcolm X Boulevard (Lenox Avenue), between 124th & 125th Streets (1-212 427 0253, www.lenoxlounge. com). Subway 2, 3 to 125th Street. **Open** noon-4am daily. **Map** p140 C3 ㊼

This classy art deco lounge, where Billie Holliday, John Coltrane, and numerous other Harlem luminaries have performed, is a true Harlem landmark and has featured in numerous films evoking Harlem's past, including *Malcolm X* and the remake of *Shaft*.

Brooklyn Bridge p162

Outer Boroughs

The Bronx

Sights & museums

Bronx Zoo/Wildlife Conservation Society

Bronx River Parkway, at Fordham Road (1-718 367 1010, www.bronxzoo.org). Subway 2, 5 to Pelham Parkway, then walk two blocks, turn left at Boston Road and bear right to the zoo's Bronxdale entrance; or Metro-North (Harlem Line local) from Grand Central Terminal to Fordham, then take the Bx9 bus to the zoo's Southern Boulevard entrance. **Open** *Apr-Oct* 10am-5pm Mon-Fri; 10am-5.30pm Sat, Sun. *Nov-Mar* 10am-4.30pm daily. **Admission** $16; $12-$14 reductions; pay what you wish Wed.
Home to more than 4,000 creatures and 650 species, the zoo shuns cages in favour of indoor and outdoor environments that mimic the natural habitats of its mammals, birds and reptiles. Nearly 100 species, including monkeys, leopards and tapirs, live inside the lush, steamy Jungle World, a re-creation of an Asian rainforest inside a 37,000sq ft building. The super-popular Congo Gorilla Forest has turned 6.5 acres into a dramatic Central African rainforest habitat. A glass-enclosed tunnel winds through the forest, allowing visitors to get close to the dozens of primate families in residence, including 26 majestic western lowland gorillas. For those who prefer cats, Tiger Mountain has six adult Siberian tigers that look particularly regal on snowy days. Madagascar!, an exhibit focused on the species-rich island off the coast of East Africa, debuted in 2008. Other recent additions include an aardvark habitat, an aquatic aviary and a butterfly garden featuring 1,000 colourful flutterers.

New York Botanical Garden

Bronx River Parkway, at Fordham Road (1-718 817 8700, www.nybg.org). Subway B, D, 4 to Bedford Park Boulevard, then Bx26 bus to the garden's Mosholu Gate;

or Metro-North (Harlem Line local) from Grand Central Terminal to Botanical Garden. **Open** 10am-6pm Tue-Sun. **Admission** $20; free-$18 reductions. *Grounds only* $6; $1-$3 reductions; grounds free Wed, 10am-noon Sat.

The serene 250 acres of the New York Botanical Garden comprise 50 gardens and plant collections, including the Rockefeller Rose Garden, the Everett Children's Adventure Garden and the last 50 original acres of a forest that once covered all of New York City. In spring, the gardens are frothy with pastel blossoms, as clusters of lilac, cherry, magnolia and crab apple trees burst into bloom, followed in autumn by vivid foliage in the oak and maple groves. On a rainy day, stay warm and sheltered inside the Enid A Haupt Conservatory, a striking glass-walled greenhouse – the nation's largest – built in 1902. It contains the World of Plants, a series of environmental galleries that take you on an eco-tour through tropical rainforests, deserts and a palm-tree oasis, as well as seasonal exhibits.

Brooklyn

Sights & museums

Brooklyn Botanic Garden
1000 Washington Avenue, at Eastern Parkway, Prospect Heights (1-718 623 7200, www.bbg.org). Subway B, Q, Franklin Avenue S to Prospect Park; 2, 3 to Eastern Parkway-Brooklyn Museum. **Open** *Mar-Oct* 8am-6pm Tue-Fri; 10am-6pm Sat, Sun. *Nov-Feb* 8am-4.30pm Tue-Fri; 10am-4.30pm Sat, Sun. **Admission** $10; free-$5 reductions; free Tue, 10am-noon Sat, Sun mid Nov-Feb.

This 52-acre haven of luscious greenery was founded in 1910. In Spring, when Sakura Matsuri, the annual Cherry Blossom Festival, takes place, prize buds and Japanese culture are in full bloom. The restored Eastern Parkway entrance and the Osborne Garden – an Italian-style formal garden – are also well worth a peek.

Brooklyn Bridge
Subway A, C to High Street; J, M, Z to Chambers Street; 4, 5, 6 to Brooklyn Bridge-City Hall.

Even if your trip to New York doesn't include a romp in the boroughs, it's worth walking to the centre of the Brooklyn Bridge along its wide, wood-planked promenade. Designed by German-born civil engineer John Augustus Roebling, the bridge was constructed in response to the harsh winter of 1867 when the East River froze over, severing connection between Manhattan and what was then the nation's third most populous city. When it opened in 1883, the 5,989ft-long structure was the world's longest bridge, and the first in the world to use steel suspension cables. From it, there are striking vistas of the Statue of Liberty, the skyline of Lower Manhattan and New York Harbor.

Brooklyn Heights Promenade
Subway 2, 3 to Clark Street, then walk 3 blocks west to the Promenade

For the best views of Manhattan, check out the Promenade on the lip of Brooklyn Heights. From this half-mile-long esplanade, you can take in the Statue of Liberty and New York Harbor, the landmark skyscrapers of the Financial District and the nearby Brooklyn Bridge. Among the many films that have shot romantic scenes here are *Saturday Night Fever*, *Moonstruck*, *She's Gotta Have It* and *Prizzi's Honor*.

Brooklyn Museum
200 Eastern Parkway, at Washington Avenue, Prospect Heights (1-718 638 5000, www.brooklynmuseum.org). Subway 2, 3 to Eastern Parkway-Brooklyn Museum. **Open** 11am-6pm Wed; 11am-10pm Thur, Fri; 11am-6pm Sat, Sun; 11am-11pm 1st Sat of mth (except Sept). **Admission** suggested donation $10; free-$6 reductions; free 5-11pm 1st Sat of mth (except Sept).

Queens' big screen

The Museum of the Moving Image has a brand new look.

Museum of the Moving Image p166

Astoria's **Museum of the Moving Image** (see p166) reopened in January 2011 after a major renovation that doubled its size and made it one of the foremost museums in the world dedicated to television, film and video. Housed in one of the buildings of the Astoria Studios complex, which served in the 1920s as the New York production headquarters of Paramount Pictures before talkies moved the industry out to Hollywood, the collection is greatly enhanced by the museum's bold new design, which announces itself at the entrance: a giant frame of transparent and mirrored glass forming the museum's name and suggesting a screen.

Upstairs, on the second floor, the MMI's brand new 264-seat main theatre screams state of the art. It features steep stadium seating and a wraparound screen formed by 1,136 panels along the ceiling and walls. Every conceivable format can be screened here, from high-definition 3-D pictures to silent classics (there's even a mini orchestra pit for musical accompaniment). It is complemented by several other new theatres, including an amphitheatre specially designed for videos, as well as a 70-seat digital screening room that is largely devoted to educational programming. Rotating exhibitions are found on the third floor, as well as the educational centre, where aspiring directors can record their own videos and post them up on the Internet in the hope that their work will go viral.

The MMI's highly popular 'Behind the Screen' exhibition, which explores all the nuances of the movie- and TV programme-making process, has been upgraded and now fills a 15,000-square-foot gallery. An interactive display, it boasts artefacts from more than 1,000 productions (including the super creepy stunt doll used in *The Exorcist*, with full head-rotating capabilities, and the famous diner booth from *Seinfeld*). Astoria Studios has come a long way from the silent era.

NEW YORK BY AREA

MoMA-P.S.1 Contemporary Art Center p166

Brooklyn's premier institution is one of the city's cultural gems. It presents a tranquil alternative to Manhattan's bigger name spaces and it's rarely crowded.

Among the museum's many assets is the third-floor Egyptian galleries (the entire collection is one of the finest outside of Egypt). Highlights include the resplendent cartonnage of the priest Nespanetjerenpere; a rare terracotta female figure from 3500-3400 BC; and the Mummy Chamber, an installation of 170 objects related to the post-mortem practice, including human and animal mummies. Also on this level, masterworks by Cézanne, Monet and Degas, part of an impressive European art collection, are displayed in the museum's skylighted Beaux-Arts Court. The Elizabeth A Sackler Center for Feminist Art on the fourth floor is dominated by American artist Judy Chicago's monumental mixed-media installation, *The Dinner Party* (1974-79); its centrepiece is a massive, triangular 'table' with 39 place settings, each representing important women down the ages. The fifth floor is primarily devoted to American works, including Albert Bierstadt's immense *A Storm in the Rocky Mountains, Mt Rosalie,* and the Visible Storage-Study Center, where paintings, furniture and other objects are intriguingly juxtaposed.

Green-Wood Cemetery

Fifth Avenue, at 25th Street, Sunset Park (1-718 768 7300, www.green-wood.com). Subway R to 25th Street. **Open** *Sept-May* 8am-5pm daily. *June-Aug* 7am-7pm daily. **Admission** free. Filled with Victorian mausoleums, cherubs and gargoyles, Green-Wood is the resting place of some half-million New Yorkers, among them Jean-Michel Basquiat, Leonard Bernstein, Boss Tweed and Horace Greeley. The spectacular, soaring arches of the main gate are carved from New Jersey brownstone, and the 1911 chapel was designed by Warren & Wetmore, the firm behind Grand Central Terminal.

Battle Hill, the single highest point in Brooklyn offering prime Manhattan skyline views, is on cemetery grounds.

New York Aquarium

610 Surf Avenue, at West 8th Street (1-718 265 3474, www.nyaquarium.com). Subway D, N to Coney Island-Stillwell Avenue; F, Q to W 8th Street-NY Aquarium. **Open** *Apr-May* 10am-5pm Mon-Fri; 10am-5.30pm Sat, Sun. *June-Aug* 10am-6pm Mon-Fri; 10am-7pm Sat, Sun. *Sept-Oct* 10am-5pm Mon-Fri; 10am-5.30pm Sat, Sun. *Nov-Mar* 10am-4.30pm daily. **Admission** $14.95; $10.95-$11.95 reductions; free under-3s. **Credit** AmEx, DC, MC, V. Should Coney Island spark hankerings for the life aquatic, ignore the beach and check out New York's foremost aquarium, just off the boardwalk. The collection is beloved for its sea lions as well as its Sea Cliffs display, a 300-ft-long stretch of rocky coastline on which penguins, walruses, seals and otters frolic. The Alien Stingers exhibit features an impressive array of jellyfish, while the brand new Conservation Hall, with its coral reefs and freshwater pools teeming with rays and anemones, is ideal for learning about the protection of endangered ecosystems.

New York Transit Museum

Corner of Boerum Place & Schermerhorn Street, Brooklyn Heights (1-718 694 1600, www.mta.info/mta/museum). Subway A, C, G to Hoyt-Schermerhorn. **Open** 10am-4pm Tue-Fri; noon-5pm Sat, Sun. **Admission** $6; $4 reductions; free under-3s; free seniors Wed. **Credit** AmEx, DC, MC, V. Located in a historic 1936 IND subway station, this is the largest museum in the United States devoted to urban public transportation history. Exhibits explore the social and practical impact of public transportation on the development of greater New York; among the highlights is an engrossing walk-through display charting the construction of the city's century-old subway system, when fearless 'sandhogs' were engaged in dangerous tunnelling. A line-up of turnstyles shows their evolution from the 1894 'ticket chopper' to the current Automatic Fare Card model. But the best part is down another level to a real platform where you can board an exceptional collection of vintage subway and El ('Elevated') cars, some complete with vintage ads.

Sights & museums

MoMA-P.S.1 Contemporary Art Center

22-25 Jackson Avenue, at 46th Avenue, Long Island City (1-718 784 2084, www .ps1.org). Subway E, M to 23rd Street-Ely Avenue; G to 21st Street-Jackson Avenue; 7 to 45th Road-Court House Square. **Open** noon-6pm Mon, Thur-Sun. **Admission** suggested donation $10; $5 reductions.

Housed in a Romanesque Revival building (a former school), P.S.1 mounts cutting-edge shows and hosts an acclaimed international studio programme. It became an affiliate of MoMA in 1999, and sometimes stages collaborative exhibitions. Reflecting the museum's global outlook, it has focused in recent years on such luminaries as Kennth Anger and Olafur Eliasson. It also hosts a popular Saturday-afternoon party, Warm Up, from July to mid September.

Museum of the Moving Image

35th Avenue, at 36th Street (1-718 784 0077, www.movingimage.us). Subway M, R to Steinway Street; N, Q to 36th Avenue. **Open** 10.30am-5pm Tue-Thur; 10.30am-8pm Fri; 10.30am-7pm Sat, Sun. **Admission** $10; free-$7.50 reductions; free admission 4-8pm Fri. No pushchairs.

After a three-year $65 million renovation, The Museum of the Moving Image reopened in January 2011. See p163 **Queens' big screen**.

Noguchi Museum

9-01 33rd Road, between Vernon Boulevard & 10th Street, Astoria (1-718 204 7088, www.noguchi.org). Subway N, Q to Broadway, then Q104 bus to 11th Street; 7 to Vernon Boulevard-Jackson Avenue, then Q103 bus to 10th Street. **Open** 10am-5pm Wed-Fri; 11am-6pm Sat, Sun. **Admission** $10; free-$5 reductions; pay what you wish 1st Fri of mth. No pushchairs. **No credit cards**.

Created by Japanese-American sculptor Isamu Noguchi (1904-88), this museum is a monument to the artist's harmonious sensibility. The building was designed, inside and out, by Noguchi as a meditative oasis carved from its gritty, industrial setting – it occupies a former photo-engraving plant that was across the street from his studio. Galleries and a garden are populated by Noguchi's sculptures, as well as painted and collaged studies, architectural models, and stage and furniture designs. A shuttle service from Manhattan ($5 each way) is available on Sundays; see website.

Queens Museum of Art

New York City Building, park entrance on 49th Avenue, at 111th Street, Flushing Meadows-Corona Park (1-718 592 9700, www.queensmuseum.org). Subway 7 to 111th Street, then walk south on 111th Street, turning left on to 49th Avenue; continue into the park and over Grand Central Parkway Bridge. **Open** Sept-June noon-6pm Wed-Sun; July, Aug 10am-6pm Mon-Thur, Sat, Sun; 10am-8pm Fri. **Admission** suggested donation $5; $2.50 reductions. **No credit cards**.

The QMA holds one of the city's most curious sights: the Panorama of the City of New York, a 9,335sq-ft scale model of all five boroughs, featuring 895,000 buildings. A modern lighting system mimics the arc of the sun as it passes over NYC. Elsewhere in the museum, contemporary and visiting exhibits have grown more bold and inventive in recent years.

Essentials

The Chatwal New York p180

Hotels

While accommodation is still more expensive in New York City than the rest of the country, it's the cheapest it's been in years. This is because hotel construction is continuing despite the economic slump, creating more rooms than there is actual demand for.

Coupled with the lowest occupancy since the 1980s, this increase has forced many existing hotels to slash rates – the average is currently under $200 a night for a double room. All the better for bargain hunting travellers.

Hotel hotspots

While Midtown contains the vast majority of New York's hotels, it is by no means your sole option. Soho and the Flatiron District are home to some of the hipper options, such as **The James New York** (see p171) and **Ace** (see p179), and the area around Ground Zero is expected to become a boom district as the World Trade Center redevelops. The Midtown hotel scene has been rejuvenated by the opening of **The Chatwal New York** (see p180) in 2010 in a glorious restored Beaux-Arts landmark augmented with a rt deco touches. It's also worth looking beyond Manhattan.

Prices & information

Although there's no doubt that visitors are currently getting more for their money, you'll probably need to plan carefully to get the best price. Rates can vary wildly according to room type and season, and those quoted here – obtained from the hotels – reflect that disparity. Unless indicated, prices are for a double room, from the cheapest in low season to the most expensive in high season.

ESSENTIALS

Of course, they're not guaranteed, but they offer a good indication of the hotel's average rack rates – what you would pay if you walked in off the street and asked for a room. Special deals are often available, especially if you book on the hotel's website. When budgeting, don't forget to factor in the hefty 14.25 per cent tax – which includes city, state and hotel-room occupancy tax – plus an extra $3.50 per night for most rooms.

Downtown

Financial District

Andaz Wall Street

75 Wall Street, at Water Street (1-212 590 1234, www.wallstreetandaz.com). Subway 2, 3, 4, 5 to Wall Street. **$$$**.
The New York outpost of this Hyatt subsidiary occupies the first 13 floors of a former Barclays Bank building. Inside, the vibe is anything but corporate: upon entering the spacious bamboo-panelled lobby-lounge, you're greeted by a free-range 'host', who acts as a combination check-in clerk and concierge. Chic, loft-style rooms are equally casual and user-friendly. The local-centric restaurant (Wall & Water), bar and spa are welcome attributes in an area with little action at weekends.

Tribeca & Soho

60 Thompson

60 Thompson Street, between Broome & Spring Streets (1-212 431 0400, 1-877 431 0400, www.60thompson.com). Subway C, E to Spring Street. **$$$$**.
An expansive, somewhat masculine second-floor lobby sets the tone for the rooms here, from the modest doubles to the spectacular duplex, the Thompson Loft. A60, the exclusive guests-only rooftop bar with magnificent city views and Moroccan-inspired decor, is equally photogenic. The modern rooms are dotted with indulgent details such as pure

SHORTLIST

Best new
- The James New York (see p171)
- The Chatwal New York (see p180)

Design statements
- Cooper Square Hotel (see p174)
- The Jane (see p177)
- Morgans (see p180)
- The Standard (see p177)

Hottest restaurants
- Ace Hotel (see p179)
- Gramercy Park Hotel (see p179)
- Greenwich Hotel (see p171)
- Hotel Elysée (see p181)

Most historical
- Algonquin Hotel (see p181)
- Hotel Chelsea (see p177)
- The Plaza (see p181)

Best budget chic
- East Village Bed & Coffee (see p174)
- Harlem Flophouse (see p182)
- New York Loft Hostel (see p175)

Best value for the location
- Abingdon Guest House (see p174)
- Cosmopolitan (see p171)
- 414 Hotel (see p180)
- SoHotel (see p173)

Most arty accommodation
- Carlton Arms Hotel (see p179)
- Gershwin Hotel (see p179)

Best pools
- Greenwich Hotel (see p171)
- Hotel Gansevoort (see p177)

Roomiest quarters
- Andaz Wall Street (see p169)

ESSENTIALS

Whatever your carbon footprint, we can reduce it

For over a decade we've been leading the way in carbon offsetting and carbon management.

In that time we've purchased carbon credits from over 200 projects spread across 6 continents. We work with over 300 major commercial clients and thousands of small and medium sized businesses, which rely upon our market-leading quality assurance programme, our experience and absolute commitment to deliver the right solution for each client.

Why not give us a call?

T: London (020) 7833 6000

www.CarbonNeutral.com

down duvets and pillows, and Kiehl's products. The hotel's acclaimed restaurant, Kittichai, serves creative Thai cuisine; in warmer months, request a table on the pavement terrace.

Cosmopolitan

95 West Broadway, at Chambers Street (1-212 566 1900, 1-888 895 9400, www.cosmohotel.com). Subway A, C, 1, 2, 3 to Chambers Street. $$.

Despite the name, you won't find the legendary pink cocktail at this well-maintained hotel in two adjacent 1850s buildings, let alone a bar in which to drink it. The Cosmopolitan is geared towards travellers with little need for extras. Open continuously since the mid 19th century, it remains a tourist favourite for its address, clean rooms and reasonable rates.

Crosby Street Hotel

79 Crosby Street, between Prince & Spring Streets (1-212 226 6400, www.crosbystreethotel.com). Subway N, R to Prince Street; 6 to Spring Street. $$$$.

In 2009, Britain's hospitality power couple, Tim and Kit Kemp, brought their super-successful Firmdale formula across the Atlantic with the warehouse-style Crosby Street Hotel. Their signature style – a fresh, contemporary take on classic English decor characterised by an oft-audacious mix of patterns, bold colours and judiciously chosen antiques – is instantly recognisable. There's a carefully selected, and predominantly British, art collection. Other Firmdale imports include a guests-only drawing room as well as a public restaurant and bar, a slick, 100-seat screening room and a verdant garden.

Duane Street Hotel

130 Duane Street, at Church Street (1-212 964 4600, www.duanestreethotel. com). Subway A, C, 1, 2, 3 to Chambers Street. $$$.

In a city with a high tolerance for hype, the Duane Street Hotel stands out by laying low and doing the simple things

well. The 45-room boutique takes its cues from its well-heeled residential neighbourhood, offering loft-inspired rooms with 11ft ceilings, oversized windows and hardwood floors. The anonymously modern decor doesn't exactly exude character, but if you appreciate cleanliness and calm (not to mention comfortable beds, free Wi-Fi and rain showerheads), you probably won't mind the lack of designer flair. Affable, unobtrusive staff round out the good value.

Greenwich Hotel

377 Greenwich Street, between Franklin & North Moore Streets (1-212 941 8900, www.thegreenwichhotel.com). Subway 1 to Franklin Street. $$$$.

'Deluxe guesthouse' might be a more fitting description of Robert De Niro's latest property, which has the vibe of a large villa located somewhere between Marrakech and Milan. Rooms are spare and comfortable, appointed with down-filled leather settees, kilims and oriental rugs, and small libraries of art books. Exquisite Moroccan tile or carrara marble envelops the bathrooms, while the main spaces feature wood-plank floors. Many rooms overlook the charming courtyard. The centrepiece of the subterranean Eastern-inspired Shibui Spa is the low-lit pool, set within the frame of a 250-year-old Kyoto farmhouse.

The James New York

NEW *27 Grand Street, at Thompson Street (1-212 526 2778, www.jameshotels.com). Subway A, C, E to Canal Street. $$$.*

Hotel art displays are usually limited to eye-catching lobby installations or forgettable in-room prints. Not so at the James, which maintains a substantial showcase of local talent. The corridor of each guest floor is dedicated to the work of an individual artist, selected by a house curator and complete with museum-style notes. Although compact, bedrooms make the most of the available space with high ceilings, wall-spanning windows and glassed off

Get the local experience

Over 50 of the world's top destinations available.

bathrooms. Natural materials warm up the clean contemporary lines, beds are piled with eco-friendly pillows, and bathroom products are courtesy of Intelligent Nutrients.. While the attractions of Soho and Tribeca beckon, the hotel also offers tempting facilities: a three-level 'urban garden' and the hot new rooftop bar Jimmy at the James.

Mercer

147 Mercer Street, at Prince Street (1-212 966 6060, 1-888 918 6060, www. mercerhotel.com). Subway N, R to Prince Street. **$$$$**.

Opened in 2001 by trendsetting hotelier André Balazs, Soho's first luxury boutique hotel still has ample attractions that appeal to a celeb-heavy clientele. The lobby, with oversized white couches and chairs, and shelves lined with colourful books, acts as a bar, library and lounge – which is exclusive to hotel guests. Loft-like rooms are large by New York standards and feature furniture by Christian Liagre. The restaurant, Mercer Kitchen, serves Jean-Georges Vongerichten's stylish version of casual American cuisine.

Chinatown, Little Italy & Nolita

SoHotel

341 Broome Street, between Bowery & Elizabeth Street (1-212 226 1482, www.thesohotel.com). Subway J, M, Z to Bowery; 6 to Spring Street. **$$**.

Thanks to new exterior coloured-light effects, this formerly modest hotel at the nexus of Chinatown, Little Italy and Nolita piques the curiosity of passers-by. A recent overhaul, including a coat of chartreuse paint, flatscreen TVs and exposed-brick walls, has given the small rooms a quirky punch. Touches such as ceiling fans, hardwood floors, skylights and vaulted ceilings place the SoHotel a rung above similarly priced establishments. SoHotel's many Regency suites ($199-$299), which can accommodate four to five guests, are the best bargain.

Lower East Side

Bowery Hotel

335 Bowery, at 3rd Street (1-212 505 9100, www.theboweryhotel.com). Subway B, D, F, M to Broadway-Lafayette Street; 6 to Bleecker Street. **$$$$**.

This fanciful boutique hotel from prominent duo Eric Goode and Sean MacPherson is the capstone in the gentrification of the Bowery. Shunning minimalism, they have created plush rooms that pair old-world touches (oriental rugs, wood-beamed ceilings, marble washstands) with modern amenities (flatscreen TVs, Wi-Fi, a DVD library).

Hotel on Rivington

107 Rivington Street, between Essex & Ludlow Streets (1-212 475 2600, www.hotelonrivington.com). Subway F to Delancey Street; J, M, Z to Delancey-Essex Streets. **$$$$**.

When the Hotel on Rivington opened in 2005, its ultra-modern glass-covered façade was a novelty on the largely low-rise Lower East Side. Now, with condos popping up on nearly every block, the building seems less out of place, but it remains one of the few luxury hotels in the neighbourhood. Rooms are super-sleek, with oh-so-hip black and white decorative touches, including velvet-covered lounge chairs, and floor-to-ceiling windows. A stylish crowd congregates in Thor; its brown leather banquettes and rock-star portraits set it apart from the traditional hotel bar.

Off Soho Suites Hotel

11 Rivington Street, between Bowery & Chrystie Street (1-212 979 9808, 1-800 633 7646, www.offsoho.com). Subway B, D to Grand Street; F to Lower East Side-Second Avenue; J, M, Z to Bowery. **$$**.

These no-frills suites have become a lot more popular since the Lower East Side emerged as a nightlife hotspot. The rates are decent value for the now-thriving location, and the spartan but spacious rooms can accommodate either two or four guests.

East Village

Cooper Square Hotel

25 Cooper Square, between 5th & 6th Streets (1-212 475 5700, www.the coopersquarehotel.com). Subway N, R to 8th Street-NYU; 6 to Astor Place. **$$$**.

Carlos Zapata's curved, 21-storey glass tower is hard to miss, but, as you approach the unmarked entrance you'll wonder what it is. A doorman ushers you into a dramatic, double-height lobby, where you should be greeted by staff (this process has been known to break down). Checking in over a glass of wine, you can admire the contemporary lodge-like library-lounge. Rooms start at a compact 250sq ft but the floor-to-ceiling windows and spare furnishings lend a sense of space. If you can stretch to it, get a high corner room for spectacular dual-aspect views.

East Village Bed & Coffee

110 Avenue C, between 7th & 8th Streets (1-212 533 4175, www.bedandcoffee. com). Subway F to Lower East Side-Second Avenue; L to First Avenue. **$**.

This East Village B&B (minus the breakfast) embodies quirky Downtown culture. Each of the guest rooms has a unique theme: for example, the 'Black and White Room' or the 'Treehouse' (with an ivory and olive colour scheme, animal-print linens and a whitewashed brick wall). Owner Anne Edris encourages guests to mingle in the communal areas, and when the weather's nice, sip your complimentary morning java in the private garden.

Hotel 17

225 E 17th Street, between Second & Third Avenues (1-212 475 2845, www. hotel17ny.com). Subway L to Third Avenue; N, Q, R, 4, 5, 6 to 14th Street-Union Square. **$-$$**.

Frayed chic is the best way to describe this hotel a few blocks from Union Square. Rooms are a study in contrast: antique dressers are paired with paisley bedspreads and vintage wallpaper.

In most cases, bathrooms are shared, but they're kept immaculately clean. Over the years, the building has been featured in numerous films – including Woody Allen's *Manhattan Murder Mystery* – and has put up Madonna and, more recently, transgender Downtown diva Amanda Lepore.

St Marks Hotel

2 St Marks Place, at Third Avenue (1-212 674 0100, www.stmarks hotel.net). Subway 6 to Astor Place. **$**.

Nestled among the tattoo parlours and cheap eateries of St Marks Place, this small hotel received a much-needed facelift in 2007; its modest rooms, which have double beds and private baths, are now bright, clean and understated and offer Wi-Fi and flatscreen TVs. Note: there is no elevator.

Greenwich Village

Washington Square Hotel

103 Waverly Place, between MacDougal Street & Sixth Avenue (1-212 777 9515, 1-800 222 0418, www.washington squarehotel.com). Subway A, B, C, D, E, F, M to W 4th Street. **$$**.

A haven for writers and artists for decades, this hotel is suited to those seeking a quiet bolt-hole. A lengthy renovation, nearly doubled the lobby size and refurbished the interiors: rooms are done up with spare art deco furnishings and an odd but pleasant colour scheme of mauve and olive; its ultra-narrow hallways are a quirky reminder of its pre-war beginnings. Rates include continental breakfast – or you can splurge on the Sunday jazz brunch at North Square, the hotel's restaurant.

West Village & Meatpacking District

Abingdon Guest House

21 Eighth Avenue, between Jane & W 12th Streets (1-212 243 5384, www. abingdonguesthouse.com). Subway A, C, E to 14th Street; L to Eighth Avenue. **$$**.

Borough boltholes

Hip scenes and low rates are luring guests across the river.

Nu Hotel

Although the growing attractions of the outer boroughs, most notably Brooklyn and Queens, have been luring visitors for several years, they haven't been seen as a base for tourists. But now that apartments in Brooklyn's prime neighbourhoods fetch millions of dollars, it was inevitable that boutique hotels would follow. The first two opened in late 2007: **Hotel Le Bleu** (370 Fourth Avenue, at 5th Street, 1-718 625 1500, www.hotellebleu.com) has easy access to the cultural and commercial riches of Park Slope, while Williamsburg's **Hotel Le Jolie** (235 Meeker Avenue, at Jackson Street, 1-718 625 2100, www.hotellejolie.com), despite its less than picturesque location on top of the Brooklyn-Queens Expressway, allows indie music fans the chance to spend the night in the hotspot after a gig. Summer 2008 saw the arrival of the chic, eco-friendly **Nu Hotel** (85 Smith Street, between Atlantic Avenue & State Street, 1-718 852 8585, www.nuhotelbrooklyn.com) on the edge of Brooklyn Heights. Those

who want to experience loft living in Bushwick's cutting-edge art enclave should check into the **New York Loft Hostel** (249 Varet Street, at Bogart Street, 1-718 366 1351, www.nylofthostel.com), which fuses the traditional dorm-style setup with a fashionable aesthetic.

Long Island City has acquired its first independent boutique hotel. Although its industrial surroundings are a bit desolate, **Ravel** (8-08 Queens Plaza South, at Vernon Boulevard, 1-718 289 6101, www.ravelhotel.com), a total rebuild of a motel, occupies a prime waterfront spot beside the Queensboro Bridge; an 8,000sq ft rooftop restaurant-bar has dazzling views of Midtown. While the room decor isn't anything special (touches such as orange faux-ostrich headboards and spacious limestone-and-granite bathrooms announce it as boutique), like any rental in New York, you get more bang for your buck in the outer boroughs – the open-plan superior rooms are a whopping 550sq ft (51 sq m).

A charming option in a charming neighbourhood: rooms in the Abingdon's two converted townhouses are done up in plush fabrics and antique furnishings, and sport homespun details such as original 1950s pine floors, hooked rugs, and four-poster or sleigh beds. All rooms have private baths, though they may not be inside the room. The small back courtyard is lovely in summer.

Hotel Gansevoort

18 Ninth Avenue, at 13th Street (1-212 206 6700, 1-877 426 7386, www.hotel gansevoort.com). Subway A, C, E to 14th Street; L to Eighth Avenue. **$$$$**.
The Gansevoort has made a name for itself as a coolhunters' hub. The lobby features four 18ft light boxes that change colour throughout the evening, while simple but elegant rooms offer a more muted colour scheme. Their real draw is floor-to-ceiling windows with incredible views, although, unfortunately, the glass is not quite thick enough to keep out noise from the street. But the mini-balconies, plush feather beds and Cutler toiletries counterbalance this minor gripe. A visit to the roof is a must: the garden has a heated pool (with underwater music) that is enclosed in winter, a bar (Plunge) and, of course, a 360-degree panorama. Jeffrey Chodorow's Tanuki Tavern serves inventive Japanese small plates.

The Jane

113 Jane Street, at West Street (1-212 924 6700, www.thejanenyc.com). Subway A, C, E to 14th Street; L to Eighth Avenue. **$-$$**.
Opened in 1907 as the American Seaman's Friend Society Sailors Home, the 14-storey landmark was a residential hotel when hoteliers Eric Goode and Sean MacPherson took it over. The wood-panelled, 50sq ft rooms were inspired by vintage train sleeper compartments – there's a single bed with built-in storage and brass hooks for hanging up your clothes, but also iPod docks and wall-mounted flatscreen TVs.

The Standard

848 Washington Street, at 13th Street (1-212 645 4646, www.standard hotels.com). Subway A, C, E to 14th Street; L to Eighth Avenue. **$$$**.
André Balazs's lauded West Coast mini-chain arrived in New York in early 2009. Straddling the High Line, the retro 18-storey structure has been configured to give each room an exhilarating view, either of the river or a Midtown cityscape. Quarters are compact (from 230sq ft) but the combination of floor-to-ceiling windows, curving tambour wood panelling and 'peekaboo' bathrooms (with Japanese-style tubs or huge showerheads) give a sense of space. Eating and drinking options include a chop house, beer garden and a top-floor bar with a massive jacuzzi.

Midtown

Chelsea

Hotel Chelsea (aka Chelsea Hotel)

222 W 23rd Street, between Seventh & Eighth Avenues (1-212 243 3700, www. hotelchelsea.com). Subway C, E, 1 to 23rd Street. **$$**.
The Chelsea has a long and infamous past – not surprising considering it's been home to artists and writers of every stripe since it opened in 1885. From *Lost Weekend* author Charles R Jackson's suicide to Nancy Spungen's fatal stabbing, it has been the site of several sordid events. The lobby's walls exude history – many of the paintings haven't moved since their installation. Room configurations are diverse, but all are generally large with high ceilings. Amenities – such as flatscreen TVs, washer-dryers and marble fireplaces – vary. In some cases, the bathrooms are shared.

Inn on 23rd

131 W 23rd Street, between Sixth & Seventh Avenues (1-212 463 0330, www.innon23rd.com). Subway F, 1 to 23rd Street. **$$**.

Home comforts

New York hotels are chucking out the check-in desk.

Cooper Square Hotel p174

When the Seattle-based owners of the **Ace Hotel** (see p179) opened an NYC outpost, they wanted to recreate the experience of staying with hip friends, so you'll find personal touches like old-school turntables in some rooms and the 'anti-design' lobby mixes vintage furniture and salvage – a panelled library from a Madison Avenue apartment defines the bar. The result is a 'lived-in' space that's inviting to both laptoppers and socialisers.

This 'home from home' approach seems to be catching on. Although Carlos Zapata's curved glass tower is a striking addition to the East Village, you could walk right past the unmarked entrance of **Cooper Square Hotel** (see p174); the doorman stationed outside suggests an upscale condo development. Inside, you won't find a check-in desk, but should be greeted by staff. Instead of standing at an airport-like counter, you'll be offered a tipple in the comfortable library-lounge, furnished by Italian design house B&B Italia, warmed by a wood-burning fire and lined with well-thumbed tomes from local charity shop Housing Works. The overall effect is of an architect's home featured in *Elle Decoration*.

Although it's a spinoff of Hyatt, **Andaz** (see p169) takes a minimal branding approach. In fact, its Wall Street property shares the building with private apartments. Upon entering, a 'host' – a combination doorman, check-in clerk, concierge and bellhop, dressed casually in New York label Theory – welcomes you. Seated in the lobby-café, they check you in using a portable 'tablet' while you sip a glass of wine or a cappuccino brewed by the on-site barista. The rooms, which look like pared-down loft apartments, are furnished with functional pieces that could have been dreamed up by a space-starved studio dweller (in some, a wardrobe 'cube' rotates to reveal a mirror or storage). And you can make unlimited gratis local calls from the cordless phone – how many friends would let you do that?

This renovated 19th-century townhouse offers the charm of a traditional bed and breakfast with enhanced amenities (a lift, pillow-top mattresses, private bathrooms, white-noise machines). Owners and Annette and Barry Fisherman have styled each bedroom with a unique theme, such as Maritime, Bamboo and 1940s. One of its best attributes is the 'library', a cosy jumble of tables and chairs where breakfast is served: it's open 24/7 to guests, should you want to relax with a cup of tea or glass of wine.

Maritime Hotel

363 W 16th Street, between Eighth & Ninth Avenues (1-212 242 4300, www.themaritimehotel.com). Subway A, C, E to 14th Street; L to Eighth Avenue. **$$$**.
Once the headquarters of the New York Maritime Union, this nautically themed hotel is outfitted with self-consciously hip details befitting a Wes Anderson film. Standard rooms are modelled on cruise cabins; lined with teak panelling and sporting a single porthole window. The hotel's busy Italian restaurant, La Bottega, also supplies room service, and the adjoining bar hosts a crowd of models and mortals, who throng the umbrella-lined patio in warmer weather. In the basement, Matsuri offers sushi, Japanese tapas and the city's only saké sommelier.

Flatiron District & Union Square

Ace Hotel

20 W 29th Street, between Fifth & Sixth Avenues (1-646 214 5742, www.acehotel.com). Subway N, R to 28th Street. **$$-$$$$**.
Bourgeois hipsters tired of crashing on couches will appreciate the New York outpost of the cool chainlet founded in Seattle by a pair of DJs. The music influence is clear: many rooms in the 1904 building have playful amenities such as functioning turntables, stacks of vinyl and gleaming Gibson guitars. And while you'll pay for the sprawling loft

spaces, there are options for those on a lower budget. The respectable 'medium rooms are outfitted with vintage furniture and original art; even cheaper are the snug bunk-bed set-ups. Chef April Bloomfield's John Dory Oyster Bar (see p114) and her Breslin Bar & Dining Room (see p112) are massively popular.

Gershwin Hotel

7 E 27th Street, between Fifth & Madison Avenues (1-212 545 8000, www.gershwinhotel.com). Subway N, R, 6 to 28th Street. **$**.
Works by Lichtenstein line the hallways, and an original Warhol soup can painting hangs in the lobby of this Pop Art-themed budget hotel. Rooms are less than pristine – especially the hostel-style dorms – but the rates are extremely reasonable for its location.

Gramercy Park & Murray Hill

Carlton Arms Hotel

160 E 25th Street, at Third Avenue (1-212 679 0680, www.carltonarms.com). Subway 6 to 23rd Street. **$**.
The Carlton Arms Art Project started in the late 1970s, when a small group of creative types brought fresh paint and new ideas to a run-down shelter. Today, the site is a bohemian backpackers' paradise and a live-in gallery – every room, bathroom and hallway is festooned with outré artwork. Themed quarters include the Money Room and a tribute to a traditional English cottage. Discounts are offered for students, overseas guests and week-long stays. Most guests share bathrooms; the pricier rooms have a private toilet. Reserve well in advance.

Gramercy Park Hotel

2 Lexington Avenue, at 21st Street (1-212 475 4320, www.gramercypark hotel.com). Subway 6 to 23rd Street. **$$$$**.
New Yorkers held their collective breath when hotelier Ian Schrager announced he was revamping the Gramercy Park

Hotel, a 1924 gem. They needn't have worried: the redesigned lobby, unveiled in 2006, retains the boho spirit with stuccoed walls, red banquettes, an enormous Venetian chandelier and artwork from Cy Twombly and Andy Warhol, among others. The eclectic elegance continues in the spacious rooms, which include tapestry-covered chairs and a Pre-Raphaelite colour palette of deep reds and blues. Guests can lounge on the private roof deck or sip cocktails at the Schnabel-designed Rose and Jade bars. Danny Meyer's new trattoria, Maialino, adds to the attractions.

Marcel at Gramercy

201 E 24th Street, at Third Avenue (1-212 696 3800, www.themarcelatgramercy.com). Subway 6 to 23rd Street. **$$$**.
Revamped in early 2008, this hotel's hip aesthetic extends from the lobby, with its marble concierge desk, sprawling leather banquette and in-house library, to the medium-sized rooms, which offer a sleek black and pewter palette, rainhead showers and Frette linens. 'inoteca – run by chefs Eric Kleinman and Steve Connaughton – serves inventive takes on classic Italian fare, while master mixologist Tony Abou-Ganim oversees the adjacent bar. Sexy subterranean lounge Polar opened in early 2010.

Morgans

237 Madison Avenue, between 37th & 38th Streets (1-212 686 0300, 1-800 334 3408, www.morganshotelgroup.com). Subway 4, 5, ,6 and 7 to 42nd Street-Grand Central. **$$$**.
New York's original boutique hotel, Morgans opened in 1984. Some 25 years later, the hotel's original designer, Andrée Putnam, returned to officiate over a revamp that has softened the stark monochrome appearance. The boxy 1930s-inspired lobby now features a hypnotic coloured-light ceiling installation and unfussy bedrooms are cast in a calming palette of silver, grey, cream and white, and hung with original Robert Mapplethorpe prints.

Theater District & Hell's Kitchen

414 Hotel

414 W 46th Street, between Ninth & Tenth Avenues (1-212 399 0006, www.414hotel.com). Subway A, C, E to 42nd Street-Port Authority. **$$**.
This is one hotel that truly deserves to be described as 'boutique'. Nearly everything about it is exquisite yet unshowy, from its power-blasted brick exterior to the modern colour scheme in the rooms that pairs grey and brown furnishings with pale walls and white bedding. Bathrooms are immaculate. 414 is twice as big as it looks, as it consists of two townhouses separated by a leafy courtyard, which in warmer months is a lovely place to sip a glass of wine or eat your complimentary breakfast.

Big Apple Hostel

119 W 45th Street, between Sixth & Seventh Avenues (1-212 302 2603, www.bigapplehostel.com). Subway B, D, F, M to 42nd Street-Bryant Park; N, Q, R, S, 1, 2, 3, 7 to 42nd Street-Times Square. **$**.
This bare-bones hostel is spotless and cheap for the location just steps from the Theater District and Times Square. If you want to get away from the crowds, you can take refuge in the breezy back patio, equipped with a grill for summer barbecues. Linens are provided, but remember to pack a towel.

The Chatwal New York

NEW *130W 44th Street, between Sixth Avenue & Broadway (1-212 764 6200, www.chatwalny.com). Subway N, R, S, 2, 3 to 42nd Street-Time Square.* **$$$**.
In a city awash with faux deco and incongruous nods to art deco style, The Chatwal New York opened in August 2010 in a Stanford White building whose interior art deco restoration is pitch perfect. Boutique hotelier Sant Chatwal entrusted the design of this 1905 beaux arts building to Thierry Despont, who worked on the centennial restoration of

the Statue of Liberty. The result is one of the most glamorous hotels in the Theater District, if not the city. The lobby is adorned with murals recalling the hotel's New York roots and theatrical pedigree – past members of the Lamb's Club have included Lionel and John Barrymore, Charlie Chaplin, Douglas Fairbanks and Fred Astaire. The elegant rooms feature vintage Broadway posters as well as hand-tufted Shifman mattresses, 400-thread count Frette linens and custom Asprey toiletries; select rooms have spacious terraces.

Fifth Avenue & around

Algonquin Hotel

59 W 44th Street, between Fifth & Sixth Avenues (1-212 840 6800, www. algonquinhotel.com). Subway B, D, F, M to 42nd Street-Bryant Park; 7 to Fifth Avenue. **$$$**.
Alexander Woollcott and Dorothy Parker swapped bon mots in the famous Round Table Room of this 1902 landmark – and you'll still find writer types holding court on the mismatched armchairs of the sprawling, old-school lobby. The Algonquin certainly trades on its literary past (cartoons from the *New Yorker* cover the hallways, commemorating Harold Ross, who secured funding for the magazine over long meetings at the Round Table), but does it work as a hotel? Yes: the modernised rooms are pleasant and comfortable, if bordering on stark; and amenities such as flatscreen TVs and free Wi-Fi are standard. Skip the impersonal Blue Bar in favour of the Oak Room, one of NYC's premier cabaret destinations.

The Plaza

768 Fifth Avenue, at Central Park South (1-212 759 3000, 1-800 759 3000, www.fairmont.com/theplaza). Subway N, R to Fifth Avenue-59th Street. **$$$$**.
This 1907 French Renaissance-style landmark building reopened in spring 2008 following a $400 million renovation. Although 152 rooms have been converted into private condo units, guests can still check into one of 282 quarters complete with Louis XV-inspired furnishings and white-glove butler service. The opulent vibe extends to the bathrooms, which feature 24-carat gold-plated sinks.

Midtown East

Four Seasons

57 E 57th Street, between Madison & Park Avenues (1-212 758 5700, 1-800 332 3442, www.fourseasons.com). Subway N, R to Lexington Avenue-59th Street; 4, 5, 6 to 59th Street. **$$$$**.
The New York arm of the luxury chain, housed in IM Pei's 52-floor tower, is synonymous with dependable luxury. Expect modern interiors and sumptuous, user-friendly design: there's room for a seat in the walk-in closet, a TV in the toilet, and the bathtub fills in 60 seconds. If you pay for a park view, you'll be treated to an unsurpassed urban vista. The hotel also houses the culinary jewel L'Atelier de Joël Robuchon.

Hotel Elysée

60 E 54th Street, between Madison & Park Avenues (1-212 753 1066, www. elyseehotel.com). Subway E, M to Lexington Avenue-53rd Street; 6 to 51st Street. **$$$**.
Since 1926, this discreet but opulent hotel has attracted luminaries. You may bump into one on the way from your antique-appointed room to the complimentary wine and cheese served every evening in the second-floor lounge, or in the exclusive Monkey Bar, *Vanity Fair* editor Graydon Carter's restaurant that shares the building. Reserve a table and your chances of eating among the power set rise from zilch to good – a few tables are set aside for guests every night.

Library Hotel

299 Madison Avenue, at 41st Street (1-212 983 4500, www.libraryhotel.com). Subway S, 4, 5, 6, 7 to 42nd Street-Grand Central; 7 to Fifth Avenue. **$$$**.

This bookish boutique hotel is as tall, thin and glossy as a coffee-table tome, with rooms carefully sorted into literary themes. Book nerds flock to the popular Fairy Tales and Paranormal rooms, where motifs are expressed through book selections and wall art; it's more clever than kitsch. In the roof garden, creative libations are inspired by Ernest Hemingway and Harper Lee, and a DVD library caters to the word-weary.

Pod Hotel

230 E 51st Street, at Third Avenue (1-212 355 0300, www.thepodhotel.com). Subway E, M to Lexington Avenue-53rd Street; 6 to 51st Street. **$$**.

As its name suggests, the rooms in this minimalist bolthole, opened in 2007 by the Mercer's owners, are small-scale. IKEA-style rooms equipped with mod cons. A third of them have shared bathrooms. The outdoor Pod Café serves treats from Balthazar Bakery.

Uptown

Upper East Side

Surrey

20 E 76th Street, between Fifth & Madison Avenues (1-212 288 3700, 1-800 978 7739, www.thesurreyhotel. com). Subway 6 to 77th Street. **$$$$**.

A stylish addition to an area thin on unstuffy accommodation, the Surrey, in a solid pre-war Beaux Arts building given a $60 million overhaul, pitches at both traditionalists and the trend-driven. Rooms are dressed in a refined palette of cream, grey and beige, with luxurious white marble bathrooms featuring products by Laura Tonatto. But the centrepiece is undoubtedly the incredibly comfortable DUX by Duxiana bed, swathed in luxurious Sferra linens. The hotel is flanked by top chef Daniel Boulud's Café Boulud and his chic cocktail destination, Bar Pleiades. The coolly elegant limestone and marble lobby showcases contemporary art.

Upper West Side

Jazz on the Park Hostel

36 W 106th Street, between Central Park West & Manhattan Avenue (1-212 932 1600, www.jazzhostels.com). Subway B, C to 103rd Street. **$**.

Jazz on the Park is one of the city's trendiest hostels, with a lounge kitted out like a space-age techno club, with a piano and pool table. The hostel also has a staffed reception 24 hours a day and no curfew. In summer, the back patio hosts a weekly barbecue for guests. Linens, towels and continental breakfast are complimentary. Visit the website for the hostel's other locations.

On the Ave Hotel

222 W 77th Street, between Broadway & Amsterdam Avenue (1-212 362 1100, 1-800 497 6028, www.ontheavenyc.com). Subway 1 to 79th Street. **$$$**.

Given the affluent area, it's hardly surprising that On the Ave's rooms are stylish (industrial-style bathroom sinks, ergonomic Herman Miller chairs). Penthouse suites have fantastic views of Central Park, and all guests have access to the verdant Adirondack balcony on the 16th floor. The hotel has two eateries: Fatty Crab and West Branch, from celebrity chef Tom Valenti.

Harlem

Harlem Flophouse

242 W 123rd Street, between Adam Clayton Powell Jr Boulevard (Seventh Avenue) & Frederick Douglass Boulevard (Eighth Avenue) (1-212 662 0678, www.harlemflophouse.com). Subway A, B, C, D to 125th Street. **$**.

The dark-wood interior, moody lighting and lilting jazz make Rene Calvo's Harlem inn feel more like a 1930s speakeasy than a 21st-century B&B. The airy suites, named for Harlem Renaissance figures such as Chester Himes and Cozy Cole, have restored tin ceilings, chandeliers and working sinks in antique cabinets.

Getting Around

Arriving and leaving

By air

John F Kennedy International Airport

1-718 244 4444, www.panynj.gov/ airports/jfk.html.

The subway ($2.25) is the cheapest option. The AirTrain ($5) links to the A train at Howard Beach or the E, J and Z trains at Sutphin Boulevard-Archer Avenue (www. panynj.gov/airports/jfk-airtrain).

New York Airport Service (1-212 875 8200, www.nyairport service.com) buses run frequently to Manhattan ($15, round trip $27), with stops near Grand Central Terminal (Park Avenue, between 41st & 42nd Streets), near Penn Station (33rd Street, at Seventh Avenue), inside the Port Authority Bus Terminal (*see p184*) and outside a number of Midtown hotels (for an extra charge). Buses also run to La Guardia ($13).

A **yellow cab** to Manhattan will charge a flat $45.50 fare, plus toll (usually $5) and tip (if service is fine, give at least $7). The fare to JFK from Manhattan is not a set rate, but is usually a little more. Check www.nyc.gov/taxi for rates.

La Guardia Airport

1-718 533 3400, www.panynj.gov/ airports/laguardia.

Seasoned New Yorkers take the **M60 bus** ($2.25), which runs to 106th Street at Broadway. The ride takes 40-60mins and runs from 4.30am to 1.30am daily. The route crosses Manhattan at 125th Street in Harlem. Get off at Lexington Avenue for the 4, 5 and 6 trains; at Malcolm X Boulevard (Lenox

Avenue) for the 2 and 3; or at St Nicholas Avenue for the A, B, C and D trains. You can also disembark on Broadway at 116th or 110th Street for the 1 train.

Less time-consuming options include **New York Airport Service** private buses (*see left*), which run frequently between Manhattan and La Guardia (one way $12, round trip $21). **Taxis** and **car services** charge about $30, plus toll and tip.

Newark Liberty International Airport

1-973 961 6000, www.panynj/airports/ newark-liberty.

The best bet is the 40min, $15 trip by **New Jersey Transit** to or from Penn Station. The airport's monorail, **AirTrain Newark** (www.airtrainnewark.com), is linked to the NJ Transit and Amtrak train systems.

Bus services operated by **Coach USA** (1-877 894 9155, www. coachusa.com) run to Manhattan, stopping outside Grand Central Station (41st Street, between Park & Lexington Avenues), and inside the Port Authority Bus Terminal ($15, round trip $25); buses leave every 15-30mins. A **car** or **taxi** will run at about $60, plus toll and tip.

By bus

Most out-of-town buses come and go from the Port Authority Bus Terminal (*see p184*). **Greyhound** (1-800 231 2222, www.greyhound. com) offers long-distance travel to destinations across North America. Its **BoltBus** (1-877 265 8287, www. boltbus.com), serves several East Coast cities. **New Jersey Transit** (1-973 275 5555, www.njtransit.com)

runs a service to nearly everywhere in the Garden State and parts of New York State. Finally, **Peter Pan** (1-800 343 9999, www.peterpanbus. com) runs extensive services to cities across the North-east; its tickets are also valid on Greyhound buses.

Port Authority Bus Terminal

625 Eighth Avenue, between 40th & 42nd Streets, Garment District (1-212 564 8484, www.panynj.gov/ bus-terminals/port-authority-bus-terminal). Subway A, C, E to 42nd Street-Port Authority.
This terminus is the hub for many commuter and long-distance services. Though it's perfectly safe, watch out for the occasional pickpocket, especially at night, and note that the food concessions don't open until around 7am.

By rail

Grand Central Terminal

42nd to 44th Streets, between Vanderbilt & Lexington Avenues, Midtown East. Subway S, 4, 5, 6, 7 to 42nd Street-Grand Central.
Grand Central is home to Metro-North, which runs trains to more than 100 stations in New York State and Connecticut.

Penn Station

31st to 33rd Streets, between Seventh & Eighth Avenues, Garment District. Subway A, C, E, 1, 2, 3 to 34th Street-Penn Station.
The national rail service, Amtrak (www.amtrak.com) departs from here as well as Long Island Rail Road and New Jersey Transit trains.

Public transport

Metropolitan Transportation Authority (MTA)

1-718 330 1234 travel information, 1-718 243 7777 updates, www.mta.info.

The MTA runs the subway and bus lines, as well as services to points outside Manhattan. News of service interruptions and MTA maps are on its website. Be warned: backpacks, handbags and large containers may be subject to random searches.

Fares & tickets

Although you can pay in cash or coins on the buses, you'll need to buy a MetroCard to enter the subway system. The standard fare across the subway and bus network on a MetroCard is $2.25. You can buy them from booths or vending machines in the stations; from the Official NYC Information Center; from the New York Transit Museum in Brooklyn or Grand Central Terminal; and from many hotels. Free transfers between the subway and buses, or between buses, are available only with a MetroCard. Up to four people can use a pay-per-use MetroCard; if you put $8 or more on the card, you'll receive a 15 per cent bonus.

However, if you're planning to use the subway or buses often, an unlimited-ride MetroCard is great value. These cards are offered in two denominations, available at station vending machines but not at booths: a seven-day pass ($29) and a 30-day pass ($104). Note that you can't share a card with travel companions.

Subway

Far cleaner and safer than it was 20 years ago, the subway system is one of the world's largest and cheapest, with a flat fare of $2.25. Trains run around the clock. If you are travelling late at night, board the train from the designated off-peak waiting area, usually near the middle of the platform; this is more secure than the ends of the platform, which are often less populated in the wee hours.

Stations are most often named after the street on which they're located. Entrances are marked with a green and white globe (open 24 hours) or a red and white globe (limited hours). Many stations have separate entrances for the uptown and downtown platforms – look before you pay. Trains are identified by letters or numbers, colour-coded according to the line on which they run. Local trains stop at every station on the line; express trains stop at major stations only.

The most current subway map is reprinted at the back of this guide; you can also ask MTA workers in service booths for a free copy, or refer to enlarged subway maps displayed in each subway station.

City buses

White and blue MTA buses are the best way to travel crosstown and a pleasant way to travel up- or downtown, as long as you're not in a hurry. They have a digital destination sign on the front, along with a route number preceded by a letter (M for Manhattan). Maps are posted on most buses and at all subway stations; they're also available from the Official NYC Information Center (*see p189*). The Manhattan bus map is printed in the back of this guide. All local buses are equipped with wheelchair lifts. The fare is payable with a MetroCard (*see p184*) or exact change ($2.25 in coins only; no pennies). MetroCards allow for an automatic transfer from bus to bus, and between bus and subway. If you pay cash, and you're travelling uptown or downtown and want to go crosstown (or vice versa), ask the driver for a transfer when you

get on – you'll be given a ticket for use on the second leg of your journey, valid for two hours. MTA's express buses usually head to the outer boroughs for a $5.50 fare.

Rail services

The following commuter trains serve NY's hinterland.

Long Island Rail Road 1-718 217 5477, www.mta.info/lirr. Rail services from Penn Station, Brooklyn and Queens to towns throughout Long Island.

Metro-North Railroad 1-212 532 4900, www.mta.info/mnr. Commuter trains serve towns north of Manhattan and leave from Grand Central Terminal.

New Jersey Transit 1-973 275 5555, www.njtransit.com. Services from Penn Station reach most of New Jersey, some points in NY State and Philadelphia.

PATH Trains 1-800 234 7284, www.panynj.gov/path. PATH (Port Authority Trans-Hudson) trains run from six stations in Manhattan to various places across the Hudson in New Jersey, including Hoboken, Jersey City and Newark. The 24-hour service costs $1.75.

Taxis

Yellow cabs are rarely in short supply, except at rush hour and during unpleasant weather. If the centre light atop the taxi is lit, the cab is available and should stop if you flag it down. Jump in and then tell the driver where you're going. (New Yorkers generally give cross-streets rather than addresses.) By law, taxis cannot refuse to take you anywhere inside the five boroughs or to New York airports. Use only yellow medallion (licensed) cabs; avoid unregulated 'gypsy cabs'.

Taxis will carry up to four passengers for the same price: $2.50 plus 40¢ per fifth of a mile or per minute idling, with an extra 50¢ charge (a new state tax), another 50¢ from 8pm to 6am and a $1 surcharge during rush hour (4-8pm Mon-Fri). The average fare for a three-mile ride is $9-$11, depending on the time and traffic. Cabbies rarely allow more than four passengers in a cab (it's illegal, unless the fifth person is a child under seven).

Not all drivers know their way around the city, so it helps if you know where you're going. If you have a problem, take down the medallion and driver's numbers, posted on the partition. Always ask for a receipt – there's a meter number on it. To complain or to trace lost property, call the **Taxi & Limousine Commission** (1-212 227 0700, 8am-4pm Mon-Fri) or visit www.nyc.gov/taxi. Tip 15-20 per cent, as in a restaurant. Most taxis now accept major credit cards.

Car services are regulated by the Taxi & Limousine Commission (see above). Unlike cabs, drivers can make only pre-arranged pickups. Don't try to hail one, and be wary of those that offer you a ride. The following companies will pick you up anywhere in the city, at any time, for a set fare.
Carmel *1-212 666 6666.*
Dial 7 *1-212 777 7777.*
Limores *1-212 777 7171.*

Driving

Car hire

You will need a credit card to rent a car, and you usually have to be at least 25 years old. All the companies listed below will add sales tax (8.875 per cent). Car hire is cheaper in the city's outskirts, and in New Jersey and Connecticut, than in Manhattan.
Aamcar *1-800 722 6923, 1-212 222 8500, www.aamcar.com;* **Alamo** *US: 1-800 462 5266, www.alamo.com. UK: 0870 400 4562, www.alamo.co.uk;* **Avis** *US: 1-800 230 4898, www.avis.com. UK: 0844 544 6666, www.avis.co.uk;* **Budget** *US: 1-800*

527 0700, www.budget.com. UK: 0844 544 3439, www.budget.co.uk;* **Dollar** *US: 1-800 800 3665, www.dollar.com. UK: 0800 252 897, www.dollar.co.uk;* **Enterprise** *US: 1-800 261 7331, www.enterprise.com. UK: 0870 350 3000, www.enterprise.co.uk;* **Hertz** *US: 1-800 654 3131, www.hertz.com. UK: 0870 844 8844, www.hertz.co.uk;* **National** *US: 1-800 227 7368, www.nationalcar.com. UK: 0116 217 3884, www.nationalcar.co.uk;* **Thrifty** *US: 1-800 847 4389, www.thrifty.com. UK: 01494 751500, www.thrifty.co.uk.*

Parking

Make sure you read parking signs and never park within 15 feet of a fire hydrant (to avoid a $115 ticket and/or having your car towed). Parking is off-limits on most streets for at least a few hours daily. The Department of Transportation provides information on daily changes to regulations (dial 311). If precautions fail, call 1-212 971 0771 or 1-212 971 0772 for Manhattan towing and impoundment information; go to www.nyc.gov for phone numbers in other boroughs.

Cycling

Aside from pleasurable cycling in Central Park, and along the wide bike paths around the perimeter of Manhattan (now virtually encircled by paths), biking in the city streets is only recommended for experienced urban riders. But zipping through bumper-to-bumper traffic holds allure for those with the requisite skills and gear.

Walking

One of the best ways to take in NYC is on foot. Most of the streets are laid out in a grid pattern and are relatively easy to navigate.

Guided Tours. See box p75.

Resources A-Z

Accident & emergency

In an emergency situation, dial 911 for an ambulance, police or the fire department, or call the operator (dial 0).

The following hospitals have emergency rooms:

Mount Sinai Hospital *Madison Avenue, at 100th Street, Upper East Side (1-212 241 6500). Subway 6 to 103rd Street.*

New York – Presbyterian Hospital/Weill Cornell Medical Center *525 E 68th Street, at York Avenue, Upper East Side (1-212 746 5454). Subway 6 to 68th Street.*

St Luke's – Roosevelt Hospital *1000 Tenth Avenue, at 59th Street, Upper West Side (1-212 523 4000). Subway A, B, C, D, 1 to 59th Street-Columbus Circle.*

Customs

US Customs allows foreigners to bring in $100 worth of gifts (the limit is $800 for returning Americans) without paying duty. One carton of 200 cigarettes (or 50 cigars) and one litre of liquor (spirits) are allowed. Plants, meat and fresh produce of any kind cannot be brought into the country. You will have to fill out a form if you carry more than $10,000 in currency. You will be handed a white form on your inbound flight to fill in, confirming that you haven't exceeded any of these allowances.

If you need to bring prescription drugs with you into the US, make sure the container is clearly marked, and bring your doctor's statement or a prescription.

Marijuana, cocaine and most opiate derivatives, along with a number of other drugs and chemicals, are not permitted: the possession of them is punishable by a stiff fine and/ or imprisonment. Check in with the US Customs Service (www. customs.gov) before you arrive if you're unsure.

UK Customs allows returning visitors to bring only £145 worth of 'gifts, souvenirs and other goods' into the country duty-free, along with the usual duty-free goods.

Disabled

Under New York City law, all facilities constructed after 1987 must provide complete access for the disabled – restrooms, entrances and exits included. In 1990, the Americans with Disabilities Act made the same requirement federal law. In the wake of this legislation, many older buildings have added disabled-access features. There has been widespread (though imperfect) compliance with the law, but call ahead to check facilities. *Access for All*, a guide to NYC's cultural institutions published by **Hospital Audiences Inc** (1-212 575 7676, www.hospaud.org) is a useful online resource. All Broadway theatres are equipped with devices for the hearing-impaired; call **Sound Associates** (1-888 772 7686, www.soundassociates.com) for details.

Electricity

The US uses 110-120V, 60-cycle alternating current rather than the 220-240V, 50-cycle AC used in Europe. The transformers that power or recharge newer electronic

ESSENTIALS

devices such as laptops are designed to handle either current and may need nothing more than an adaptor for the wall outlet. Other appliances may also require a power converter. Adaptors and converters can be purchased at airport shops, pharmacies, department stores and at branches of electronics chain Radio Shack (www.radioshack.com).

Embassies & Consulates

Australia *1-212 351 6500.*
Canada *1-212 596 1628.*
Great Britain *1-212 745 0200.*
Ireland *1-212 319 2555.*
New Zealand *1-212 832 4038.*

Internet

NYCWireless (1-212 592 7000, www.nycwireless.net) has established dozens of hotspots in the for free wireless access. (For example, most parks below 59th Street are covered.)
Branches of the **NYPL** (www.nypl.org.) are great places to get online for free, offering both Wi-Fi and computers for public use. (Ask for an out-of-state card, for which you need proof of residence, or a guest pass.) One of the three libraries with the most computers available for public internet access are the **Science, Industry & Business Library**, 188 Madison Avenue, at 34th Street (with about 50 computers). All libraries have a computer limit of 45 minutes per day.
Cyber Café 250 W 49th St, between Broadway & Eighth Avenue, Theater District (1-212 333 4109). Subway C, E, 1 to 50th Street; N, R, Q to 49th Street. **Open** 8am-11pm Mon-Fri; 8.30am-11pm Sat, Sun.
Starbucks (www.starbucks.com) Many branches offer up to two hours of free wireless access per day through AT&T, with activation of a Starbucks card (which you purchase in-store).

Opening hours

These are general guidelines.
Banks 9am-6pm Mon-Fri; generally also Sat mornings.
Businesses 9am or 10am to 5pm or 6pm Mon-Fri.
Pubs & Bars 4pm-2am Sun-Thur, noon-4am Fri, Sat (hours vary widely).
Shops 9am, 10am or 11am to 7pm or 8pm Mon-Sat (some open at noon and/or close at 9pm). Many are also open on Sun, usually 11am or noon to 6pm.

Police

The NYPD stations below are in central, tourist-heavy areas of Manhattan. For the location of your nearest police precinct or information about police services, call 1-646 610 5000.
Midtown North Precinct *306 W 54th Street, between Eighth & Ninth Avenues, Hell's Kitchen (1-212 760 8300).*
17th Precinct *167 E 51st Street, between Third & Lexington Avenues, Midtown East (1-212 826 3211).*
Midtown South Precinct *357 W 35th Street, between Eighth & Ninth Avenues, Garment District (1-212 239 9811).*
Central Park Precinct *86th Street & Transverse Road, Central Park (1-212 570 4820).*

Post

Post offices are usually open 9am-5pm Monday-Friday (a few open as early as 7.30am and close as late as 8.30pm); some are open Sat until 3pm or 4pm. The **James A Farley Post Office** (421 Eighth Avenue, between 31st & 33rd Streets, Garment District, 1-800 275 8777 24hr information, www.usps.com) is open 24 hours daily for automated services.

Smoking

The 1995 NYC Smoke-Free Air Act makes it illegal to smoke in virtually all indoor public places, including the subway and cinemas. A law went into effect in 2011 that also bans smoking in public parks.

Telephones

As a rule, you must dial 1 + the area code before a number, even if the place you are calling is in the same area code. The area codes for Manhattan are 212 and 646; Brooklyn, Queens, Staten Island and the Bronx are 718 and 347; 917 is now mostly for mobile phones and pagers. Numbers preceded by 800, 877 and 888 are free of charge when dialled from within the US. To dial abroad, dial 011 followed by the country code, then the number. For the operator dial 0. Mobile phone users from other countries will need a tri-band handset. Public pay phones take coins and credit cards. The best way to make long-distance calls is with a phone card, available from the post office, chain stores such as Duane Reade and Rite Aid.

Time & dates

New York is on Eastern Standard Time. This is five hours behind Greenwich Mean Time. Clocks are set forward one hour in early March for Daylight Saving Time (Eastern Daylight Time) and back one hour at the beginning of November. Going from east to west, Eastern Time is one hour ahead of Central Time, two hours ahead of Mountain Time and three hours ahead of Pacific Time.

Tipping

In restaurants, it's customary to tip at least 15 per cent, and a quick way to calculate the tip is to double the tax. For taxi tipping (*see p183*).

Tourist information

Official NYC Information Center
810 Seventh Avenue, between 52nd & 53rd Streets, Midtown (1-212 484 1222, www.nycgo.com). Subway B, D, E to Seventh Avenue. **Open** 8.30am-6pm Mon-Fri; 9am-5pm Sat, Sun.

What's On

The weekly *Time Out New York* magazine, which hits newsstands on Wednesdays, is NYC's essential arts and entertainment guide. The best sources for all things gay is *Next* (www.netmagazine.com); girls should pick up the monthly *Go* (www.gomag.com) magazine.

Visas

Some 36 countries participate in the Visa Waiver Program (VWP; www.cbp.gov/esta) including citizens of Australia, Ireland, New Zealand, and the UK. Citizens of the 36 currently participating countries do not need a visa for stays in the US shorter than 90 days (business or pleasure) as long as they have a machine-readable passport (e-passport) valid for the full 90-day period, a return ticket, and authorisation to travel through the ESTA (Electronic System for Travel Authorization) scheme. Visitors must fill in the ESTA form at least 24 hours before travelling (72 hours in advance is recommended though) and pay US$14 for processing; the form can be found at www.cbp.gov/xp/cgov/travel/id_visa/esta/).

If you do not qualify for entry under the VWP, you will need a visa; leave plenty of time to check before travelling.

ESSENTIALS

Index

Sights & Areas

ESSENTIALS

ESSENTIALS